Bloom's Modern Critical Interpretations

Bloom's Modern Critical Interpretations

Joseph Heller's

Catch-22
New Edition

Edited and with an introduction by
Harold Bloom
Sterling Professor of the Humanities
Yale University

BLOOM'S
LITERARY CRITICISM
An imprint of Infobase Publishing

Editorial Consultant, Matthew J. Bruccoli

Bloom's Modern Critical Interpretations: Joseph Heller's *Catch-22*—New Edition

Copyright ©2008 by Infobase Publishing

Introduction ©2008 by Harold Bloom

Bloom's Literary Criticism
An imprint of Infobase Publishing
132 West 31st Street
New York NY 10001

Library of Congress Cataloging-in-Publication Data

Joseph Heller's Catch-22 / edited by Harold Bloom. — New ed.
    p. cm. — (Modern criticial interpretations)
  Includes bibliographical references and index.
  ISBN 978-0-7910-9617-8 (acid-free paper : alk. paper)
   1. Heller, Joseph. Catch-22. 2. World War, 1939–1945—Literature and the war. 3. War stories, American—History and criticism. I. Bloom, Harold.
PS3558.E476C334 2008
813'.54—dc22   2007042768

Bloom's Literary Criticism books are available at special discounts when purchased in bulk quantities for businesses, associations, institutions, or sales promotions. Please call our Special Sales Department in New York at (212) 967-8800 or (800) 322-8755.

You can find Bloom's Literary Criticism on the World Wide Web at
http://www.chelseahouse.com.

Cover design by Ben Peterson

Printed in the United States of America

Bang BCL 10 9 8 7 6 5 4 3 2 1

This book is printed on acid-free paper.

All links and web addresses were checked and verified to be correct at the time of publication. Because of the dynamic nature of the web, some addresses and links may have changed since publication and may no longer be valid.

Contents

Contents

Editor's Note

My Introduction amiably consigns *Catch-22* to the vast heap of Period Pieces, a strange dumping-ground on the moon of a planet in another solar system. There Heller's extended joke joins other celebrated fictions that will be forgotten, including *On the Road, Beloved,* and the sacred seven Harry Potter tediums.

There are twenty or so contributors to this volume who do not agree with me, but that does not disturb the aged canonical critic, the pariah of his self-slain profession.

I can single out Robert Brustein, Christopher Buckley, and Sanford Pinsker for keeping some sense of balance in this volume. Alas, I myself find nothing in *Catch-22* that might provoke balance. It will not last, and there's an end on it.

HAROLD BLOOM

Introduction

Joseph Heller's *Catch-22* (1961)

Catch-22 (1961) after more than forty years is definitive of what is meant by a Period Piece, a work not for all time, but for the 1960s and 1970s. If *Catch-22* prophesied anything, it was the spirit of the Counter-Culture that began in the late 1960s and was dominant in the 1970s. By now, the Counter-Culture has been assimilated and co-opted; its principal organ is *The New York Times*. In the aura of an official Counter-Culture, *Catch-22* can be read with nostalgia (though not by me) or with the qualified patience that a four-hundred-fifty-page extended joke demands if it is to be read at all.

Heller's half-dozen subsequent books were scarcely readable; his time had passed. World War II ended in 1945: to parody it before 1960–61 would have been in poor taste. Whether it could be parodied then, or now, is a problematic question, to which the likely answer is "No." Heller's perspective is that of individual survival, which is jeopardized by a war being run as a racket. Any perspective upon killing and being killed is legitimate, but Yossarian is not Sir John Falstaff and Joseph Heller was not Shakespeare. Madness is mocked by *Catch-22*, but the mockery loses control and enters the space of literary irreality, where only a few masters have been able to survive. Heller was not one of them.

I remember going to a performance of Heller's play, *We Bombed in New Haven*, featuring Ron Leibman, in New Haven, though I cannot recall the year. Before the intermission, I was gone, irritated by the same qualities that caused my incredulity when reviewers proclaimed *Catch-22* "an apocalyptic masterpiece." It is neither apocalyptic nor a masterpiece, but a tendentious

1

burlesque, founded upon a peculiarly subjective view of historical reality. Subjectivity, to be persuasive, requires lucidity, and nothing in *Catch-22* is lucid. Compare Heller to the great parodist Nathanael West, and Heller vaporizes. One need not invoke *Miss Lonelyhearts;* the cheerfully savage *A Cool Million*, read side-by-side with *Catch-22*, easily eclipses Heller. After many rereadings, I uneasily laugh and wince my way through *A Cool Million*. *Catch-22*, zanily comic in its motion-picture guise, no longer induces either laughter or shock.

Rather than continue to drub *Catch-22*, which will for perhaps another decade still find an audience, I prefer to meditate briefly upon the sub-literary phenomenon of Period Pieces. The Harry Potter books manifestly are for a time only; they simply are too poorly written and too weakly characterized to survive as classics of children's literature. There are permanent works of popular literature, like the detective novels of Agatha Christie, but I doubt that *Catch-22* will achieve Christie's status. Period Pieces have several distinguishing stigmata. Either they are satires or parodies whose targets have faded away (or become unassailable) or they embody stances and attitudes that reflect the spirit of a particular moment or two.

Yossarian's war ends with his departure for Sweden, a desertion that Heller presents as a triumph, which it has to be, if the war as aptly characterized by Heller's parodistic cast of con-men, schemers, profiteers, and mad commanders. War is obscene, necessarily, but the war against Hitler, the SS, and the death camps was neither World War I nor the Viet Nam debacle. Heller isolates the reader from the historical reality of Hitler's evil, yet nevertheless the war against the Nazis was also Yossarian's war.

ROBERT BRUSTEIN

The Logic of Survival in a Lunatic World

"The man who declares that survival at all costs is the end of existence is morally dead, because he's prepared to sacrifice all other values which give life its meaning."

— Sidney Hook

"... It's better to die on one's feet than live on one's knees," Nately retorted with triumphant and lofty conviction. "I guess you've heard that saying before." "Yes, I certainly have," mused the treacherous old man, smiling again. "But I'm afraid you have it backward. It is better to live on one's feet than die on one's knees. That is the way the saying goes."

— Catch-22

Like all superlative works of comedy—and I am ready to argue that this is one of the most bitterly funny works in the language—Catch-22 is based on an unconventional but utterly convincing internal logic. In the very opening pages, when we come upon a number of Air Force officers malingering in a hospital—one censoring all the modifiers out of enlisted men's letters and signing the censor's name "Washington Irving," another pursuing tedious conversations with boring Texans in order to increase his life span by making time pass slowly, still another storing horse chestnuts in his cheeks to

New Republic, 13 November 1961, pp. xx–xx. © 1961 *The New Republic*.

give himself a look of innocence—it seems obvious that an inordinate number of Joseph Heller's characters are, by all conventional standards, mad. It is a triumph of Mr. Heller's skill that he is so quickly able to persuade us 1) that the most lunatic are the most logical, and 2) that it is our conventional standards which lack any logical consistency. The sanest looney of them all is the apparently harebrained central character, an American bombardier of Syrian extraction named Captain John Yossarian, who is based on a mythical Italian island (Pianosa) during World War II. For while many of his fellow officers seem indifferent to their own survival, and most of his superior officers are overtly hostile to his, Yossarian is animated solely by a desperate determination to stay alive:

> It was a vile and muddy war, and Yossarian could have lived without it—lived forever, perhaps. Only a fraction of his countrymen would give up their lives to win it, and it was not his ambition to be among them.... That men would die was a matter of necessity; which men would die, though, was a matter of circumstance, and Yossarian was willing to be the victim of anything but circumstance.

The single narrative thread in this crazy patchwork of anecdotes, episodes, and character portraits traces Yossarian's herculean efforts—through caution, cowardice, defiance, subterfuge, strategem, and subversion, through feigning illness, goofing of, and poisoning the company's food with laundry soap—to avoid being victimized by circumstance, a force represented in the book as *Catch-22*. For *Catch-22* is the unwritten law which empowers the authorities to revoke your rights whenever it suits their cruel whims; it is, in short, the principle of absolute evil in a malevolent, mechanical, and incompetent world. Because of *Catch-22*, justice is mocked, the innocent are victimized, and Yossarian's squadron is forced to fly more than double the number of missions prescribed by Air Force code. Dogged by *Catch-22*, Yossarian becomes the anguished witness to the ghoulish slaughter of his crew members and the destruction of all his closest friends, until finally his fear of death becomes so intense that he refuses to wear a uniform, after his own has been besplattered with the guts of his dying gunner, and receives a medal standing naked in formation. From this point on, Yossarian's logic becomes so pure that everyone thinks him mad, for it is the logic of sheer survival, dedicated to keeping him alive in a world noisily clamoring for his annihilation.

According to this logic, Yossarian is surrounded on all sides by hostile forces: his enemies are distinguished less by their nationality than by their ability to get him killed. Thus, Yossarian feels a blind, electric rage against the Germans whenever they hurl flak at his easily penetrated plane; but he feels an equally profound hatred for those of his own countrymen who exercise an arbitrary power over his life and well-being. Heller's huge cast of characters, therefore, is dominated by a large number of comic malignities, genus Americanus, drawn with a grotesqueness so audacious that they somehow transcend caricature entirely and become vividly authentic. These include: Colonel Cathcart, Yossarian's commanding officer, whose consuming ambition to get his picture in the Saturday Evening Post motivates him to volunteer his command for every dangerous command, and to initiate prayers during briefing sessions ("I don't want any of this Kingdom of God or Valley of Death stuff. That's all too negative.... Couldn't we pray for a tighter bomb pattern?"), an idea he abandons only when he learns enlisted men pray to the same God; General Peckem, head of Special Services, whose strategic objective is to replace General Dreedle, the wing commander, capturing every bomber group in the US Air Force ("If dropping bombs on the enemy isn't a special service, I wonder what in the world is"); Captain Black, the squadron intelligence officer, who inaugurates the Glorious Loyalty Oath Crusade in order to discomfort a rival, forcing all officers (except the rival, who is thereupon declared a Communist) to sign a new oath whenever they get their flak suits, their pay checks, or their haircuts; Lieutenant Scheisskopf, paragon of the parade ground, whose admiration for efficient formations makes him scheme to screw nickel-alloy swivels into every cadet's back for perfect ninety degree turns; and cadres of sadistic officers, club-happy MPs, and muddleheaded agents of the CID, two of whom, popping in and out of rooms like farcical private eyes, look for Washington Irving throughout the action, finally pinning the rap on the innocent chaplain.

These are Yossarian's antagonists, all of them reduced to a single exaggerated humor, and all identified by their totally mechanical attitude towards human life. Heller has a profound hatred for this kind of military mind, further anatomized in a wacky scene before the Action Board which displays his (and their) animosity in a manner both hilarious and scarifying. But Heller, at war with much larger forces than the army, has provided his book with much wider implications than a war novel. For the author (apparently sharing the Italian belief that vengenace is a dish which tastes best cold) has been nourishing his grudges for so long that they have expanded to include the post-war American world. Through the agency of grotesque comedy, Heller has found a way to confront the humbug, hypocrisy, cruelty, and sheer stupidity of our mass society—qualities which have made the few other Americans who care almost speechless with baffled rage—and through some miracle of prestidigitation, Pianosa has become a satirical microcosm for many of the macrocosmic idioicies of our time. Thus, the author flourishes his Juvenalian scourge at government-subsidized agriculture (and farmers, one of whom "spent every penny he didn't earn on new land to increase the amount of alfalfa he did not grow"); at the exploitation of American Indians, evicted from their oil-rich land; at smug psychiatrists; at bureaucrats and patriots; at acquisitive war widows; at high-spirited American boys; and especially, and most vindictively, at war profiteers.

This last satirical flourish, aimed at the whole mystique of corporation capitalism, is embodied in the fantastic adventures of Milo Minderbinder, the company mess officer, and a paradigm of good-natured Jonsonian cupidity. Anxious to put the war on a businesslike basis, Milo has formed a syndicate designed to corner the world market on all available foodstuffs, which he then sells to army messhalls at huge profits. Heady with success (his deals have made him Mayor of every town in Sicily, Vice-Shah of Oran, Caliph of Baghdad, Imam of Damascus, and the Sheik of Araby), Milo soon expands his activities, forming a private army which he hires out to the highest bidder. The climax of Milo's career comes when he fulfills a contract with the Germans to bomb and strafe his own outfit, directing his planes from the Pianosa control tower and justifying the action with the stirring war cry: "What's good for the syndicate is good for the country." Milo has almost succeeded in his ambition to preempt the field of war for private enterprise when he makes a fatal mistake: he has cornered the entire Egyptian cotton market and is unable to unload it anywhere. Having failed to pass it off to his own messhall in the form of chocolate-covered cotton, Milo is finally persuaded by Yossarian to bribe the American government to take it off his hands: "If you run into trouble, just tell everybody that the security of the country requires a strong domestic Egyptian cotton speculating industry." The Minderbinder sections—in showing the basic incompatibility of idealism and economics by satirizing the patriotic cant which usually accompanies American greed—illustrate the procedure of the entire book: the ruthless ridicule of hypocrisy through a technique of farce-fantasy, beneath which the demon of satire lurks, prodding fat behinds with a red-hot pitchfork.

It should be abundantly clear, then, that *Catch-22*, despite some of the most outrageous sequences since A Night at the Opera, is an intensely serious work. Heller has certain technical similarities to the Marx Brothers, Max Schulman, Kingsley Amis, Al Capp, and S.J. Perelman, but his mordant intelligence, closer to that of Nathanael West, penetrates the surface of the merely funny to expose a world of ruthless self-advancement, gruesome cruelty, and flagrant disregard for human life—a world, in short, very much like our own as seen through a magnifying glass, distorted for more perfect accuracy. Considering his indifference to surface reality, it is absurd to judge Heller by standards of psychological realism (or, for that matter, by conventional artistic standards at all, since his book is as formless as any picaresque epic). He is concerned entirely with that thin boundary of the surreal, the borderline between hilarity and horror, which, much like the apparent formlessness of the unconscious, has its own special integrity and coherence. Thus, Heller will never use comedy for its own sake; each joke has a wider significance in the intricate pattern, so that laughter becomes a prologue for some grotesque revelation. This gives the reader an effect of surrealistic dislocation, intensified by a weird, rather flat, impersonal style, full of complicated reversals, swift transitions, abrupt shifts in chronological time, and manipulated identities (e.g. if a private named Major Major Major is promoted to Major by a faulty IBM machine, or if a malingerer, sitting out a doomed mission, is declared dead through a bureaucratic error, then this remains their permanent fate), as if all mankind was determined by a mad and merciless mechanism.

Thus, Heller often manages to heighten the macabre obscenity of total war much more effectively through its gruesome comic aspects than if he had written realistic descriptions. And thus, the most delicate pressure is enough to send us over the line from farce into phantasmagoria. In the climactic chapter, in fact, the book leaves comedy altogether and becomes an eerie nightmare of terror. Here, Yossarian, walking through the streets of Rome as though through an inferno, observes soldiers molesting drunken women, fathers beating ragged children, policemen clubbing innocent bystanders until the whole world seems swallowed up in the maw of evil:

> The night was filled with horrors, and he thought he knew how Christ must have felt as he walked through the world, like a psychiatrist through a ward of nuts, like a victim through a prison of thieves. . . . Mobs . . . mobs of policemen. . . . Mobs with clubs were in control everywhere.

Here, as the book leaves the war behind, it is finally apparent that Heller's comedy is his artistic response to his vision of transcendent evil, as if the escape route of laughter were the only recourse from a malignant world.

It is this world, which cannot be divided into boundaries or ideologies, that Yossarian has determined to resist. And so when his fear and disgust have reached the breaking point, he simply refuses to fly another mission. Asked by a superior what would happen if everybody felt the same way, Yossarian exercises his definitive logic, and answers, "Then I'd be a damned fool to feel any other way." Having concluded a separate peace, Yossarian maintains it in the face of derision, ostracism, psychological pressure, and the threat of court martial. When he is finally permitted to go home if he will only agree to a shabby deal whitewashing Colonel Cathcart, however, he finds himself impaled on two impossible alternatives. But his unique logic, helped along by the precedent of an even more logical friend, makes him conclude that desertion is the better part of valor; and so (after an inspirational sequence which is the weakest thing in the book) he takes off for neutral Sweden—the only place left in the world, outside of England, where "mobs with clubs" are not in control.

Yossarian's expedient is not very flattering to our national ideals, being defeatist, selfish, cowardly, and unheroic. On the other hand, it is one of those sublime expressions of anarchic individualism without which all national ideals are pretty hollow anyway. Since the mass State, whether totalitarian or democratic, has grown increasingly hostile to Falstaffian irresponsibility, Yossarian's anti-heroism is, in fact, a kind of inverted heroism which we would do well to ponder. For, contrary to the armchair pronouncements of patriotic ideologues, Yossarian's obsessive concern for survival makes him not only not morally dead, but one of the most morally vibrant figures in recent literature—and a giant of the will beside those wary, wise, and wistful prodigals in contemporary novels who always accommodate sadly to American life. I believe that Joseph Heller is one of the most extraordinary talents now among us. He has Mailer's combustible radicalism without his passion for violence and self-glorification; he has Bellow's gusto with his compulsion to affirm the unaffirmable; and he has Salinger's wit without his coquettish self-consciousness. Finding his absolutes in the freedom to be, in a world dominated by cruelty, carnage, inhumanity, and a rage to destroy itself, Heller has come upon a new morality based on an old ideal, the morality of refusal. Perhaps - now that Catch-22 has found its most deadly nuclear form—we have reached the point where even the logic of survival is unworkable. But at least we can still contemplate the influence of its liberating honesty on a free, rebellious spirit in this explosive, bitter, subversive, brilliant book.

Nelson Algren

The Catch

There was only one catch and that was *Catch-22*, which specified that a concern for one's own safety in the face of dangers that were real and immediate was the process of a rational mind. Orr was crazy and could be grounded. All he had to do was ask; and as soon as he did, he would no longer be crazy and would have to fly more missions. He would be crazy to fly more missions and sane if he didn't, but if he was sane he had to fly them. Yossarian was moved very deeply by the absolute simplicity of this clause and let out a respectful whistle:

"That's some catch, that Catch-22," he observed.
"It's the best there is," Doc Daneeka agreed.

Yossarian was moved deeply day and night and what moved him more deeply than anything else was the fact that they were trying to murder him.

"Who's '*they*'?" Clevenger wanted to know. "Who, specifically, is trying to murder you?"
"Every one of them," Yossarian told him.
"Every one of *whom*?"
"Every one of whom do you think?"

The Nation (4 November 1961): pp. 357–358. © 1961 *The Nation*.

"I haven't any idea."

"Then how do you know they aren't?"

Yossarian had proof, because strangers he didn't know shot at him with cannons every time he flew up into the air to drop bombs on them, so it was of no use for Clevenger to say "No one is trying to kill you."

"Then why are they shooting at me?"

"They're shooting at everyone."

"And what difference does that make?"

"I'm not going to argue with you," Clevenger decided, "you don't know who you hate."

"Whoever is trying to poison me."

"Nobody is trying to poison you."

"They poisoned my food twice, didn't they? Didn't they put poison in my food at Ferrara and during the Great Big Siege of Bologna?"

"They put poison in everybody's food," Clevenger explained.

"And what difference does that make?"

There was no established procedure for evasive action. All you needed was fear, and Yossarian had plenty of that. He bolted wildly for his life on each mission the instant his bombs were away. When he fufilled the thirty-five missions required of each man of his group, he asked to be sent home.

Colonel Cathcart had by then raised the missions required to forty. When Yossarian had flown forty he asked to be sent home. Colonel Cathcart had raised the missions required to forty-five—there *did* seem to be a catch *somewhere*. Yossarian went into the hospital with a pain in his liver that fell just short of being jaundice. If it became jaundice the doctors could treat it. If it didn't become jaundice and went away they could discharge him. Yossarian decided to spend the rest of the war in bed by running a daily temperature of 101. He had found a catch of his own.

To preserve his sanity against the formalized lunacy of the military mind in action, Yossarian had to turn madman. Yet even Yossarian is more the patriot than Sgt. Minderbinder, the business mind in action. Even Yossarian has to protest when Minderbinder arranges with the Germans to let them knock American planes down at a thousand dollars per plane. Minderbinder is horrified—"Have you no respect for the sanctity of a business contract?" he demands of Yossarian, and Yossarian feels ashamed of himself.

Below its hilarity, so wild that it hurts, *Catch-22* is the strongest repudiation of our civilization, in fiction, to come out of World War II. *The Naked and the Dead* and *From Here to Eternity* are lost within it. That the horror and the hypocrisy, the greed and the complacency, the endless cunning and the endless stupidity which now go to constitute what we term Christianity are dealt with here in absolutes, does not lessen the truth of its repudiation. Those happy few who hit upon Terry Southern's *The Magic Christian* will find that, what Southern said with some self-doubt, Heller says with no doubt whatsoever. To compare *Catch-22* favorably with *The Good Soldier Schweik* would be an injustice, because this novel is not merely the best American novel to come out of World War II; it is the best American novel that has come out of anywhere in years.

JOHN WAIN

A New Novel About Old Troubles

It now seems a certainty that *Catch-22*[1] will pass into literature, i.e., break through the invisible but tough wall that separates the volcanic flow of 'recent books'—mere merchandise to be weighed, transported, labelled and commented on by bleary-eyed hacks—from the tiny residue of permanent work that each age deposits. Its reception was ecstatic, and the usual limbs were gone out on; the dust-jacket gives a few samples, for instance that one reviewer called it 'the greatest satirical work in English since *Erewhon*.' I don't think I could go this far, because surely *Animal Farm* is better satire than *Catch-22:* just as poignant, just as far-reaching and inclusive, but much more elegant and economical. Elegance and economy are odd virtues to bring up in connection with *Catch-22*, which rather magnificently spurns both; still, they are virtues nevertheless.

On the other hand, I do agree with Nelson Algren's claim that '*The Naked and the Dead* and *From Here to Eternity* are lost within it.' As a book about war, written from the viewpoint of the fighting man, it is entirely credible, very moving, and—I expect to find—unforgettable. Most of it is pitched in the key of bitterly exuberant farce, a farce through which fear and *ennui* are always perceptible. But now and again the custard-pies are quietly laid aside, and we are given a deadly serious passage which proves that Mr. Heller, if he had wanted to, could have written a Jones or a Mailer into the

The Critical Quarterly, Vol 5, Number 2 (Summer 1963): pp 168–173. © Blackwell Publishers.

ground. (If you happen to have the book by you, and are interested enough
to want an example long enough to prove the point and therefore too long
to quote in a review, I am thinking of such things as the description of
Snowdon's death on pp. 426-430.)

Of course Snowdon's death has been mentioned a number of times,
and even partly narrated; it is typical of the book's narrative method that
we should have to wait till page 426, a bare twenty pages or so from the
end, before getting the full details. Broadly speaking, this method is half-way
between straight narrative and what the Elizabethans would have called an
'anatomy'. Instead of taking us in a straight line from one point in time to
another, the story zigzags considerably, ending up only a very little further
on from where it began. A tremendous amount of incident, a huge gallery
of portraits, and an ambitiously wide range of emotions and effects lie in
between. No wonder this book took eight years to write, and was gestated for
eight before that! Thus we are told, for instance, that the hero, Yossarian, one
day appeared on parade stark naked. Various comic pseudo-explanations of
this are given, but the real reason—that his uniform had been drenched with
Snowdon's blood and guts on that terrible occasion, that he had peeled it off
hysterically, and continued for some time in a state of shock, refusing to wear
a uniform again—is held back until we are ready for it. And so on, throughout
scores of intertwined episodes. And be it noted that the construction is circu-
lar or spiral, like that of *Finnegans Wake:* it opens with Yossarian in hospital,
having a conversation with the chaplain, and ends with Yossarian again in
hospital and talking to the same chaplain.

This method of scrambling the narrative has one disadvantage at the
beginning; it reminds the reader too forcibly of the dozens of other scrambled
narratives through which he has had to pick his dazed, irritated way. To a
certain kind of modern novelist, regular progression and a clearly-indicated
time-sequence add up to an admission of weakness. The reader must be kept
guessing, and if the writer's vision of life, his understanding of his characters,
are not profound enough to make the reader work hard, then he must be tied
up in the plot: information must be kept back, the story must stop, start, and
go backwards, till the reader becomes so engrossed in the struggle to make
out what is happening that he submissively concedes the book's right to be
called difficult, *avant-garde* and 'advanced.' For a few pages, *Catch-22* recalls
this familiar annoyance. But only for a few pages. After that, it becomes clear
that the method is completely justified. To these bomber-pilots, life does not
flow in a regular, unfolding ribbon, experience following on from experience,
as it does in even the most tumultuous life in peace-time. It teeters round
and round in a continual stalemate. Each time they wait to fly on another
mission, everything has to stand still until they know whether or not they are
going to survive. The experiences they have in the meantime, all the escapist

drinking, whoring and quarrelling, may be intense, but they are static and self-contained. They issue from nowhere and lead nowhere, being enclosed in a staff cast of anxiety. And this gives us the strong impression that the lives of fighting men are utterly and helplessly different, cut off and set apart from normal lives. Which is, of course, what *erat demonstrandum*.

In the last few pages, the story suddenly shakes itself, gets up and moves. Hungry Joe, who had seemed dementedly immortal, dies. Orr has reached Sweden by paddling on a raft. And all of a sudden Yossarian realizes the carefully planned method behind Orr's madness. Up to that time, Orr had seemed to Yossarian, and therefore to the reader, as no more than a helpless grotesque:

> Orr was an eccentric midget, a freakish, likable dwarf with a smutty mind and a thousand valuable skills that would keep him in a low income group all his life. He could use a soldering iron and hammer two boards together so that the wood did not split and the nails did not bend. He could drill holes. He had built a good deal more in the tent while Yossarian was away in the hospital. He had filed or chiseled a perfect channel in the cement so that the slender gasoline line was flush with the floor as it ran to the stove from the tank he had built outside on an elevated platform. He had constructed andirons for the fireplace out of excess bomb parts and had filled them with stout silver logs, and he had framed with stained wood the photographs of girls with big breasts he had torn out of cheesecake magazines and hung over the mantelpiece. Orr could open a can of paint. He could mix paint, thin paint, remove paint. He could chop wood and measure things with a ruler. He knew how to build fires. He could dig holes, and he had a real gift for bringing water for them both in cans and canteens from the tanks near the mess hall. He could engross himself in an inconsequential task for hours without growing restless or bored, as oblivious to fatigue as the stump of a tree, and almost as taciturn. He had an uncanny knowledge of wildlife and was not afraid of dogs or cats or beetles or moths, or of foods like scrod or tripe.

Just before this description, Orr has made Yossarian an offer. "'You ought to try flying a few missions with me when you're not flying lead. Just for laughs. Tee-hee.' Orr gazed up at Yossarian through the corners of his eyes with pointed mirth."

Yossarian simply does not bother to consider the idea, Orr being notoriously accident-prone, and it is only in the closing pages that he, and we, realize that Orr has been devotedly practising crash-landing, pancaking on to the water, etc., so as to put himself in a position to get to neutral territory and be interned in comfort. The moment he does realize this, Yossarian experiences a great wave of positiveness, decides that his apparently insuperable problems can be solved if only he is man enough to run away from them, and deserts. Whereupon the story ends.

A war-novel which ends with the desertion of the hero is obviously not heroic, and *Catch-22* is in fact a pretty thorough debunking job. Every senior officer who appears in the story is either a maniacal sadist or a blundering oaf, and those characters who show any great zeal for their duties are plainly tick-eted as floperoos, duped into playing the game of General Dreedle, General Peckem, Lieutenant Scheisskopf and the rest of the Dickensian crew. We get a pretty fair idea of the book's objectives from the conversation—obviously a set-piece, written in as exposition and not thrown up by the organic life of the story—between Nately and the old man in the whorehouse (p. 238 ff.), of which this is a specimen:

> "Well, frankly, I don't know how long America is going to last," he proceeded dauntlessly. "I suppose we can't last forever if the world itself is going to be destroyed someday. But I do know that we're going to survive and triumph for a long, long time."
>
> "For how long?" mocked the profane old man with a gleam of malicious elation. "Not even as long as the frog?"
>
> "Much longer than you or me," Nately blurted out lamely.
>
> "Oh, is that all! That won't be very much longer then, considering that you're so gullible and brave and that I am already such an old, old man."
>
> "How old are you?" Nately asked, growing intrigued and charmed with the old man in spite of himself.
>
> "A hundred and seven." The old man chuckled heartily at Nately's look of chagrin. "I see you don't believe that either."
>
> "I don't believe anything you tell me," Nately replied, with a bashful mitigating smile. "The only thing I do believe is that America is going to win the war."
>
> "You put so much stock in winning wars," the grubby iniquitous old man scoffed. "The real trick lies in losing wars, in knowing which wars can be *lost*. Italy has been losing wars for centuries, and just see how splendidly we've done nonetheless. France wins wars and is in a continual state of crisis. Germany loses and prospers. Look at our own recent history. Italy won a war in Ethiopia and promptly stumbled into serious trouble. Victory gave us such insane delusions of grandeur that we helped start a world war we hadn't a chance of winning. But now that we are losing again, everything

has taken a turn for the better, and we will certainly come out on top again if we succeed in being defeated."

Nately gaped at him in undisguised befuddlement. "Now I really don't understand what you're saying. You talk like a madman."

"But I live like a sane one. I was a fascist when Mussolini was on top, and I am an anti-fascist now that he has been deposed. I was fanatically pro-German when the Germans were here to protect us against the Americans and now that the Americans are here to protect us against the Germans I am fanatically pro-American. I can assure you, my outraged young friend"—the old man's knowing, disdainful eyes shone even more effervescently as Nately's stuttering dismay increased "that you and your country will have a no more loyal partisan in Italy than me-but only as long as you remain in Italy."

"But," Nately cried out in disbelief, "you're a turncoat! A timeserver! A shameful, unscrupulous opportunist!"

"I am a hundred and seven years old," the old man reminded him suavely.

When Nately points out that Italy, having been occupied by the Germans and currently occupied by the Americans, can't be said to be doing very well in the war, the old man replies, 'Italian soldiers are not dying any more. But American and German soldiers are. I call that doing extremely well'.

And so we come round again to the eternal discussion about values and about honour. 'Who hath it? He that died a Wednesday.' Is the war a just one? Is it worth giving your life for? Personally I have every sympathy with anyone who takes the same line as the old man, that survival is the great test of fitness to survive. On the other hand, I admire and even revere men brave enough to give their lives for a cause they believe in. An out-and-out pacifist book, debunking 'war' on the grounds that 'war' kills people, never seems to me to give the whole picture, though it arouses deep and sympathetic echoes in me. Perhaps these questions are too hard for one person to solve. Certainly Mr. Heller side-steps them' He sets his story at a time when the war is nearing its close, when the Germans, and the Japanese, cannot hold out much longer. At such a time, to fight bravely is merely to serve the interests of the military higher-ups. And since the novel portrays those higher-ups as subhuman nuisances, unfit to clutter the earth's surface, the answer is evident. Yossarian is right to desert, Orr is right to ditch his plane and paddle to Sweden. Still, the nagging questions remain, and Mr. Heller tries rather clumsily to push them back where they can't do any serious harm to his story. In the closing scene, Yossarian has a conversation with Major Danby, one of the very few sympathetic senior officers, in which he justifies himself.

With deliberate amiability he said, "Danby, how can you work along with people like Cathcart and Korn? Doesn't it turn your stomach?"

Major Danby seemed surprised by Yossarian's question.

"I do it to help my country," he replied, as though the answer should have been obvious. "Colonel Cathcart and Colonel Korn are my superiors, and obeying their orders is the only contribution I can make to the war effort. I work along with them because it's my duty. And also," he added in a much lower voice, dropping his eyes "because I am not a very aggressive person."

"Your country doesn't need your help any more," Yossarian reasoned without antagonism. "So all you're doing is helping them."

"I try not to think of that," Major Danby admitted frankly. "But I try to concentrate on only the big result and to forget that they are succeeding, too. I try to pretend that they are not significant."

"That's my trouble, you know," Yossarian mused sympathetically, folding his arms. "Between me and every ideal I always find Scheisskopfs, Peckems, Korns and Cathcarts. And that sort of changes the ideal."

"You must try not to think of them," Major Danby advised affirmatively. "And you must never let them change your values. Ideals are good, but people are sometimes not so good. You must try to look up at the big picture."

Yossarian rejected the advice with a skeptical shake of his head. "When I look up, I see people cashing in. I don't see heaven or saints or angels. I see people cashing in on every decent impulse and every human tragedy."

"But you must try not to think of that." Major Danby insisted. "And you must try not to let it upset you."

"Oh, it doesn't really upset me. What does upset me, though, is that they think I'm a sucker. They think that they're smart, and that the rest of us are dumb. And, you know, Danby, the thought occurs to me right now, for the first time, that maybe they're right."

"But you must try not to think of that too," argued Major Danby. "You must think only of the welfare of your country and the dignity of man."

"Yeah," said Yossarian.

"I mean it, Yossarian. This is not World War One. You must never forget that we're at war with aggressors who would not let either one of us live if they won."

"I know that," Yossarian replied tersely, with a sudden surge of scowling annoyance. "Christ, Danby, I earned that medal I got, no matter what their reasons were for giving it to me. I've flown seventy goddam combat missions. Don't talk to me about fighting to save my country. I've been fighting all along to save my country. Now I'm going to fight a little to save myself. The country's not in danger any more, but I am."

"The war's not over yet. The Germans are driving towards Antwerp."

"The Germans will be beaten in a few months. And Japan will be beaten a few months after that. If I were to give up my life now, it wouldn't be for my country. It would be for Cathcart and Korn. So I'm turning my bombsight in for the duration. From now on I'm thinking only of me."

I quote the whole of this conversation because it makes clear not only the central evasiveness of the book, its one serious flaw, but also Yossarian's role as hero. Yossarian is the hero of every modern novel; he is the man who looks up towards an ideal and sees, thrusting in between him and it, the phonies, liars and exploiters. 'What does upset me is that they think I'm a sucker.' And so he is. That's why Yossarian is the hero. Because he's the fall guy. It runs right through the centre of modern literature, like a vein in quartz: this conviction that the life we live, in the society we have made, is a deep swindle, that you can't win if you are handicapped with decency and humanity: so you concentrate on losing: gracefully, humorously, resistantly, but always losing. That, at any rate, is what the bulk of Western literature says; and there is plenty of indirect evidence that Eastern literature, if it were free to say anything at all, would say the same thing. Does this reflect the true state of man in our time? Or is it just the writer, enmeshed in the world of the technocrat, who sees himself, and everything he loves, as bound to go down?

Note

1. *Catch–22*. Joseph Heller. Jonathan Cape, 1962, 21s.

FREDERICK R. KARL

Joseph Heller's Catch-22: Only Fools Walk in Darkness

What we yearn for in the post-war generation is fiction that seems "true"—or suggests whatever passes for truth—in its specifics as well as its generalities. While we all agree that the older great writers still move us profoundly, their vision in its particulars cannot appeal to us: Dostoyevsky was a reactionary, religious fanatic; Conrad, an anti-liberal; Lawrence, for blood, not social action; Mann, a disillusioned nationalist; Hesse, a mystic who recommended asceticism. We are still obviously affected by their psychological vision of man and the world, but repelled by what they offer in return, disturbed by the fact that they do not seem one of us. Perhaps because we have so assimilated their vision, we no longer turn to them for advice. They offer only a diagnosis, not a course of action true in its details. We read them with admiration, respect, even involvement. What they say is intensely true. But when we turn away from their printed pages, we face a different world. They are too idealistic for us. They want too much change, and at best they offer only spiritual rewards.

On the other hand, a novel like *Catch-22*, trailing recollections of Joyce, Nathanael West, and early, "funny" Céline, speaks solidly to those who are disaffected, discontented, and disaffiliated, and yet who want to react to life positively. With its occasional affirmations couched in terms of pain and cynical laughter, it makes nihilism seem natural, ordinary, even appealing. The

Contemporary American Novelists, ed. Harry T. Moore (Carbondale, Ill.: Southern Illinois University Press, 1965), pp. 134–142. Copyright © 1964 by Southern Illinois University Press.

very zaniness of its vision constitutes its attraction even to those who have compromised with most of the absurdities it exposes.

Catch-22 obviously appeals to the student, who beneath his complacency and hipster frigidity is very confused and afraid. It appeals to the sophisticated professional—the educator, lawyer, professor—who must work at something he cannot fully trust. It appeals to the businessman, who does not really believe that his empire primarily serves the public good. It certainly appeals to all the new professionals—the advertisers, publicity men, television writers—whose world is little different from the absurd one Heller presents.

Wartime life on Pianosa—whatever the veracity of its details—is a replica of life within any organization. Whether one is a lawyer, teacher, doctor, judge, union member, white-collar worker, or writer attached to a magazine, advertising agency, newspaper, or television station, he finds himself in a similar kind of world. It is not simply a neurotic reaction to his surroundings that gives one this sense of absurdity: the absurdity is an actual fact, the consequence of many conflicting interests interacting and creating a world unfit for the individual.

This point is of course true of all good service fiction, but it is particularly true of *Catch-22*, beginning with its catchy title, its sense that the individual must always relinquish part of himself to the organization which chews him up and then eliminates him. Most people try to prevent becoming waste matter. The novel appeals to all those who want the good life and nevertheless reject its particularities, or even fear defining them. Beneath the surface, all its avid readers are afraid that "life"—whatever it is—is dribbling away from them in ways they can never dam. Calling themselves social animals, and arguing that every individual must be part of society, they bate society and distrust any individual who is a social animal.

For those who find given life nauseating, frustrating, and demeaning—that is, our sane citizens—*Catch-22* provides, at least temporarily, a moral, affirmative way out. So far do people diverge from their public image that their frustrated longings often consume their entire existence. They may wish to do right, but are compromised by the wrongness of their situation. They see themselves as defeated victims, but are forced to carry themselves as victors They want to love, but find that hate is more sophisticated, and viable. They want to pursue self, but are admonished and shamed into embracing the public good. They desire to aid society, but are warned that only a fool puts self last. They wish for authenticity, good faith, decency, but find that inauthenticity brings immediate and often sensational results. Trying to believe, they more frequently are mocked by the very forces they desire to accept. Wishing to embrace the great world, they find themselves successes in the little.

What American novel of the last decade has spoken better to this type of individual—perhaps to all of us?—than *Catch-22?* Its surface extravagance masks a serious purpose: that in an impossible situation, one finally has to honor his own self; that in an absurd universe, the individual has the right to seek survival; that one's own substance is infinitely more precious than any cause, however right; that one must not be asked to give his life unless *every-body* is willing to give *his.*

It is the latter point—a kind of Kantian categorical imperative applied to survival—that has generally been neglected. When Yossarian decides that his life does count, he is making a moral decision about the sanctity of human existence. Life must not be taken lightly, either by others (military men, business manipulators, world leaders) or by oneself. Yossarian is a hero by virtue of his sacred appraisal of his future. To himself he is as valuable as a general or a president. Since he is so valuable, he has a right, an inviolable right, to save himself once he has done his share of the world's dirty business. The individual must consider himself supreme. What could be more democratic, American, even Christian!

Heller's point is always moral. The fact that many outraged readers saw Yossarian as immoral, cowardly, or anti–American simply indicates what falsely patriotic hearts beat sturdily beneath seemingly sophisticated exteriors. Yossarian is a great American—if we must have this point—an American of whom we should all be proud, even if Heller makes him an Assyrian (at times he seems like a young Turk hiding behind an Armenian name).

The morality, in fact, both implied and stated, is somewhat pat. Despite the presence of so many seemingly "evil" characters, Heller believes implicitly in the goodness of man. Even the former (Cathcart, Dreedle, Milo, *et al.*), however, are not really evil in any sinister way: rather, they simply react to the given chance, the proffered opportunity. They could be professors, or even ministers. They are men on the make, and such is the quality of modern life—*all* men are waiting for their chance. There are millions of Eichmanns, Hannah Arendt tells us. Yossarian is a Jesus among the money-lenders, without the mean sense of righteousness of a potential Messiah.

Yossarian is the man who acts in good faith, to use Sartre's often-repeated phrase. In Yossarian's situation—one in which war has turned all men into madmen—people float uneasily in a foreign world where human existence is feeble, contradictory, and contingent upon an infinity of other forces. Nothing, here, is certain except the individual's recurring assurance of his own response. All he can hope to know is that he is superior to any universal force (man-made or otherwise), and all he can hope to recognize is that the universal or collective force can never comprehend the individual. The only sure thing in a swamp of absurdity is one's own identity. "I think, therefore I am" has never seemed truer, distorted though Descartes' phrase may have become in the twentieth century.

Accordingly, the true hero of our era is the man who can accept absolute responsibility. He must act alone, and his faith—not in God, but in himself—must be good, honest, pure. If, as Nietzsche said, all the gods are dead, then man must become mature enough to assume the role. Yossarian's decision that life must pre-empt all other considerations is precisely this moral act of responsibility. In choosing life, Yossarian shows himself to be reflective, conscious, indeed free. All the others are slugs living in the swampy depths of self-deception; not bad men necessarily, they are simply unaware, and unaware they cannot be free.

When Yossarian strikes for freedom at the end of the novel (the fact that it is Sweden demonstrates Heller's concern with the good society made by good men), his act symbolizes more than defiance, certainly not cowardice. He has done his duty—Heller is careful to keep before us Yossarian's many missions (the word itself indicates a high calling). He has shown his responsibility to society at large, and has given his physical energy and his nervous sweat. Now he must seek a meaningful life, try to make order out of chaos. He must overcome nausea. In this respect, Sweden seems like Paradise: sane people, plenty of good sex, a benevolent government, jolly drunkenness. In Sweden, the individual seems to have a chance, what Yeats felt in part about his mythical Byzantium.

It is no more immoral for Yossarian to seek Sweden than for Yeats to have searched for Byzantium. Both places indeed are more a state of mind than a real place. We can be sure that when Yossarian reaches Sweden, he will be disappointed, even frustrated. Not all the tall, blonde women will capitulate, not all the people will be sane; the government will even expect him to work, and liquor will be expensive. Yet Sweden remains valid as an idea—one certainly has the right to seek it as an alternative to death. It may prove a false Eden, but man in his desperation may still desire Paradise. It is a mark of his humanity that he does.

There is, except for Sweden, really no community that Yossarian can join. An open character in a closed society, he must shun everyone to retain his identity: appear naked among the clothed, refuse to acquiesce to ill-motivated orders, avoid love while seeking sex, reject a mission that is no longer his. In virtually every situation, he is alone—his name, his racial origin, his integrity all indicate his isolation. Like an ancient hero rather than a modem *schlemiel*, he goes through his solitary ordeal, and the ordeal, as Heller presents it, is eminently worthwhile: to defy death in the name of reason and life.

A good deal of the humor of the novel derives from Yossarian's very openness in a society closed to authenticity and good faith. When an open character—responsive, sensitive, decent—throws himself upon a closed society—unresponsive, fixed, inflexible—very often the result can be tragic. What keeps Yossarian comic, however, is the fact that he never tries to change the society he scorns; he is quite willing to accept its absurdity if it will leave him alone. Never a revolutionary, rarely a rebel, unintentionally a hero, only occasionally a young Turk, Yossarian is more often a rank conformist. The only sanity he desires is his own, not the world's; the only joys he seeks are those he can himself generate; the only rewards he covets are the compensations, not of glory, but of full lips, breasts, and thighs. He is more Sancho than Don. The comedy of Yossarian is the comedy of a romantic, Rousseauistic natural man forced to do the dirty work of the world.

Yet this twentieth-century natural man is "with it," not against it. He is able to adapt to the forces that would otherwise destroy. He retains his naturalness (integrity, sexual balance, coolness) in situations that have frustrated and smashed men more rebellious and affirmative than he. What both impresses and dismays us is Yossarian's adaptability; his views do not cause rigidity, and without rigidity there can be only personal comedy. Tragedy is always "out there," involving those who try to fight the system or those who are trapped by a system they never understood (Clevinger, Nately, Snowden). Like Yossarian, Milo is of course comic because he *knows* about the system; he is the very fellow who masterminds systems.

The two extremes Yossarian must avoid include the avarice and egoism of Milo and the innocence and naïveté of Nately ("new-born") and Snowden (pure whiteness). As Heller presents the alternatives, a person must be in the know in all the particulars of life or else he cannot be true to himself. Only a fool walks in darkness. Yossarian is an honest man because Yossarian understands that the way to righteousness is through balance: he must assure his own survival without the help of others. Thus, Heller condemns both Nately and Milo; the latter obviously stands for a base, commercial acquisitiveness, while the former attempts to be Jesus Christ in a situation that calls for an instinctive sense of survival.

Those who have felt the tragic overtones of the novel often find it difficult to place its tragic center. Clearly, *Catch-22* is not simply a comic novel full of puns, high jinks slapstick, witty dialogue, and satirical asides. It has these in abundance—perhaps, on occasion, in overabundance—but its purpose and execution are fully serious, what we feel in Saul Bellow's work, to mention a contemporary American whom Heller comes closest to. At the center of the tragedy is Heller's awareness of a passing era, an era that perhaps never existed but one that might have if people and situations had gone differently. Heller's is the nostalgia of the idealist—such a writer's style is usually jazzed-up, satirical, somehow surrealistic—the idealist who can never accept that moral values have become insignificant or meaningless in human conduct. This heritage, what we find in Nathanael West, early Céline, and a whole host of similar writers, derives from the tragic undertones of Ecclesiastes with its monody against vanity, egoism, hypocrisy, folly—those qualities which have, unfortunately, become the shibboleths of the twentieth century.

Heller's recoil from these false qualities takes the form of his attack upon religion, the military, political forces, commercial values—as C. Wright Mills indicates, the whole power formation of a country successful in war and peace. What is left is the only true thing remaining for all men—sex: healthy, robust, joyful sex. Not love—Heller carefully draws the distinction—for love means entanglements and involvements that will eventually lead to phoniness. It is not so curious that love itself falls victim to a society in which true feeling had better stop at orgasm. Heller's non-treatment of love is of course indicative of his [140] attitude, not of an inability: love is martyred amidst people whose every feeling is promiscuous. To expect more from them, even from Yossarian, is to accept their folly as truth.

The nightmarish scenes of *Catch-22* which convey its tragic sense culminate in the cosmic nightmare of Chapter XXXIX, "The Eternal City." Once glorious, Rome is now a "dilapidated shell," as though modern Goths and Vandals had destroyed everything in their path; or as if a modern God had visited his wrath upon it. The monuments are shattered, the streets contain surrealistic nightmares, the people seem the husks and shards of humanity. All values are overturned, all hopes and dreams made valueless; sanity itself becomes a meaningless term. Everything visible—an emblem of what lies beneath—is off balance, out of key. The center of western religion is godless. Here we have Heller's immoral world, a scene from Hieronymus Bosch's Hell, in which Aarfy can freely rape and kill while Yossarian is picked up for lacking a pass. Caught in such a dark world, Yossarian can only run toward the light. If he stays, he will—like Milo and the others—eat and sleep well at the expense even of those who share his ideals.

An early version of *Catch-22* was itself much more nightmarish in its development than the published book. Evidently strongly influenced by *Ulysses*, Heller had originally tried to make the narrative typically Joycean: that is, full of intermittent streams of consciousness and involutions of time. Further, he suggested the narrative through recurring symbols of devastation and doom, eliminating in several places orthodox plot structure.

As a consequence, the reader who missed the significance of the symbols—and they were by no means clear, even peripherally—was lost in a surrealistic forest of words from which there was no escape. Added to the stream, the symbols, and the involutions of time was an impressionistic treatment of characters and events, a half-toned, half-tinted development that seemed neither to go forward nor to remain still. [141]

For the final version, Heller retained in its entirety only the first chapter of the original and then in part straightened out both the narrative line and the character development. Words themselves became a kind of language midway between evocation and denotation; at its worst, the language overextends itself, but at its best it suits Heller's zany, absurd world. So often misunderstood, his language would not of course fit a rational theme-it is itself an attempt to convey a world beyond the logic of the word.

For Heller, the war is a perfect objective correlative, as it was for Hemingway in *A Farewell to Arms.* Both, however, are war novels only in limited ways. The war gave Heller, even more than it did Hemingway, the community against which Yossarian can operate. The military becomes an entire society, looming so large that it casts its shadow on the horizon and blocks out everything beyond. Such is the nature of the curse, and it is this—the indefinable character of what one is a part of—that Heller can exploit. The war or the military (not the enemy) provides the conflict, makes anything possible. The norm is no longer any determinable quality: each action gives birth to a norm of its own. Unlike the fixed roles that people assume in civilian life, in war they hide behind masks (uniforms) and redefine themselves, like the protean creatures in Ovid's *Metamorphoses.* Here, Yossarian—the ancient Assyrian, the modern Armenian, but really a wandering New York Jew—can give vent to his disgust and revulsion, and through laughter show us that our better selves may still turn up in Sweden. [142]

MINNA DOSKOW

The Night Journey in Catch-22

Sanford Pinsker in his article on *Catch-22* characterizes Heller's hero as a *puer eternis.*[1] As a result, he sees Yossarian refusing the "traditional journey of learning in manhood,"[2] and the ending of the novel becomes Yossarian's escape from reality to Sweden, a kind of never-never land. Although Yossarian may be innocent, as Mr. Pinsker claims, at the beginning of the novel, and his belief that he can work within the establishment using their rules for his own ends is incredibly naive, he does, I believe, learn better, and after his symbolic journey to the underworld, represented by his trip through the dark streets of Rome, he comes to a new recognition of the meaning of his experience and reaches a new knowledge in the hospital after his near death, achieving what one could perhaps call an informed innocence. His flight to Sweden is not an escape but an alternative as he himself tells us: "I'm not running *away* from my responsibilities. I'm running *to* them."[3] Thus, a definite and meaningful pattern of action emerges from the novel, and one which is startlingly similar to the archetypal pattern that characterizes classical epic or romance. Heller's hero, like those of *The Odyssey, The Aeneid* and *The Divine Comedy,* is involved in a struggle with an alien force which he must and eventually does overcome in order to survive. He too reaches a crisis in his struggle, undertakes a journey to the underworld, emerges with new knowledge, and is finally

Twentieth Century Literature, Vol. 12, No. 4 (January 1967), pp. 186–193. © Hofstra University.

29

victorious, prevailing against the forces marshalled against him. From the outset of the novel, Yossarian struggles against a hostile establishment and the code it maintains for controlling the society it rules, that is, Catch-22, the principle of power which states "they have a right to do anything we can't stop them from doing." (416) However, the confrontation reaches its climax and emerges most clearly and intensely in the night journey episode of the last chapters, and in the action that follows from it. A close analysis of these chapters (39–42) will show how Yossarian through his participation in the archetypal pattern of the descent and renewal of the romance hero achieves his new perception which culminates quite logically in his flight to Sweden:

When Yossarian goes AWOL to Rome in an attempt to save the kid sister of Nately's whore, we witness a crisis in his continuous battle with the establishment. In his previous conflicts with those forces, Yossarian was consistently foiled by 'Catch-22.' However, his absolute and unconditional refusal to fly any more missions after Nately's death indicates a new and complete break with the code 'Catch-22' typifies. In the subsequent trip to Rome his efforts are not only directed at saving his own life, but also those of future generations represented by the still virginal twelve year old sister. "Every victim," he tells us in explaining his action, "was a culprit, every culprit a victim, and somebody had to stand up sometime to try to break the lousy chain of inherited habit that was imperiling them all." (414) He is out to break the "mind-forged manacles" that imprison men. While this enemy is far different from the medieval dragon or classical monster whom the romantic hero must overcome, yet it is equally menacing to human life, can prove equally fatal, and Yossarian must overcome it in order to achieve his own renewal.

As he plunges into Rome, a city of universal destruction, Yossarian begins his symbolic descent to the underworld. At first he tries to enlist the aid of the authorities in control. But his initial naive attempt to work with the Roman police is blasted by their essential indifference and by Milo Minderbinder's preference for black-market tobacco profits to the salvation of little girls. Yossarian, realizing that the police will not help him, then begins the journey on his own. However, since it is a journey born out of pure frustration it is cast in a somber and ironic rather than a truly romantic mode. He has already learned that he can expect no help from the police, and before his journey is over he will further discover that the police themselves are the enemy and that he must protect himself from them.

His emergence from the police station leaves him at the bottom of a hill in a "dark tomblike street," obviously suggestive of an entrance into the underworld with its murky atmosphere smelling of death. However, it is not an otherworldly or spiritual hell but the hell that man has created both spiritually and physically here on earth that Yossarian enters. And what the reader sees as he accompanies Yossarian on his harrowing night journey through the labyrinthine streets of this Roman hell is:

> all the shivering stupefying misery in a world that never yet had provided enough heat and food and justice for all but an ingenious and unscrupulous handful. (421)

Nevertheless, the striking atmosphere of misery and pain leads to the inevitable comparison with hell which becomes more relevant and forceful as Yossarian travels further along the streets encountering sickness, hunger, poverty, sadistic cruelty and coercion and viewing an entire gallery of mutilated bodies and warped souls.

The pervasive gloom through which Yossarian travels resembles Dante's City of Dis or Homer's City of Perpetual Mist in its absence of penetrating light. In scene after scene of his journey, from the yellow light bulbs that "sizzled in the dampness like wet torches" (421) immediately outside the police station, to the "ghostly blackness," and "dense impenetrable shadows of a narrow winding side street," (423) through the "drizzling, drifting, lightless, nearly opaque gloom," (426) the darkness remains impenetrable. Even the apparent sources of light cannot shatter the gloom. The yellow light bulbs do not enable Yossarian to look around him, and the "flashing red spotlight" (423) attached to the M.P.'s jeep only adds a lurid glow to the picture of the young lieutenant in convulsions. Nor do the amber fog lights of the ambulance which is used to incarcerate the helpless victims of the police light up the scene, and even the street lights themselves appear as "curling lampposts with eerie shimmering glare surrounded by smoky brown mist." (423) The only exception, the piercing white light of Tony's restaurant, is expressly forbidden to the ordinary inhabitants of Rome and to Yossarian as well and is clearly marked "KEEP OUT."

Not only is Yossarian cast into a world without light, but the city itself appears strangely distorted and out of perspective. "The tops of the sheer buildings slanted in weird surrealistic perspective and the street seemed tilted." (421) The lampposts seem to curl, and together with the mists the shadows succeed in "throwing everything visible off-balance." (423) The shimmering uncertainty of forms helps to upset Yossarian's equilibrium and enhance the unearthly quality of the scene through surrealistic distortion.

Even the elements conspire to intensify the hostile and bizarre nature of the setting. From the outset Yossarian finds himself pelted by a frigid rain, exposed and vulnerable, denied shelter and forced to huddle for warmth and protection against the raw night. Moreover, the rain does not, as might be expected in another region, cleanse what it touches, but only besmirches it.

Thus the street is "rain-blotched," (423) the mist is "smoky brown," (423) and Yossarian stumbles upon "human teeth lying on the drenched glistening pavement near splotches of blood kept sticky by the pelting raindrops poking each one like sharp finger nails." (424) The rain lends this street a bloody luminescence intensifying the gory and grotesque scene, and the drops themselves seem to sharpen the probing cruelty.

The distortion of the visible world surrounding Yossarian is accompanied by an equal distortion of all that is audible. Just as the yellow bulbs outside the police station lend the street an eerie light, so do the sizzling sounds they emit echo the effect. However, the most common sounds that Yossarian hears as he travels through the streets of Rome are human cries, the sobs and screams of the victims of hell. The scream of the child being beaten, the sympathetic weeping of a woman in the crowd, the "snarling, inhuman voices" (423) of the spectators, the cries of the women being raped begging "Please don't," or in drunken variation "Pleeshe don't," (423) the scream of the man being clubbed by the police, "Police! Help! Police!" (415) all swell the chorus of pain, the cacophony of hell. In addition, the accents of the torturers are also audible and add to the clamour. We hear the hellish accents of the M.P.'s who mock and jeer at the suffering young lieutenant in "raucous laughter." (423)

Even inanimate objects take on the disturbing characteristics of their surroundings. Announcing its arrival with jangling clamour, the ambulance is distorted into an engine of torture, not a vehicle of mercy, and it comes not to aid the soldier with the mutilated mouth, but to incarcerate the screaming civilian who clasps his books to him in an uneven struggle with the club-wielding policemen arresting him. The fountain which Yossarian hopes will help guide him out of hell is dry, and becomes a perfect symbol of the aridity and barren aspect of the surrounding wasteland. The "haunting incongruous noise" (423) that Yossarian hears of a snow shovel scraping against a rain soaked street adds a weirdly surrealistic note suggesting the meaningless and endless labor of some modern Sisyphus.

The labor of hell is characteristically unproductive, endless and pointless. Thus, the labor represented by the sound of the scraping shovel is adapted to its location as is the aimless action of the six soldiers trying to help the epileptic young lieutenant. In their well-intentioned impotence they only succeed in moving him from car hood to sidewalk and back again achieving nothing. The realization of the futility of their attempts to alleviate his pain and help their friend and of the inevitable isolation of the suffering man cause "A quiver of moronic panic [to] spread from one straining brute face to another." (422) Their effort is unproductive and his isolation remains unaffected.

The only actions that yield results in hell are cruelty and coercion, While the soldiers are powerless to relieve the suffering of their sick friend, the M.P.'s can mock it and so intensify it. And, in the same way, the sympathetic woman is powerless to stop the man from beating his dog and must retreat "sheepishly with an abject and humiliated air" (424) from the sadist's stick which can easily be turned against her. The crowd watching the child being beaten has already recognized the limits of action, and thus no one moves in even a futile attempt to stop the beating. No one here still hopes to avert the surrounding cruelty, and the sympathetic only weep "silently into a dirty dish towel." (424)

As Yossarian proceeds further and further into hell on his journey, he witnesses a progression in the inhumanity and brutality that surrounds him. The figures he sees become more horribly maimed, the mutilation becomes more inclusive and extensive, and the possibility for action more limited. The imagery proceeds in a crescendo of distortion and pain until it excludes all possibility of redemption or love, and even the futile attempts to help that he observed toward the beginning of his journey are absent. Yossarian, much like Dante in his progress through the Inferno, thus passes through the various levels of hell necessary for his final emergence as a new person having learned his proper course of action on the verge of entering a new realm. Moreover, accompanying the progression in Yossarian's surroundings, is a progression in Yossarian's own role in the action, again necessary if he is to learn from his hell journey.

Although Yossarian is, from the beginning, haunted by his surroundings and feels compassion for the souls he sees in torment, he is not an integral part of the hell he walks through. He is an alien observer proceeding in "lonely torture, feeling estranged," (422) isolated although not insulated from his surroundings. He feels a sense of his own difference and of alienation from those around him.

> . . . he thought he knew how Christ must have felt as he walked
> through the world, like a psychiatrist through a ward full of nuts,
> like a victim through a prison full of thieves. (424)

The perception fills him with dread and he tries to escape from the world surrounding him. However, despite his efforts to flee, there is no escape until he has gone through all of hell and until his isolation too has been broken down. In spite of all his efforts not to see and not to hear what is around him, he cannot avoid the sights and sounds of torment, and each turning only takes him farther into the labyrinthine hell of the Roman streets. Even when he sights a familiar landmark, the dry fountain, which he believes will guide him to the officer's quarters, he manages only to come upon another instance of brutality: the man beating the dog. Unlike Raskolnikov, whose dream this scene reminds him of, Yossarian cannot dispel the terror by awakening. The nightmare world is his reality and he must go on in this world observing repeated torments until he recognizes this and recognizes his own involvement in that world as well.

Only after Yossarian comprehends the warning shout uttered by one of the victims of the police:

> 'Police! Help! Police! . . . a heroic warning from the grave by a doomed friend to everyone who was *not* a policeman with a club and a gun and a mob of other policemen with clubs and guns to back him up. (425)

when he recognizes the forces that control the world for what they are, does a distinct change occur in his role. For the first time in his journey, Yossarian ceases to be the alien observer isolated from his surroundings. He feels the threat extended to himself as well as to the others around him, identifying him somewhat with them. He also recognizes a direct possibility for action, a distinct opportunity to help the old woman of eighty with the bandaged ankles who is chasing the burly woman half her age. But he responds in the same way as the other inhabitants of hell. Like the passive crowd watching the beating of the child, he does nothing. His failure to act identifies him more closely with the shade-like victims he has observed, and now he no longer observes the action from outside but from within it. This change in his role makes him flee not in dread this time, but in shame since he recognizes his identity with those around him and shares their guilt. Thus, "he darted furtive, guilty glances back as he fled in defeat." (426) He, like all the other inhabitants of Rome, has given in to the forces in control and is defeated since he has allowed the principles ruling hell to rule him as well. Brought to acknowledge that "mobs with clubs were in control everywhere," (426) he also now admits that he has neither the power nor the will to oppose them. This explicit recognition of his defeat foreshadows his later capitulation to the Colonels (the ruling minions of that enormous and organized "mob with clubs"—the army) who embody the extension of the ruling principle in the hellish world beyond Rome.

Yossarian, no longer separated from the world around him, is tortured in the same way as the figures he has passed. The only image that he can salvage from the picture of universal corruption is the memory of Michaela, the plain, simple-minded and hard working maid who served in the officers' apartment and who had somehow retained her innocence amid her savage surroundings. His rush towards her is a last attempt to save himself from complete despair. However, only her violated and mutilated body lying on the pavement is there to welcome him, "the pitiful, ominous, gory spectacle of the broken corpse." (427) Aarfy has already raped and murdered her. Thus, the one apparent departure from the picture of universal deformity and perversion has become the sacrificial victim of that deformity and perversion. The demonic distortion that has corrupted the world culminates in the image of Michaela's maimed body, the rape and killing of the one girl associated with the army who was not a whore, and the final resolving chord in the demonic crescendo that has been building throughout the journey is sounded.

In a further change of role which reiterates his position at the inception of the journey, Yossarian, no longer the observer, no longer passive, challenges the world around him in a last appeal for justice and order, for the vindication of humane ideals. He shouts: "you can't take the life of another human being and get away with it, even if she is just a poor servant girl." (428) It is inevitable that this appeal be denied by the forces in control. Thus, morality is finally and completely turned inside out; moral law or justice has completely degenerated into rule through naked power; the "mobs with clubs" are in full control, and "mere anarchy is loosed upon the world." As the agents of retribution are heard on the stairs and Aarfy slowly turns green in anticipation of punishment, Yossarian's absurd hope that order will be restored to the chaos he has been wandering in all night is blasted. The "two large brawny M.P.'s with icy eyes and firm sinewy unsmiling jaw" (429) who appear act in perfect consistency with hellish logic and with 'Catch-22.'

> They arrested Yossarian for being in Rome without a pass.
> They apologized to Aarfy for intruding and led Yossarian away
> between them, gripping him under each arm with fingers as hard
> as steel manacles. (429)

As if to emphasize the metamorphosis of humane law into its demonic opposite, the M.P.'s no longer retain even their superficial humanity; their flesh having turned to steel, they resemble unyielding machinery rather than men.

After Yossarian has personally experienced the rule of the demonic principles as well as observed their universal application, he consents to become a part of this rule. Thus, as his actions in relation to the old woman of eighty have intimated, he accepts Colonel Korn's and Colonel Cathcart's "odious deal," knowing it is disgusting and deceitful. At this moment he is rechristened with a hellish name, taking on a new and appropriate identity. "Everyone calls me Yo-Yo!" (440) he tells us, accepting a name he once found noxious.

When he accepts the Colonels' deal after his return from Rome, Yossarian is for the first time in the novel in complete harmony with his environment. He has joined in the devilish conspiracy that holds sway over the world and whose undisguised sinister image has been evident throughout the novel, although most clearly and intensely seen in the night journey episode.

Having then sunk into hell itself, no longer resisting its influence but becoming part of it, a lost soul himself, Yossarian approaches the absolute depths of the abyss and glimpses a demonic phantom. This is the "strange man with the mean face," the "spiteful scowl," the sharp fingers, the "nasty smirk" and "malicious laugh" who eludes Yossarian's grasp and will only say, "We've got your pal, buddy. We've got your pal." (442) Nor will he elucidate when Yossarian, with a flicker of sardonic humor on Heller's part, inquires "What the *hell* are you talking about?" (445) (Italics are Heller's.) However, we must remember that Yossarian is still anesthetized at the moment of his vision. Thus, his physical state of induced unconsciousness partially accounts for his new submissive attitude. It also corresponds to his spiritual or moral state in which consciousness has as well been put to sleep temporarily, as exemplified in his acceptance of the "odious deal." In this state he can see the devil without really recognizing him or perceiving the meaning of his message. The vision is nevertheless vital to any new perception Yossarian will be able to achieve after the both literal and figurative anesthesia wears off.

After his vision, Yossarian once more rebels and refuses the Colonels' deal. He emerges, in this way, from unconsciousness and from the abyss into whose depths he had to descend before his renewal or resurrection could occur. Just as Dante descends into the nethermost region of hell, passes Satan himself, and uses the devil to pull himself out of hell, so Yossarian uses his Satanic vision to extricate himself from his hell in order finally to approach a place where there still is hope. In both cases the contact with the devil is mandatory. As Virgil tells Dante, "There is no way/but by such stairs to rise above such evil."[4]

After he passes the devil whose words recall Snowden's death to him, Yossarian glimpses the truth which gleams from the haunting memory: "The spirit gone, man is garbage." (450) He now realizes that it is necessary to retain some other quality along with the mere existence that he has been struggling to preserve since the beginning of the book and that he had guaranteed through his "deal." Armed by his recent experience in hell and his emergence from it through the recognition of what life means, he has once more achieved the strength to say no to the tyrants in control. "I'm not making any deals with Colonel Korn," (450) he tells us. Unlike his earlier instinctive rebellion, his new denial is informed by the experience of the depths of hell and by his new recognition. Only through his exploration of the abyss has he reached the perception which may lead to his eventual salvation. And it is possible salvation that is offered by Yossarian's projected plan of flight to Sweden. Perhaps it is only Purgatory that Yossarian will gain (as Dante does at this point in his progress), but it is a world where life is at least possible.

Yossarian now realizes that accepting the Colonels' deal would be, in his words, "a way to lose myself," (456) would be, that is, his own damnation through complete surrender to the demonic powers in control. But what he is searching for is a way to "save" himself (to use his own words again) in a world that both he and Major Danby, the university professor turned army officer, agree contains "no Hope." (458) This last phrase is reiterated throughout their entire discussion of escape so that we can hardly fail to think of the cardinal feature of hell and also of the motto that Dante tells us is inscribed over the gates of hell. In addition, Heller's language heightens our awareness of the scene's implications. The words "lose," "save," and "no hope" echo rather forcefully the conventional religious language describing the soul's struggle for salvation. From the latter we know that hell is a place of no hope and that it is a spiritual state as well as a geographical location. We know that the lost soul goes to hell and conversely, that hell is the condition of the lost soul. And finally, we know that the soul can only achieve salvation by recognizing evil and resisting or overcoming it. It is obvious how appropriately this describes Yossarian's progress in the novel, shown most clearly in the chapters just discussed.

Thus, Yossarian's departure for Sweden is the concrete external representation of his spiritual renewal that expressed itself first in his recognition of man's nature and in his subsequent refusal of the "deal." As Yossarian knows, Sweden is no paradise or utopia; there are no such things in the world this novel depicts. In escaping to Sweden, Yossarian also recognizes that he is "not running away from responsibilities," (461) but toward them, that salvation entails responsibility, and that he will have to be ever-vigilant in order to remain free of the demonic powers of the world he is forsaking. Thus he leaves taking the necessary risks and exulting in the new feeling of freedom and hope that he now has. If it is a miracle as the chaplain claims, then it is a miracle achieved through Yossarian's own will and conscience and one which leaves him open to ambush and knife attack from such characters as Nately's whore. It is she who marks his departure from the demonic realm, his crossing of the gulf, she who is herself caught in the endlessly repeated and repeatedly unsuccessful actions characteristic of hell, and who thus represents the threats that Yossarian will have to overcome on his new course.

NOTES

1. Sanford Pinsker, "Heller's *Catch-22:* The Protest of *a Puer Etetnis," Critique,* VII (Winter 1964–1965): pp. 150–162.

2. *Ibid.,* p. 151.

3. Joseph Heller, *Catch-22* (New York, 1962), p. 461. All quotations and page references are from the Dell edition.

4. Dante Alighieri, *The Inferno,* trans. John Ciardi (New York, 1954), Canto XXXIV, 11: pp. 83–84.

JOSEPH HELLER

Catch-22 *Revisited*

Where the airfield stood, there is nothing. The planes are gone, the tents are gone. It's almost as though there had never been an American air base here on the eastern shore of Corsica. It's almost, in fact, as though there had never been a war. . . .

Bastia, the largest city in Corsica, was empty, hot and still when we arrived. It was almost one o'clock, and the people in Corsica, like those in Italy, duck for cover at lunchtime and do not emerge until very late in the afternoon, when the harsh and suffocating summer heat has begun to abate. The hotel in Île Rousse, on the other side of the island, had sent a taxi for us. And driving the taxi was François, a sporty, jaunty, chunky, barrel-chested, agreeable ex-cop. He was in his forties, and he wore a white mesh sport shirt, neat slacks and new leather sandals.

There were two roads from Bastia to Île Rousse, a high road and a low road. "Take the low road," said my wife, who has a fear of dying.

"*D'accord*," François agreed, and began driving straight up. In a minute or two the city of Bastia lay directly below us.

"Is this the low road?" asked my wife.

It was the high road, François informed us. He had decided, for our own good, that we should take the scenic high road to Île Rousse and then, if we still insisted, the low road coming back. François was indeed an

Holiday Magazine (April 1967): pp. 44–61, 120, 141–142, 145.

agreeable person; he agreed to everything we proposed and then did what he thought best.

I had remembered from my military service that there were mountains in Corsica, but I had never appreciated how many there were or how high they rose. For the record, there is one peak 9,000 feet high and eight more than 8,000. It was one of these 8,000-foot mountains we were now crossing. The higher we drove, the more the land began to resemble the American West. We soon saw cactus growing beside the road, and then eagles wheeling in the sky—down below us!

After about two hours we had crossed the island and came to the other coast, still riding high above it. We drove southward now, passing, on a small beach, some German pillboxes no one had bothered to remove. Soon we saw Île Rousse resting in a haze below us between the mountains and the shore. The road descended slowly. We continued through the town and out to the hotel, which stood almost at the end of a narrow spit.

My main purpose in coming to Corsica again was to visit the site of our air base, to tramp the ground where our tents had stood and see what changes had occurred to the airstrip on which our planes had taken off and landed so many times. This was not in Île Rousse but back on the other side of the island, about fifty miles south of Bastia. I had come to Île Rousse now because it's a summer resort, and because the Air Force had a rest camp there during the war. I was disappointed in what I found now. The Napoléon Bonaparte, the large luxury hotel that had accommodated the officers, was not open. The hotel in which enlisted men had stayed was dilapidated. There was not, of course, any of the wartime noise, energy and excitement. With the exception of Rome and Naples, almost all the towns and cities I was to visit that were associated with my war experiences brought me the same disappointment. They no longer had any genuine connection with the war, but it was only through the war that I was acquainted with them.

We went swimming that afternoon. A jukebox at the beach played records by Bob Dylan, the Beatles, the Rolling Stones and Nancy Sinatra. At the tables were a number of teen-age girls and boys, good-looking and ultra cool, down for the season from Nice, Marseilles and even Paris. They were inert and blasé, determinedly paying no more attention to us than they did to each other.

That evening I was taken to dinner by a man who had been an important public official in Île Rousse for eighteen years and would be one still if he had not grown weary of the honor. We drove down the coast several miles to the village of Algajola, where we had dinner in a small new hotel perched on a hill overlooking the water. He introduced me to an old man who had worked at the Hotel Napoléon Bonaparte as a bartender when it was an American rest camp. The old man had nothing unpredictable to offer in the way of recollections. There was much liquor and few women, except for occasions when Army nurses were brought in for dances from other parts of Corsica.

More interesting than the rest camp was my host himself, a stout, generous, dark-complexioned man in his fifties who had been in his youth an authentic *bon vivant*. He had gone to school in Paris and had planned to spend the rest of his life there in pleasure and idleness. Then, in a short period, he had lost his father, uncles and grandfather, and it was necessary for him to return to Corsica to take charge of the family's business affairs. He had lived in Corsica ever since. He really loved Corsica, he told me without conviction, although he missed the opera, the ballet, the theater, literature, good food and wine, and the chance to talk about these things with others who enjoyed them as much as he did. He smiled frequently as he spoke, but his geniality was clouded with a tremendous regret. He had a grown son who was supposed to return for us with the car at ten o'clock. He would arrive here on time, I was assured. And precisely at ten his son appeared.

"He is always on time," my host remarked sorrowfully as we rose to go. "He does not even have enough imagination to come late once in a while." Here, in a small village in Corsica, I had found Ethan Frome, for this was truly a tale of blasted hopes and wasted years that he had related.

Early the next day we headed back across the island in search of the old air base. François made us listen as he sounded the horn of the car. It was a Klaxon. He had installed it for the journey back over the low road, so that we all might be more at ease. Each time we whizzed into a blind curve, I instructed François, *"Sonnez le Klaxon,"* and he was delighted to oblige.

The low road from Île Rousse was very high for part of the way. But the land soon leveled out, and we found ourselves whizzing along comfortably on flat ground. Jokingly, I remarked to François that I might bring him back with me to New York, where I knew he would excel in the Manhattan traffic. François pounced so readily on this chance at the big time that I had to discourage him quickly. A New York taxi driver, I told him, works for other people, makes little money and *n'est pas content, jamais content,* and only someone very rich, like Alan Arkin, could afford his own car and chauffeur. While François was still pondering this information solemnly, the fan belt snapped, and a wild clatter sounded from the front of the car. François eased the car softly to a stop at the side of the road, in back of a small truck already parked there. Two men lifted grease-stained faces from beneath the truck's open hood and looked at us questioningly. It turned out that we had been forced to come to a stop, purely by chance, directly in front of the only garage in miles.

In minutes we were ready to proceed. François, while asking directions to the old American air base, chanced to mention that I was one of the officers who had been stationed there. Both mechanics turned to me with huge grins, and one of them called for his wife to come out of the house to see me. To François this reaction was electrifying; it had not occurred to him that he was driving a potential dignitary whose presence could enlarge his own importance. Chest out, the cop in authority again, he pushed his way between me and this welcoming crowd of three, keeping them back as he screened their questions. After a minute he declared abruptly, to us as well as to them, that it was necessary for us to go. They waved after us as we went driving away.

I was unable to spy anything more familiar than the Mediterranean. Instead of the ageless landmarks I recalled, I saw Fire Island cottages that *I know* had not been there during the war. We did, however, find the crossroad to Cervione, another mountain village to which we used to drive in a jeep every now and then for a glass of wine in a cool, darkened bar. The bar was still there. It was larger now, and much brighter. Coca-Cola was advertised, and a refrigerated case offered *gelati alemagne*, German ice cream, direct from Leghorn, in Italy. The several patrons inside were a generation or two younger than the silent, brown, old men in work clothes I remembered. These wore summer sport shirts and wash-and-wear trousers.

François entered first and announced to all in the room that he had brought them an American officer who had been stationed at the airfield below and had returned for a visit after so many years because he loved Corsica and loved the people of Cervione. The response was tumultuous. Ice cream and cold soda appeared for my wife and children; beer, wine and other flavorful alcoholic drinks appeared for me. I was, it turned out, the only American from the air base who had ever returned, which helped account for the exuberant celebration. My wife asked through the noise whether we could have lunch in Cervione. A meal was ordered by telephone, and we walked to the restaurant ten minutes later, following François, who swaggered ahead with such inflated self-importance that I was certain he had exaggerated enormously the part I had played in beating Hitler and vanquishing Japan.

The only restaurant in Cervione was on the second floor of the only hotel, and it seemed to be part of the living quarters of the family who ran it. A large table had been made ready for us in the center. Food began arriving the moment we sat down, and some of the things looked pretty strange.

"Don't drink the water," my wife warned the children, who ignored her, since they were thirsty, and no other suitable beverage was available.

"Don't drink the water," François said to me, and popped open a bottle of wine.

My wife and children got by on cooked ham, bread and cheese. I ate everything set before me and asked for more. The main dish was a slice of what seemed like pan-broiled veal, which was probably goat, since kid is a specialty of the island.

Back at the bar we had coffee, and then a strange and unexpected ceremony took place. The entire room fell silent while a shy, soft-spoken young man stepped toward us hesitantly and begged permission to give us a *cadeau*, a gift, a large, beautiful earthenware vase from the small pottery shop from which he gained his livelihood. It was touching, sobering; I was sorry I had nothing with which to reciprocate.

After Cervione, the airfield, when we finally found it, was a great disappointment. A lighthouse that had served as a landmark for returning planes left no doubt we had the right place, but there was nothing there now but reeds and wild bushes. And standing among them in the blazing sunlight was no more meaningful, and no less eccentric, than standing reverently in a Canarsie lot. I felt neither glad nor sorry I had come; I felt only foolish that I was there.

"Is this what we came to see?" grumbled my son.

"The airfield was right here," I explained. "The bombers used to come back from Italy and France and land right out that way."

"I'm thirsty," said my daughter.

"It's hot," said my wife.

"I want to go back," said my son.

"We aren't going back to Île Rousse," I said. "We're spending the night in Bastia." "I mean back to New York!" he claimed angrily. "I'm not interested in your stupid airfield. The only airfield I want to see is John F. Kennedy."

"Be nice to Daddy," my daughter said to him, with a malicious twinkle. "He's trying to recapture his youth."

I gave my daughter a warning scowl and looked about again, searching for a propeller, a wing, an airplane wheel, for some dramatic marker to set this neglected stretch of wasteland apart from all the others along the shore. I saw none; and it would have made no difference if I had. I was a man in search of a war, and I had come to the wrong place. My war was over and gone, and even my ten-year-old son was smart enough to realize that. What the grouchy kid didn't realize, though, was that *his* military service was still ahead; and I could have clasped him in my arms to protect him as he stood there, hanging half outside the car with his look of sour irritation.

"Can't we go?" he pleaded.

"Sure, let's go," I said, and told François to take us straight to Bastia.

François shot away down the road like a rocket and screeched to a stop at the first bar he came to. He had, he mumbled quickly, to go see his aunt, and he bounded outside the car before we could protest. He was back in thirty seconds, licking his upper lip and looking greatly refreshed. He stopped three more times at bars on the way in, to see his mother-in-law, his best friend and his old police captain, returning with a larger smile and a livelier step from each brief visit.

François was whistling, and we were limp with exhaustion, by the time we arrived in the city, where the heat was unbearable. Add humidity to Hell, and you have the climate of Bastia in early July.

François and I went to the nearest bar for a farewell drink. He was jaunty and confident again. "New York?" he asked hopefully.

I shook my head. He shrugged philosophically and lifted his glass in a toast. *"Tchin-tchin,"* he said, and insisted on paying for the drinks.

The first time I came to Corsica was in May, 1944, when I joined the bomb group as a combat replacement. After four days I was assigned to my first mission, as a wing bombardier. The target was the railroad bridge at Poggibonsi.

Poor little Poggibonsi. Its only crime was that it happened to lie outside Florence along one of the few passageways running south through the Apennine Mountains to Rome, which was still held by the Germans. And because of this small circumstance, I had been brought all the way across the ocean to help kill its railroad bridge.

The mission to Poggibonsi was described to us in the briefing room as a milk run—that is, a mission on which we were not likely to encounter flak or enemy planes. I was not pleased to hear this. I wanted action, not security. I wanted a sky full of dogfights, daredevils and billowing parachutes. I was twenty-one years old. I was dumb. I tried to console myself with the hope that someone, somewhere along the way, would have the good grace to open fire at us. No one did.

As a wing bombardier, my job was to keep my eyes on the first plane in our formation, which contained the lead bombardier. When I saw his bomb-bay doors open, I was to open mine. The instant I saw his bombs begin to fall, I would press a button to release my own. It was as simple as that—or should have been.

I guess I got bored. Since there was no flak at Poggibonsi, the lead bombardier opened his bomb-bay doors early and took a long, steady approach. A lot of time seemed to pass. I looked down to see how far we were from the target. When I looked back up, the bombs from the other planes were already falling. I froze with alarm for another second or two. Then I squeezed my button. I closed the bomb-bay doors and bent forward to see where the bombs would strike, pleading silently for the laws of gravitational acceleration to relax just enough to allow my bombs to catch up with the others.

The bombs from the other planes fell in an accurate, concentrated pattern that blasted a wide hole in the bridge. The bombs from my plane blasted a hole in the mountains several miles beyond.

It was my naïve hope that no one would notice my misdemeanor; but in the truck taking us from the planes a guy in a parachute harness demanded: "Who was the bombardier in the number two plane?"

"I was," I answered sheepishly.

"You dropped late," he told me, as though it could have escaped my attention. "But we hit the bridge."

Yeah, I thought, but I hit the mountain.

A few days after I returned to Italy from Corsica with my family, we rode through Poggibonsi on our way south to Siena to see an event there called the Palio. The railroad bridge at Poggibonsi has been repaired and is now better than ever. The hole in the mountains is still there.

As soon as we checked in at our busy hotel in Siena, a flushed, animated woman in charge smiled and said, "Watch out for pickpockets! They'll steal your money, your checks, your jewelry and your cameras! Last year we had three guests who were robbed!"

She uttered this last statistic in a triumphant whoop, as though in rivalry with another hotel that could boast only two victims. The woman cradled an infant in her arms, her grandchild; her daughter, a tall, taciturn girl in her twenties, worked at a small tabulating machine. Our own children, in one of those miraculous flashes of intuition, decided not to attend the Palio but to remain at the hotel.

Something like 40,000 people packed their way into the standing-room section of the public square to watch the climax of this traditional competition between the city's seventeen *con-trade,* or wards. Soon many began collapsing from heat exhaustion and were carried beneath the stands by running teams of first-aid workers. Then, up behind the last row of seats in our section, there appeared without warning a big, fat, bellowing, intoxicated, 200-pound goose with crumbs in his mouth and a frog in his throat. He was not really a goose but an obese and obnoxious drunk who wore the green and white colors of his own *contrada,* which was, I believe, that of the goose or duck or some other bird. He had bullied his way past the ticket taker to this higher vantage point, from which to cheer his *contrada* as it paraded past and to spray hoarse obscenities at the others. Immediately in back of us, and immediately in front of him, was a row of high-school girls from North Carolina, touring Europe under the protection of a slender young American gentleman who soon began to look as though he wished he were somewhere else. One of the girls complained steadily to him in her Southern accent.

"How do you say policeman in Italian? I want you to call that policeman, do you hear? That Italian is spitting on me every time he yells something. And he smells. I don't want that smelly Italian standing up here behind me."

With us at the Palio were Prof. Frederick Karl, the Conrad authority from City College in New York, and his beautiful wife, the Countess
D'Orestiglio, who is an Italian from Caserta.

The countess, who has a blistering temper, was ready to speak out impe-
riously, but could not decide to whom. She found both principals in this situation equally offensive. Before she could say anything, the horse race started,
and a great roar went up from the crowd that closed off conversation.

We did not see who won, and we did not particularly care. But the out-
come apparently made a very big difference to other people, for as soon as the
race was over three men seized one of the losing jockeys and began to punch
him severely. Suddenly fist fights were breaking out all over, and thousands
of shouting people were charging wildly in every direction. Here was the
atmosphere of a riot, and none of us in the reserved seats dared descend. As
we sat aghast, as exposed and helpless on our benches as stuffed dolls in a
carnival gallery, a quick shriek sounded behind me, and then I was struck by
a massive weight.

It was the drunken goose, who had decided to join his comrades below
by the most direct route. He had simply lunged forward through the row of
girls, almost knocking the nearest ones over, and tumbled down on us. With
instinctive revulsion, Professor Karl and I rolled him away onto the people
in the row ahead of us, who spilled him farther down, on the people below
them. In this fashion our drunken goose finally landed sprawling at the bottom. He staggered to his feet with clenched fists, looking for a moment as
though he would charge into us, but then allowed himself to be swept along
by the torrents of people.

Somehow, after ten or twenty minutes, all the fighting resolved itself
into a collective revelry in which people from different *contrade* embraced
each other, joined in song and pushed ahead to take part in a procession
through the city behind the victorious horse. The sense of danger faded. In
a little while we went down and moved toward the exit, passing pasty-faced
people lying on stretchers and an occasional Peeping Tom staring up solemnly at the legs of women who were still in the stands. Once outside, we
kept near the walls of the buildings, clutching our money, jewelry and cameras, and returned to the hotel, where our two bored and rested children told
us they wanted to return to Florence that same night, and where the woman
in charge was exclaiming rapturously about the race and the three men who
had beaten up a jockey.

While my wife went upstairs to pack, I drew the woman aside to talk to
her about the war. Tell me about it, I asked; you were here. No, she wasn't.
She was in Bologna during the war, which was even better; she was at the
railroad station there with her little girl the day American bombers came to
destroy it in a saturation attack. She ran from the station and took shelter

on the ground somewhere beside a low wall. When the attack was over and she returned to the station, she could not find it. She could not distinguish the rubble of the railroad station from the rubble of the other buildings that had stood nearby. Only then did she grow frightened. And the thought that terrified her—she remembered this still—was that now she would miss her train, for she did not know when it would leave, or from where.

But all that was so far in the past. There was her little girl, now grown up, tall and taciturn at the adding machine, and the woman would much sooner talk about the Palio or about Siena, which at the request of the Pope had been spared by both sides during the war—for Siena is the birthplace of Saint Catherine, patron saint of Italy. So the Germans made their stand a bit farther north, at Poggibonsi, which was almost completely leveled.

Poor Poggibonsi. During those first few weeks we flew missions to rail and highway bridges at Perugia, Arezzo, Orvieto, Cortona, Tivoli and Ferrara. Most of us had never heard of any of these places. We were very young, and few of us had been to college. For the most part, the missions were short—about three hours—and relatively safe. It was not until June 3, for example, that our squadron lost a plane, on a mission to Ferrara. It was not until August 3, over Avignon, in France, that I finally saw a plane shot down in flames, and it was not until August 15, again over Avignon, that a gunner in my plane was wounded and a copilot went a little berserk at the controls and I came to the startling realization—*Good God! They're trying to kill me, too!* And after that it wasn't much fun.

When we weren't flying missions, we went swimming or played baseball or basketball. The food was good—better, in fact, than most of us had ever eaten before—and we were getting a lot of money for a bunch of kids twenty-one years old. Like good soldiers everywhere, we did as we were told. Had we been given an orphanage to destroy (we weren't), our only question would have been, "How much flak?" In vehicles borrowed from the motor pool we would drive to Cervione for a glass of wine or to Bastia to kill an afternoon or evening. It was, for a while, a pretty good life. We had rest camps at Capri and Île Rousse. And soon we had Rome.

On June 4, 1944, the first American soldiers entered Rome. And no more than half a step behind them, I think, must have come our own squadron's resourceful executive officer, for we received both important news flashes simultaneously: the Allies had taken Rome, and our squadron had leased two large apartments there, one with five rooms for the officers and one with about fifteen rooms for the enlisted men. Both were staffed with maids, and the enlisted men, who brought their food rations with them, had women to cook their meals.

Within less than a week friends were returning with fantastic tales of pleasure in a big, exciting city that had girls, cabarets, food, drinking, enter-

tainment and dancing. When my turn came to go, I found that every delicious story was true. I don't think the Colosseum was there then, because no
one ever mentioned it.

Rome was a functioning city when the Germans moved out and the Allies moved in. People had jobs and homes, and there were shops, restaurants,
buses, even movie theaters. Conditions, of course, were far from prosperous;
food, cigarettes and candy were in short supply, and so was money. Clothing
was scarce, although most girls succeeded in keeping their dresses looking
pretty. Electric power was rationed, limiting elevator service, and there was a
curfew that drove Italian families off the street—men, women, children and
tenors—just as they were beginning to enjoy the cool Roman evenings.

Then, as now, the busiest part was the area of the Via Veneto. What
surprised me very strongly was that Rome today is pretty much the same as
it was then. The biggest difference was that in the summer of 1944 the people
in uniform were mainly American and the civilians all Italian, while now
the people in uniform were Italian and the civilians mainly American. The
ambience there was one of pleasure, and it still is. This was vastly different
from Naples, where it was impossible to avoid squalor, poverty and human
misery, about which we could do nothing except give a little money. In this
respect, Naples too is unchanged.

On the Via Veneto today the same buildings stand and still serve pretty
much the same purpose. The American Red Cross building, at which we
would meet for breakfast and shoeshines, was in the Bernini-Bristol Hotel,
at the bottom of the Via Veneto; American rest camps were established in
the Eden, the Ambasciatori and, I think, the Majestic. The Hotel Quirinale
on Via Nazionale was taken over by New Zealanders, and a man at the desk
still neatly preserves a letter of praise he received from their commander. The
men who now work in the motor pool at the American embassy are the same
men who worked as civilian chauffeurs for the American military command
then, and they are eager to relate their war experiences as automobile drivers during the liberation. They could not agree on the location of the Allied
Officers Club, a huge nightclub and dance hall whose name, I think, was
Broadway Bill's. For the war itself, one must go outside the center of the city,
to the Fosse Ardeatine, where more than 300 Italian hostages were massacred by German soldiers.

During the war we came from Corsica by plane and stayed five or six days
each time. Often we would take short walks during the day in search of curios-
ities and new experiences. One time on a narrow street, a sultry, dark-eyed girl
beckoned seductively to me and a buddy from behind a beaded curtain cover-
ing the entrance to a store. We followed her inside and got haircuts. Another
time we were seized by a rather beefy and aggressive young man, who pushed
and pulled us off the sidewalk into his shop, where he swiftly drew caricatures

of our heads on printed cartoon torsos. He asked our names and titled the pictures *Hollywood Joe I and Hollywood Joe II*. Then he took our money, and then he threw us out. The name of the place was the Funny Face Shop, and the name of the artist was Federico Fellini. He has made better pictures since.

Only once in all the times I came there as a soldier did I attempt any serious sight-seeing; then I found myself on a bus with gray-haired majors and with Army nurses who were all at least twenty years older. The stop at the catacombs was only the second on the schedule, but by the time we moved inside, I knew I'd already had enough. As the rest of the group continued deeper into the darkness, I eased myself secretly back toward the entrance and was never heard from again.

Today, of course, it's a different matter in Rome, for the great presence there, I think, is Michelangelo. He complained a lot, but he knew what he was doing. His *Moses* is breathtaking, particularly if you can see it before the groups of guided tourists come swarming up and the people in charge give the same apocryphal explanations of the horns on the head and the narrow sear in the marble of the leg. The story about the latter is that Michelangelo, overwhelmed by the lifelike quality of his statue, hurled his ax at it and cried, "Speak! Why won't you speak?"

The story isn't true. I have seen that statue, and I know that if Michelangelo ever hurled an ax at it, Moses would have picked up the ax and hurled it right back.

With the ceiling of the Sistine Chapel, however, I have recurring trouble. The gigantic fresco has been called the greatest work ever undertaken by a single artist. No summer tourist will ever be able to tell, for no summer tourist will ever be able to see it, his view obstructed by hundreds of others around him. The lines outside are as long as at Radio City Music Hall, and the price of admission is high. Once inside, you walk a mile to get there. And once you arrive, you find yourself in a milling crush of people who raise a deafening babble. Women faint and are stretched out to recover on the benches along the side. Attendants shout at you to keep quiet or keep moving. Jehovah stretches a hand out to Adam and pokes his finger into the head of the Korean in front of you. If you do look up, you soon discover it's a pain in the neck. The ideal way to study the ceiling would be to lie down in the center of the floor. Even then the distance is probably too great for much sense to be made of that swirling maelstrom above. E. M. Forster defined a work of art as being greater than the sum of its parts: I suspect that just the reverse may be true of the Sistine ceiling, that it is much greater in its details than in total.

However, Michelangelo's fresco of the *Last Judgment*, on a wall in the same chapel, is another matter entirely. The wall is forty-four feet wide and forty-eight feet high, and the painting is the most powerful I know. It is the best motion picture ever made. There is perpetual movement in its violent rising and failing, and perpetual drama in its agony and wrath. To be with Michelangelo's *Last Judgment* is to be with Oedipus and King Lear. I want that wall. I would like to have enough money and time someday to fly to Rome just to look at it whenever I felt a yearning to. I know it would always be worth the trip. Better still, I would like to put that wall in my own apartment, where it would always be just a few steps away. But my landlord won't let me.

After Rome was captured by my squadron executive officer, the fighting rapidly moved northward. By the middle of June French forces captured Leghorn, where broken blocks of stone from the battle still lie near the docks and will probably remain forever. On August 13 the Americans were in Florence. Before the Germans evacuated the city and moved up into the mountains beyond, they blew up the bridges across the Arno River; they hesitated about the Ponte Vecchio and then blew the approaches instead, leaving the old bridge standing. The damage at both ends of the Ponte Vecchio has been restored with buildings of stone and design similar to those around them, and only a searching eye can detect that the destruction of the war ever touched there.

Perugia, Arezzo, Orvieto, Siena and Poggibonsi were all on our side of the action now. Pisa was captured on September 2, and the Germans pulled back along the flat coastal land to take positions in the mountains past Carrara. This was the Gothic Line now, extending clear across the country to the Adriatic; they were able to hold it all through the winter and far into the following spring. It was not until the middle of April that the Allies were able to push through to Bologna, and by then the war in Europe was all but over.

Rome, Siena and Florence had all been given over by the Germans in fairly good condition. In the tiny village of Saint Anna, high up in the mountains, past the marble quarries of Carrara, some 700 inhabitants, the entire population, were massacred by the German army in reprisal for the killing of two soldiers. When the deadline came and the town did not produce the guilty partisans, every house was set on fire, and the people were gunned down as they fled into the streets. One can only wonder why people so indifferent to the lives of other human beings would be so sparing of their cities. Perhaps it's because they expected to come back.

Every spring now they do come back, as German tourists thirsting for the sun. Unmarried girls, I have heard, descend in great aggressive crowds on Rimini and other spots along the Adriatic shore in a determined quest for sunburns, sex and sleep, in that order. On the western coast, where we stayed for several weeks on a fourteen-mile stretch of sandy beach known as the Versilian Riviera, menus, signs, notices and price lists are printed in four languages—Italian, English, French and German. This area includes

Viareggio, Camaiore, Pietrasanta, Forte dei Marmi. There was no doubt in June that German families were the main visiting group. By the beginning of July, they had all but vanished. Every year, we were told, they come early and depart before July. The Tuscans, who dislike the Germans with well-guarded propriety, sometimes hint that the Germans leave so soon because the high season starts and rates go up. I suspect there is something more. By July Italy turns hot; there is warm weather closer to home.

The Hotel Byron in Forte dei Marmi is an inexpensive jewel of a family hotel. The rooms are comfortable, the food is meticulously prepared, and the setting is beautiful; but more delightful than any of these are the owner, the manager, the concierge and the entire staff of maids and waiters, who are all exquisitely sweet, polite, accommodating and sympathetic. They would fall to brooding if I snapped at my daughter or my son looked unhappy. A brief compliment to any one member of the staff was enough to bring us grateful smiles from all the rest. This was true in almost every restaurant and hotel in Italy. In Italy a word of praise, particularly for an endeavor of personal service, goes a very long way toward creating happiness.

The owner of the hotel had served in Africa with the Italian army and could tell me nothing from his own experience about the war in Italy. I did not tell anyone at the hotel about mine, for we had flown many missions to targets in this area. We bombed the bridges at Viareggio at least once, those at Pietrasanta at least four times.

I was soon very curious to visit Pietrasanta because of a strange war memorial near the road bridge there. The bridge was new and smooth and spanned a shallow river no wider than a city street, which helped explain why it had been bombed so frequently—it was so easy to repair. The war memorial was a bombed-out house that the people of Pietrasanta had decided to leave standing as an eternal reminder of the German occupation. I almost smiled at the incongruity, for the building stood so close to the bridge that it must certainly have been destroyed by bombs from American planes. On the new bridge was a memorial of another kind, which I found more moving—a small tablet for a girl named Rosa who had been killed there by an automobile not long before.

One day my wife thought she recognized Henry Moore, the famous English sculptor, having lunch at the hotel. The manager confirmed it. It was indeed Henry Moore. He owned property in Forte dei Marmi and had many acquaintances around Viareggio and Pietrasanta. Shortly after that we met Stanley Bleifeld, a sculptor from Weston, Connecticut, and his wife. That made two sculptors we had come upon in a short period of time, and Bleifeld told us about others—Jacques Lipchitz, who owns a spectacular mountain villa on the way to Lucca, and Bruno Lucchesi, who sells, it is said with envy, everything he produces, and many more sculptors who come to this part of

Italy every summer to work and play. They work in bronze, which is cast in Pietrasanta in the foundry of Luigi Tommasi, who thinks they are crazy.

He thinks they are crazy because of the work they do and the money they pay him to have it finished. Tommasi is a smiling, handsome man of about forty in blue Bermuda shorts and dust. His basic source of income is religious objects and, I suppose, leaning towers of Pisa—good, durable items of established appeal. But he is happy to set this work aside every summer when his artists arrive. Neither he nor his workers can convince themselves that the clay models they receive are deliberate; he has, however, given up trying to correct the errors he sees, for he has found in the past that such good intentions have not been appreciated. His foundry is a striking treasure house of works in various stages of progress. As we walked through, Bleifeld could not restrain himself from flicking out nervously with his thumbnail at a piece of residue on a casting of one of his own works, while a young laborer regarded him coolly. In the yard stood a tall and swarming statue by Lipchitz, a fecund and suggestive work of overpowering force and beauty that will soon stand before a building in California.

Florence is the nearest large city to Forte dei Marmi, and we went there often to revisit the masterpieces of Michelangelo and Botticelli and to buy earrings for my daughter. Florence is the best city in the world in which to have nothing to do, for it offers so much that *is* worth doing. Except to my son; he had nothing to do but review all the uncomfortable places he had visited. One evening in Florence we all went to the race track to watch the trotters. Children are admitted, and many play politely on the grass in back of the grandstand or sit on the benches with their parents and watch the horses run. The minimum bet is small. The race track is a family affair, social and safe. My son picked four straight winners and came out eight dollars ahead. The next day he no longer wanted to go home. He wanted to go back to the race track. There were no races that night, so I took him to the opera instead. After that he wanted to go home.

Soon he was a step nearer, for we were leaving Italy by train, on our way to Avignon. We arrived in a debilitating heat wave that settled for days over all of southern Europe. My family had never heard of Avignon before from anyone but me, just as most of us in Corsica had never heard of Avignon before the day we were sent there to bomb the bridge spanning the River Rhône. One exception was a lead navigator from New England who had been a history teacher before the war and was overjoyed in combat whenever he found himself in proximity to places that had figured importantly in his studies. As our planes drew abreast of Orange and started to turn south to the target, he announced on the intercom:

"On our right is the city of Orange, ancestral home of the kings of Holland and of William III, who ruled England from 1688 to 1702."

"And on our left," came back the disgusted voice of a worried radio gunner from Chicago, "is flak."

We had known from the beginning that the mission was likely to be dangerous, for three planes had been assigned to precede the main formations over the target, spilling out scraps of metallic paper through a back window in order to cloud the radar of the antiaircraft guns. As a bombardier in one of those planes, I had nothing to do but hide under my flak helmet until the flak stopped coming at us and then look back at the other planes to see what was happening. One of them was on fire, heading downward in a gliding spiral that soon tightened into an uncontrolled spin. I finally saw some billowing parachutes. Three men got out. Three others didn't and were killed. One of those who parachuted was found and hidden by some people in Avignon and was eventually brought safely back through the lines by the French underground. On August 15, the day of the invasion of southern France, we *flew* to Avignon again. This time three planes went down, and no men got out. A gunner in my plane got a big wound in his thigh. I took care of him. I went to visit him in the hospital the next day. He looked fine. They had given him blood, and he was going to be all right. But *I* was in terrible shape; and I had twenty-three more missions to fly.

There was the war, in Avignon, not in Rome or Île Rousse or Poggibonsi or even Ferrara, when I was too new to be frightened; but now no one in Avignon wanted to talk about anything but the successful summer arts festival that was just ending. More people had come than ever before, and the elated officials in charge of this annual tourist promotion were already making plans for doing still better the following year. Avignon subsists largely on tourism, I was told, and this surprised me, for the city is small. It is so small that the windows of our bedrooms, at the rear of the building, were right across a narrow street from what I took to be a saloon and what the people at the hotel hinted was a house of ill repute. A woman with a coarse, loud voice laughed and shouted and sang until four in the morning. When she finally shut up, a baker next door to her began chopping dough. The following day I asked to have our rooms changed, and the man at the desk understood and advised me not to visit the place across the street from the back of the hotel.

"It is a very bad place," he observed regretfully, as though he was wishing to himself that it were a much better one. He transferred us to rooms in the front of the hotel, overlooking a lovely dining patio with an enormous tree in the center that shaded the tables and chairs.

A day later we were traveling by train again, my tour of battlefields over. It had brought me only to scenes of peace and to people untroubled by the threat of any new war. Oddly, it was in neutral little Switzerland, after I had given up and almost lost interest, that I finally found, unexpectedly, my war. It came to me right out of the blue, from a portly, amiable middle-aged Frenchman whom we met during our trip on one of those toylike Swiss trains that ply dependably over and through the mountains between Montreux and Interlaken.

He spoke no English and smoked cigarettes incessantly, and he stopped us at one station from making a wrong change of trains. He was going to Interlaken, too, to spend his vacation with a friend who owned a small chalet in a village nearby. That morning he had parted from his wife and son in Montreux; they had boarded the train to Milan to visit Italy, where his son wanted to go.

He volunteered this information about his family so freely that I did not hesitate to inquire when he would be rejoined by his wife.

Then it came, in French, in a choked and muffled torrent of words, the answer to the questions I hadn't asked. He began telling us about his son, and his large eyes turned shiny and filled with tears.

His only boy, adopted, had been wounded in the head in the war in Indochina and would never be able to take care of himself. He could go nowhere alone. He was only thirty-four years old now and had lain in a hospital for seven years. "It is bad," the man said, referring to the wound, the world, the weather, the present, the future. Then, for some reason, he said to me, "You will find out, you will find out." His voice shook. The tears were starting to roll out now through the corners of his eyes, and he was deeply embarrassed. The boy was too young, he concluded lamely, by way of apologizing to us for the emotion he was showing, to have been hurt so badly for the rest of his life.

With that, he turned away and walked to the other end of the car. My wife was silent. The children were subdued and curious.

"Why was he crying?" asked my boy. "What did he say?" my daughter asked me.

What can you tell your children today that will not leave them frightened and sad?

"Nothing," I answered.

It took Joseph Heller eight years to complete "Catch-22," but since 1961 it has been translated into twelve languages, become a best-seller in Czechoslovakia, and sold more than 3,500,000 copies.

JAN SOLOMON

The Structure of Joseph Heller's Catch-22

On the whole, the reviewers and critics who judged *Catch-22* in the fall and winter of 1961 were not entirely enthusiastic. One observation common to favorable and unfavorable notices alike was that *Catch-22* lacked structure. According to *Time:* "Heller's talent is impressive, but it is also undisciplined, sometimes luring him into bogs of boring repetition. Nearly every episode in *Catch-22* is told and retold."[1] In *The New York Times Book Review* repetition is again noted: "its material is repetitive and monotonous." Further, the novel "gasps for want of craft and sensibility;" in fact, "the book is no novel."[2] *The New Yorker* echoes the "no novel" judgment: *Catch-22* "is not really a book. It doesn't even seem to have been written; instead it gives the impression of having been shouted onto paper."[3] The more favorable reviews as well expressed some uneasiness about the form. Orville Prescott tempered his admiration by commenting that the book was "not an entirely successful novel" and "not even a good novel by conventional standards."[4] But Robert Brustein's review-essay on *Catch-22* is most instructive. Despite his enthusiasm for and his unique insight into Heller's novel, Mr. Brustein too charges *Catch-22* with formlessness: "Considering his indifference to surface reality, it is absurd to judge Heller by standards of psychological realism (or, for that matter, by conventional artistic standards at all, since his book is as formless as any

Critique, Vol. 9 (1967): pp. 46–57. © Heldref Publications.

picaresque epic)." Formlessness in this case is not to be considered a weakness and the charge is dismissed as being inconsequential in regard to a novel worthy of being described as "one of the most bitterly funny works in the language."[5]

While the success of *Catch-22* was not immediate, the novel soon began to gain in importance. The English publication of the book in the spring of 1962 brought very favorable notices and within one week it was first on the English best-seller list.[6] Soon *Time* was including paragraphs on Heller in its occasional reports on the literary scene, and even *Vogue* printed his picture above some coy copy and under the puzzling title of "The New Veers." Popular articles on the absurd in American fiction were incomplete without a consideration of *Catch-22*.[7] Finally, *Heller* became an entry in the Twentieth Century American section of the *PMLA Annual Bibliography* with a scattering of articles in the professional journals listed beneath it. Arrived, admired, and analyzed, *Catch-22* is now something of an institution; there are no more comments on its formlessness. The novel has been accepted as some sort of gifted example of what in literature must be thought to approximate the drip-and-smear school of modern painting.

But *Catch-22 is* a novel, and fine, formless novels are a rare species. A careful examination of Heller's novel reveals not only that it has form, but that this form is carefully constructed to support the pervasive theme of absurdity, in fact to create its own dimension of absurdity.

The most significant aspect of the structure of *Catch-22* is its chronology. Behind what appear to be merely random events lies a careful system of time-sequences involving two distinct and mutually contradictory chronologies. The major part of the novel, focussed on Yossarian, moves forward and back from a pivotal point in time. Yossarian, like many other anti-heroes of modern fiction from Leopold Bloom to Moses Herzog, lives in a world dominated not by chronological but by psychological time. Yossarian's time is punctuated, if not ordered, by the inexorable increases in the number of missions and by the repetitious returns to the relative safety and sanity of the hospital where, "they couldn't dominate Death . . . but they certainly made her behave."[8]

While the dominant sequence of events shifts back and forth from the present to the past treating any period of time as equally present, equally immediate, a counter-motion controls the time of the history of Milo Minderbinder. Across the see-saw pattern of events in the rest of the novel Minderbinder moves directly forward from one success to the next. In the solid fashion of nineteenth-century fiction, he begins the novel as a hardworking young hopeful dreaming of a syndicate and ends wielding absolute power. Independently, each chronology is valid and logical; together, the two time-schemes are impossible. By manipulating the points at which the different systems cross, Heller creates a structural absurdity enforcing the absurdity of character and event in the novel.

Examining first the part of *Catch-22* dominated by Yossarian, we find a fairly complex chronology. The novel opens at a point midway in the development of the situation, so that "past" events, those preceding the opening scene, must be revealed to the reader. These past eventsd are slowly unfolded as the "present" action progresses, but they are not related through conventional flash-backs. At first numerous, brief references to an event are inserted into the current action; then somewhat fuller allusions; and finally, fo reach specific important episode, a fairly extended direct narration. This method of weaving past and present time is, of course, what has been labeled repetition. These episodes are never related with any sense of their having become distant in time, but are told with freshness and immediacy, suggesting the effect they continue to have on Yossarian. Since any scene in the novel seems equally "present", all sense of chronological relativity is denied to the reader who thus fails to attain any solid vantage point in time. The sense of time is undermined and with it one hold on the rational.

The net-work of present and past events builds toward a psychological effect in Yossarian, and in the reader. With the gradual unfolding of such "past" events as The Glorious Loyalty Oath Crusade and The Great Big Siege of Bologna develops the tension that reaches its peak at the end of the novel in the scene of Snowden's death. The negation of the significance of chronology is particularly apparent here; the critical event of the novel—Snowden's death and the revelation of "his secret"—actually occurs some months before the opening of the book.

Time, in this complex system of narration, is marked out for us by two closely linked devices, Yossarian's stays in the hospital and the continual raising of the number of missions. Yossarian's constant retreats to the hospital enforce the reversal of values in the world of Pianosa, where the hospital represents the high-water mark of the safe and the reasonable. These escapes maek as well the stages in Yossarian's insubordination; each self-imposed hospitalization is a response to the raising of the required number of missions. Insubordination, the refusal to play the game, has begun in the "past" time of the novel. After the death of Snowden, Yossarian goes naked rather than wear a uniform stained by Snowden's mortality. Naked, he attends Snowden's funeral, and naked, he receives a medal. But the acts of insubordination toward the end of the novel become increasingly dangerous to authority. Yossarian refuses to fly further missions, a decision he enforces by walking backwards and carrying a gun. His punultimate gesture of revolt takes him AWOL to Rome, and at last he deserts. The psychological development to revolt in Yossarian significantly does not depend on the actual chronology of the events. The cause and effect pattern of increased missions and flights to the hospital is the first indication of rebelliousness the novel presents. The more absurd and intense insubordination of nakedness predates any of Yossarian's Pianosa hospitalizations; yet, although it is alluded to early on in the book, it is not fully recounted until Chapter 24, more than half way through the novel, where it fits into the pattern of Yossarian's growing psychological unrest. The events do make a pattern, not in terms of chronology but in terms of the order which they are related. Again the significance of real time is negated.

In Yossarian's final insubordination, his desertion, chronology and the narrative order if events combine. The chronological order of events has brough Yossarian into dangerous conflict with Colonels Cathcart and Korn. Thus, present events motivate him. But past events are equally forceful, for at this point in the novel the death of Snowden is narrated in full and horrible detail. Snowden's death occurred months before, but it is described at the end of the novel so that it may have its ultimate effect in the ultimate action of the novel, the desertion. There is, of course, psychological validity; past events can motivate present actions, but more important is the insistent denial of the typical novelistic convention which locates causes in immediately antecedent events.

In the structural economy of *Catch-22*, the raising of the missions and Yossarian's flights to the hospital not only serve the psychological development of Yossarian but also permit us to follow the time-scheme of the novel. When the novel opens, the missions have been raised to 45 and Yossarian has responded by escaping to the hospital on the pretext of his liver condition. This opening hospital scene admits the reader to the history of Yossarian *in medias* res and at the same time initiates certain key events such as Yossarian's friendship with the chaplain, the creation of Washington Irving, mysterious signer of letters and documents, and the appearance of The Soldier in White. Driven from the ward by a cheerful Texan, Yossarian returns to duty, only to find the missions raised to 50; he flees once more to the hospital. When he leaves the hospital again, the action proper of the novel begins.

In the first three or four chapters references to past events reveal that many of the novel's most significant episodes have already taken place. Avignon and Ferrara have been bombed. All the "Great" and "Glorious" events have occurred: The Glorious Atabrine Insurrection, The Glorious Loyalty Oath Crusade, and The Great Big Siege of Bologna. Furthermore, Snowden, Kraft, and Clevinger, as well as other less significant characters have already died. For two-thirds of the novel, about 300 pages, the disclosure of these past events forms a considerable part of the texture of narration; the last third of the novel moves steadily forward at an increased pace directly relating the events of the present.

Catch-22 falls into three nearly equal parts separated by the rhythmic repetition of hospital scenes. In the first section, although the narration dwells primarily on the past, a few events do occur in the present to advance the action somewhat. The missions are raised from 45 to 50 and to 55, at which point Yossarian goes to Major Major Major Major with his grievance. When Yossarian finally manages to see this elusive figure, he is offered the option of flying only milk-runs. Yossarian turns the offer down, foreshadowing his similar refusal of the Colonels' deal at the end of the novel. This kind of narrative rhythm is another of Heller's structural devices, and we see it again when Yossarian flees from the terrors of the Bologna mission to a Rome populated by soldiers and whores, a flight to be repeated at the climax of the novel.

In the first section of *Catch-22* primary attention is paid to introducing us to the major characters of the novel and to adding more information of past events to the framework of knowledge being built around Yossarian and Pianosa. Occasionally in the early chapters past events are told in the form of extended straight narration, not, however, any of the events occurring on Pianosa, but only those histories that took place in the more distant past: Yossarian and Clevinger at Santa Ana (particularly the trial of Clevinger) and the biography of Major Major Major Major. Otherwise, by hints and allusions we receive some information about Avignon, Ferrara, Bologna and about the interpersonal affairs of the men on Pianosa: Orr and Appleby and the ping-pong fight, the war between Flume and Chief Halfoat, the fistfight between Huple's cat and Hungry Joe. Not until the end of this section does the narration tend to concentrate on one major past event, The Great Big Siege of Bologna. The first third of the novel ends with the second run over Bologna and Yossarian's night in Rome with Luciana, after which, on returning to Pianosa, he finds the missions raised to 40. Yossarian rushes to the hospital.

The second passage of hospital scenes, beginning with Chapter 16, marks the division between the first two sections of the novel and establishes circularity and repetition by bringing together several points in time. Yossarian leaves the hospital after ten days, but again the missions are raised, now to 45, and again he returns. The manipulation of time has brought us back to the opening of the novel: Yossarian in the hospital with the missions at 45.

Chapter 17 is entitled "The Soldier in White" and now further grotesque description magnifies the horror of his symbolic depersonalization. From this series of hospitalizations the narrative moves back in time to others. Reference is made to Yossarian in North Africa with venereal disease. A passage follows about Yossarian's first hospitalization, a form of malingering that began back at Lowry Field, where Yossarian so much enjoys spending Thanksgiving in bed that he attempts to remain there by imitating the symptoms of The Soldier Who Saw Everything Twice. As a result, when this soldier dies, Yossarian is forced into impersonating him for the benefit of his visiting family. The device of exchanged and confused identities will, like The Soldier in White, recur.

The second section of *Catch-22* is again approximately 150 pages, or one-third of the novel, and again appears framed in hospital scenes. This section contains somewhat more action in the present time. The problems of the chaplain with Colonel Cathcart, Corporal Whitcomb, and the Washington Irving Investigation are developed. Then, as the missions are raised to 60, Dobbs conceives his plan to kill Colonel Cathcart. In Rome more attention is paid to the whores and to the old man with whom a frustrated Nately passionately debates the principles of the American dream. Past events in this section focus primarily on the events of Avignon, the moaning at the briefing, Snowden's death (still given in only fragmentary detail), and Snowden's funeral with a naked Yossarian in attendance in a tree. Since Avignon preceded Bologna, the events most concentrated on in the first section, we have yet another denial of chronology.

Yossarian, at the end of this second section, returns to the hospital, not this time as a malingerer but as a casualty. He has been wounded as a result of Aarfy's poor navigation on returning from Parma. At this point, the issue of confused identities is repeated. Dunbar has become A. Fortiori, a feat accomplished by taking over A. Fortiori's bed. Dunbar suggests that Yossarian drive one Lumley, a lower-ranking soldier, out of his bed, thereby assuming Lumley's identity. This action has unfortunate ramifications; Yossarian, certified at last by the hospital psychiatrist as crazy enough to be sent home, is jubilant. The orders arrive; they are for A. Fortiori.

In the final section of the novel, which, except for the full narration of the death of Snowden, concentrates on events in the present, the tempo of horrors increases. The chief officers become even more self-seeking and incompetent. Lt. Scheisskopf arrives from California, soon becomes a General, and takes over Special Services from General Dreedle at the moment when Special Services takes over the control of combat. More of Yossarian's fellows die, and their deaths are more bizarre. McWatt buzzes the raft and cuts Kid Sampson in half; guilt drives McWatt to fly his plane into a mountain. Doc Daneeka, supposedly on that plane, dies on paper, a death that proves just as effective as a more mortal end. Chief Halfoat dies of pneumonia, as predicted, and Hungry Joe smothers under Huple's cat. New young soldiers arrive and commit the weirdest of murders by removing the effects of the dead man, Mudd, from Yossarian's tent. Even Orr, shot down again, is missing. As the missions skyrocket to 80, the chaplain is arrested and questioned about Washington Irving in a scene that repeats the earlier mad trial of Clevinger. Dunbar "is disappeared", and finally Nately dies, his whore becoming a ubiquitous assassin threatening Yossarian.

In the increased pace of the final section there is an additional reminder of the hospital. The careful rhythm is not disrupted although it is not Yossarian who is hospitalized but Nately whose nose Yossarian has broken in a wild Thanksgiving revel. All morality is corrupted now as even the chaplain appears in the hospital with "Wisconsin Shingles", finding at last the delights of sin in his malingering: "The chaplain had sinned, and it was good." (356) Most disturbingly, there appears in the ward another Soldier in White, another faceless, featureless, characterless mummy absorbing liquid through one tube and evacuating liquid through a second tube attached to the first. Neither the soldiers nor the reader can be sure that it is not the same spectral soldier who appeared at the opening of the novel.

Finally, Yossarian's rebellion takes a more aggressive form; wearing a gun and walking backwards, he refuses to fly. He goes AWOL to Rome where, after passing like an impotent Dante through the Eternal City which has become a modern Inferno, he finds that Aarfy has murdered a whore. The M.P.s arrive and arrest not Aarfy, the murderer, but Yossarian, the AWOL soldier. When the Colonels offer Yossarian and themselves an out, an opportunity for him to return home and to advertize the goodness and intelligence of his officers, Yossarian wavers, accepts, and then, attacked by Nately's whore, is hospitalized. The novel ends as it began, in the hospital. Here Yossarian learns of Orr's escape to Sweden and the reader learns the details of Snowden's death. Yossarian turns down the deal, as he had turned down Major Major Major Major's earlier offer, and deserts.

The chronology of the Yossarian portion of the novel, then, moves between present and past from the point at which the novel opens, marking off divisions in the novel by returns to the hospital, and creating ever-increasing tension through the narrated order, not the actual chronology, of events. *Catch-22* is not simply an anti-novel in the sense that it avoids the more simple and direct chronological and causal chain of events that makes up the traditional novel. Heller is interested as well in presenting us with his particular vision of the absurd and he accomplishes this too through the time-structure of the book.

The absurd is structurally expressed through the confrontation of the psychological time in which Yossarian's history is told and the chronological time in which Milo Minderbinder's history is told. Minderbinder is introduced to us after Yossarian is released from the hospital at the beginning of the novel, that is, *after* many of the events in the novel have taken place, notably after Avignon and the death of Snowden and after The Great Big Siege of Bologna. Minderbinder enters the novel at the very outset of his career, when he has just been made mess sergeant and when, on first meeting Yossarian, he talks of "the syndicate I'd like to form someday. . ." (65)

Heller, however, begins immediately to confuse the two chronologies. As we are told that Minderbinder is just starting out, so we are also presented with a series of past events, mentioned early in the novel, that include some of Minderbinder's more infamous exploits, the bridge at Orvieto—when Milo's planes attacked and Milo's guns defended—and Milo's bombing and strafing of his own squadron on Pianosa. The incompatibility of the chronological and causal relationships of events is apparent at once; for these sinister exploits are explained as the necessary economic results of the financial embarrassment occasioned Minderbinder by his cornering the world cotton-market. Since Milo's plunge into cotton cannot have occurred when we first meet him, obviously neither Orvieto nor the bombing of the squadron can have yet taken place. In the narrative order of events Heller makes this quite clear; the cornering of the cotton market is related in Chapter 22, the bombing of the squadron in Chapter 24. Nevertheless, the network of references to events preceding the opening of the novel deliberately confounds the time-sequence.

A great deal seems to hinge on the actual time of the cornering of the cotton-market in relation to other events, but Heller avoids establishing this time. His technique here depends on the subtle manipulation of transitions. He presents us with an event which is placed in the time-scheme of the novel; then he compares this to a second event, one which we cannot place in relation to the time of any other happening. The rhetoric of comparison conceals the shift. Finally, the reader shuttles back and forth between events unable to tell which came first.

In the instance of the cotton-market, we are told of Dobb's eagerness to kill Colonel Cathcart as a result of the missions having been raised to 60. Since the missions establish relative time in the novel, there is no difficulty. Dobb's emotional condition at this time is then compared to Orr's at the time when Orr and Yossarian joined Milo on a tour. This buying trip takes them to Cairo and to the ticker-tape machine which introduces Minderbinder to cotton. The confounding of our time sense is subtly accomplished, and we cannot know whether this tour preceded or followed the period when the missions were raised to 60.

> Dobbs was in even worse shape than Hungry Joe, who could at least fly missions when he was not having nightmares. Dobbs was almost as bad as Orr, who seemed happy as an undersized, grinning lark with his deranged and galvanic giggle and shivering warped buck teeth and who was sent along for a rest leave with

Milo and Yossarian on the trip to Cairo for eggs when Milo bought cotton instead and took off at dawn for Istanbul with his plane packed to the gun turrets with exotic spiders and unripened red bananas. (224)

This narrative sleight-of-hand conceals the fact that Heller is building a chronological impossibility. For the cotton caused the bombing of the squadron and the bombing of the squadron is related as one of the events preceding the opening of the novel—at 45 missions—as preceding, in fact, The Great Big Siege of Bologna (see pages 30–31), while in fact Milo only initiates his career when the novel begins, shortly after Bologna.

The irreconcileability of the two chronologies serves the effect of absurdity, and the two time-schemes operate to enforce thematic considerations, principally the repudiation of the business ethic. The separate time-lines of the novel exist simultaneously, moving, like lines of polyphonic music, into occasional shocking dissonance. As Yossarian develops increasing rebelliousness through events of past and present, so Minderbinder increases his financial empire step by chronological step. The dissonance sounds when a step in Milo's success occurs simultaneously with the relating of an event in the "past" time of Yossarian's story. The dissonances, moreover, tend to fall at moments when one of Minderbinder's greatest successes coincides with one of the more grotesque moments in the decay of Yossarian's world. The logic of connection between cynical success and Moral decay supersedes the logic of chronology.

Heller's technique becomes most apparent in two scenes which bring together Milo's progress and the details of Snowden's death and funeral. Chapter 24 tells of the funeral with Yossarian naked in a tree. He is joined in the tree by an immaculately attired Minderbinder, who wants Yossarian to taste his latest ingenious attempt to unload the now chocolate-covered cotton. Of course, the chronology is impossible; Minderbinder was not mess sergeant, was not apparently even on Pianosa, at the time of Avignon and Snowden's death. Nevertheless, the logic is inescapable, the symbolic juxtaposition of death and business.

> "Look at that!" [Minderbinder] exclaimed in alarm. . . . "That's a funeral going on down there. . . ."
>
> Yossarian answered him slowly in a level voice. "They're burying that kid who got killed in my plane over Avignon the other day. Snowden."
>
> "What happened to him?" Milo asked in a voice deadened with awe.
>
> " He got killed."

"That's terrible," Milo grieved, and his large brown eyes filled with tears. "That poor kid. It really is terrible." He bit his trembling lip hard, and his voice rose with emotion when he continued, "And it will get even worse if the mess halls don't agree to buy my cotton." (257–258)

More significantly anachronistic and more markedly cynical is the juxtaposition of Minderbinder and Snowden when the details of Snowden's death are finally revealed. The details are horrible, and Yossarian's humanity, his revulsion at the sight of Snowden, his careful binding of the wrong wound, only draw the agony finer. To Snowden's continued complaint of cold, Yossarian murmurs comfort, and at last, reaching for the morphine, finds that there is none.

There was no morphine in the first-aid kit, no protection for Snowden against pain but the numbing shock of the gaping wound itself. The twelve syrettes of morphine had been stolen from their case and replaced by a cleanly lettered note that said: "What's good for M & M Enterprises is good for the country. Milo Minderbinder." (426)

The chronological illogicality fades into insignificance beside the appropriateness of the final example of Milo's rapacity and the cruel impersonality of the now enormous syndicate. Heller makes his final thrust with the revelation of Snowden's secret: "Man is matter". Men (Yossarian, Snowden, Nately, Clevinger, and the others) make their tentative way through a complex pattern of past and present; there is no possibility of progress, only the near certitude of death. But Milo Minderbinder moves consistently, inexorably forward—against nations, against wars, against time itself.

The conclusion of *Catch-22* is frequently criticized, and the third section of the novel, with its comparatively straight-forward narration of present events, undoubtedly lacks the force of the earlier sections. The optimism, even the euphoria, of Yossarian's desertion is also difficult to accept. Nevertheless, Yossarian's flight is fitting, even necessary. Minderbinder can build an empire in the world of the novel, the microcosm of Pianosa; for his success depends on the venality and self-interest of others. Milo faces nomoral dilemmas. He operates according to the accepted ethics of Pianosa, the sanctity of business, and he avoids the one deadly sin, doing business with the Communists. For Yossarian, the world of Pianosa becomes the world of impossible alternatives In which he must either betray himself by playing along with the Colonels or face court-martial and prison. Even though Yossarian is innocent, he will be proven guilty, because "They can get all the witnesses they need simply by persuading them that destroying you is for the good of the country." (433) "The good of the country", the ultimate sanction of Minderbinder's ethics, is turned against Yossarian. There is no percentage and not even any valor in remaining to fight this offense against justice and morality, for there are no more moral imperatives in this world and no more concepts of justice. The slogans alone remain and even the slogans have been bought up by M & M Enterprises.

NOTES

1. *Time*, Oct. 27, 1961, p. 97.
2. Richard G. Stern, *The New York Times Book Review*, Oct. 22, 1961, p. 50.
3. Whitney Balliett, *The New Yorker*, Dec. 9, 1961, p. 247.
4. Orville Prescott, *The New York Times*, Oct. 23, 1961, p. 27.
5. Robert Brustein, *The New Republic*, Nov. 13, 1961, pp. 13, 11.
6. As reported by R. Walters in *The New York Times Book Review*, Sept. 9, 1962, p. 8. See also Howard Taubman, *The New Statesman*, June 15, 1962, p. 871; and *The Spectator*, June 15, 1962, p. 801.
7. *Time*, Feb. 1, 1963, pp. 82–84; *Time*, Feb. 12, 1965, pp. 94–95; *Vogue*, Jan. 1, 1963, p. 112; *The New York Times Book Review*, June 6, 1965, pp. 3, 28, 30.
8. Joseph Heller, *Catch-22* (New York, 1961), p. 164. All other page references to *Catch-22* will be noted parenthetically in the text.

DOUG GAUKROGER

Time Structure in Catch-22

T he most striking feature of *Catch-22*[1] is the novel's unusual structure,
more specifically its time structure. The rapid changes between events back
and forth in time with seemingly little regard for the reader's ability to follow the action clearly has confused some and delighted many. Therefore, it
seems strange that in the eight years since the novel's publication only one
article has appeared (*Critique*, 1967) which attempts to examine its intricate
chronological structure. This article by Jan Solomon sought to illuminate
the structure and sort out to some extent the juxtaposed and carefully dis-
ordered time sequence of *Catch-22*.[2] Unfortunately, Mr. Solomon's article is
flawed by a number of grave textual errors and misreadings; so grave in fact
as to subvert entirely his main thesis. I hope to refute points put forth in the
Solomon essay, and following this, to lay out for the first time the events
in the novel in their proper chronological order. This latter step is, I feel,
made necessary by two considerations. First, it offers an alternative to Mr.
Solomon's faulty interpretation of the time structure. Second, it will facilitate
an examination of some minor inconsistencies which appear in the novel.

A brief summary of Mr. Solomon's thesis and his arguments in support
of it will be necessary before we begin to examine and ascertain its validity.
He begins by telling us that he is going to examine the novel's form and that
the form is most heavily influenced by the time structure.

Critique: Studies in Modern Fiction, Volume XII, No. 2 (1967): pp. 70–85. © Heldref
Publications.

A careful examination of Heller's novel reveals not only that it has form, but that this form is carefully constructed to support the pervasive theme of absurdity. . . .

The most significant aspect of the structure of *Catch-22* is its chronology. Behind what appears to be merely random events lies a careful system of time-sequences involving two distinct and mutually contradictory chronologies. The major part of the novel, focussed on Yossarian, moves forward and back from a pivotal point in time. Yossarian, like many anti-heroes of modern fiction from Leopold Bloom to Moses Herzog, lives in a world dominated not by chronological but by psychological time. Yossarian's time is punctuated, if not ordered, by the inexorable increases in the number of missions and by the repetitious returns to the relative safety and sanity of the hospital. . . .

While the dominant sequence of events shifts back and forth from the present to the past treating any period of time as equally present, equally immediate, a counter-motion controls the time of the history of Milo Minderbinder. Across the see-saw pattern of events in the rest of the novel Minderbinder moves directly forward from one success to the next. . . . Independently, each chronology is valid and logical; *together, the two time-schemes are impossible.* By manipulating the points at which the different systems cross, Heller creates a structural absurdity enforcing the absurdity of character and event in the novel.[3] (italics mine)

This thesis, then, states that Yossarian and Milo Minderbinder, while they appear and interact together throughout the novel, actually exist in two different time structures and that it is (at times) impossible for these two time structures to meet. It is further claimed that two events in the novel could not possibly have occurred; the first is Milo climbing the tree to join the naked Yossarian who is watching Snowden's funeral (pp. 255–261), and the second involves the missing styrettes of morphine (in the B-25's first aid kit when Yossarian tries to treat Snowden's wound) which have been replaced by signs reading "What's good for M & M Enterprises is good for the country. Milo Minderbinder" (p. 426). These two events are impossible because Milo supposedly does not arrive on Pianosa until Yossarian's hospital visit, described in Chapter I of the novel at the time when Yossarian had 38 missions to his credit.[4] Yossarian, by this reading, does not meet Milo until shortly after this hospital visit. But this particular hospital stay did not occur until after the Avignon mission and Snowden's death and funeral. How then could Yossarian talk to Milo in the tree at a time prior to their first meeting? How could Milo have stolen the morphine for his syndicate when his syndicate had not yet been formed? Such obviously impossible events are explainable only as conscious devices used by Heller in an effort to cause the structure of the novel to coincide with and "support the pervasive theme of absurdity, . . . and to create its own dimension of absurdity."[5]

If all the smoke-screening found in the notions of the two time sequences, the "psychological time" of Yossarian and the "chronological time" of Milo Minderbinder, is cleared away we find that Solomon's article relies totally on two "facts" which he has gleaned from his textural analysis. One is that Yossarian does not meet Milo until after the hospital visit and that Milo has not yet begun his syndicate. The other "fact" is the impossibility of determining at which point in the chronology Yossarian and Orr join Milo on the buying trip which results in his cornering the world cotton market. If these two assertions are disproven and it is shown that Yossarian met Milo before Snowden's death, that the cotton market cornering took place before Avignon, then arguments for an impossible time sequence crumble.

Let us begin by taking a look at Yossarian's first meeting with Milo which Heller describes in Chapter VII and attempts to determine whether it actually did take place after the hospital visit described in Chapter I, when Yossarian had 38 missions.

> "What's this?" Milo had cried out in alarm, when he came upon the enormous corrugated carton filled with packages of dried fruit and cans of fruit juices and desserts that two of the Italian laborers Major — — de Coverley had kidnapped for his kitchen were about to carry off to Yossarian's tent.
>
> "This is Captain Yossarian, sir," said Corporal Snark with a superior smirk. Corporal Snark was an intellectual snob who felt he was twenty years ahead of his time and did not enjoy cooking down to the masses. "He has a letter from Doc Daneeka entitling him to all the fruit and fruit juices he wants."
>
> "What's this?" cried out Yossarian, as Milo went white and began to sway.
>
> "This is Lieutenant Milo Minderbinder, sir," said Corporal Snark with a derisive wink. "One of our new pilots. He became mess officer *while you were in the hospital this last time*." (pp. 59–60) (italics mine)

Milo, then, became mess officer and hence began planning his syndicate while Yossarian was "in the hospital this last time." Nothing in this statement, nor in any statement before or after, would suggest that "this last time" refers to the opening hostal scene. The handling of the chronological structure in Chapter VIII gives the impression that all events are equally present in time, and thus a superficial reading makes it appear that Yossarian does indeed meet Milo for the first time after his hospital visit at 38 missions. A closer reading, however, reveals that this conclusion is unjustified and that in reality Chapter VII offers no clue at all as to when the first meeting did take place. Later I hope to demonstrate that while one cannot determine *exactly* when Yossarian and Milo first met, one can show that they did indeed meet before 38 missions, probably at a time previous to The Great Big Siege of Bologna.

If one assumes that Milo's career did not begin until after first met Yossarian at the time when Colonel Cathcart was demanding 45 missions, then two events (the missing morphine over Avignon, and Snowden's funeral), both of which involve a wealthy Milo in some way, are rendered chronologically impossible because they occur prior to the time of the 45 missions. These two alleged chronological impossibilities, then, are said to "serve the effect of absurdity, while the two time schemes operate to enforce thematic considerations, principally the repudiation of the business ethic".[6] Excluding the fact that one cannot prove that Yossarian first met Milo at the time of 45 missions (when Yossarian had 38 missions), a large number of other events involve Milo before this time. If only two events were out of time, as has been suggested, a case might be made for a dual time scheme; however, *all* the events involving Milo occurred at a time prior to the period of 45 missions. This suggests to me either that Heller made a colossal error in his plotting or that Solomon is guilty of overlooking or misreading a great number of events in *Catch-22*. I believe the latter to be the case and the only real impossibility in the time sequence is Solomon's interpretation of it. Heller repeatedly states in the novel that Milo was doing his dirty work long before Yossarian's hospital visit of Chapter I when he had 38 missions. Let us look at some examples.

At the time when Yossarian first meets Milo (p. 61), Milo asks Yossarian if he knows why Corporal Snark has been demoted.

> [Milo speaking] "Incidentally, do you happen to know why he was busted to private and is only a corporal now?"
> "Yes," said Yosarrian. "He poisoned the squadron."
> Milo went pale again. "He did what?"
> "He mashed hundreds of cakes of GI soap into the sweet potatoes just to show that people have the taste of Philistines and don't know the difference between good and bad. Every man in the squadron was sick. Missions were cancelled." (p. 63)

Actually there were two poisonings. This is the first and occurred during the missions to Ferrara (p. 19) before Milo arrived on Pianosa. The second poisoning occurs during The Great Big Siege of Bologna when Milo had already been made mess officer.

> "Please find out from Corporal Snark if he put laundry soap in the sweet potatoes again," he requested furtively. "Corporal Snark trusts you and will tell you the truth if you give him your word you won't tell anyone else. As soon as he tells you, come and tell me,"
>
> "Of course I put laundry soap in the sweet potatoes," Corporal Snark admitted to Yossarian. "That's what you asked me to do, isn't it? Laundry soap is the best way."
>
> "He swears to God he didn't have a thing to do with it," Yossarian reported back to Milo. (p. 123)

Milo, apparently, became mess officer between the two poisonings, as he did not know about the first but had become mess officer by the second. The second poisoning occurred during The Great Big Siege of Bologna when Yossarian had 31 missions and the Colonel wanted 35 (p. 163). Bologna occurred before the Chapter I hospital visit when Yossarian had 38 missions; yet here we have Yossarian talking to Milo both before and during the second mess hall poisoning which happened a full seven missions previous to the time they supposedly met.

Solomon's further assertion that,

> A great deal seems to hinge on the actual time of the cornering of the cotton market in relation to the other events, but Heller avoids establishing this time . . . This buying trip takes them to Cairo and to the ticker tape machine which introduces Minderbinder to cotton . . . we cannot know whether this tour preceded or followed the period when the missions were raised to 60[7]

also proves quite false. On the contrary, we *can* accurately establish the time when Yossarian, Orr, and Milo flew to Cairo and cornered the cotton market. The reader has merely to turn to pages 120–121 and examine the conversation between Yossarian and Wintergreen. Wintergreen, who is in competition with Milo, comes to Pianosa "to learn if it was really true about Milo and the Egyptian cotton" (p. 120). While Wintergreen is on Pianosa, Yossarian begs him to save the squadron from the fate of flying to Bologna.

> Yossarian suddenly seized his [Wintergreen's] arm. "Couldn't you forge some official orders on that mimeograph machine of yours *and get us out of flying to Bologna?*" (pp. 120–121) (Italics mine)

Milo bought the Egyptian cotton, then, just before The Great Big Siege of Bologna which was at the time of 35 missions when Yossarian had flown 31. This means that Milo bought the cotton before Mudd was killed at Avignon, and not afterward as we have been led to believe.

Another misreading is found in Solomon's statement that "Since Avignon preceded Bologna . . . we have yet another denial of chronology".[8] The Avignon mission did *not* precede Bologna; it was flown about three weeks and perhaps four missions later. Yossarian's 32nd mission was the second mission to Bologna after which he fled directly to Rome (p. 151). We learn that Snowden is also in Rome at the time Yossarian trips over his duffel bag, just before he finds the maid in the lime-green panties (pp. 132, 162). If Snowden is still alive at this time, the only conclusion that can be drawn is that the Avignon mission must have been flown after Bologna, probably during the six missions Yossarian flew between hospital visits at 32 and 38 missions.

Many other examples show Milo going about the business of building an empire long before the time he supposedly arrived on Pianosa. Milo begins his air empire by tempting Major — — de Coverley with visions of a fresh egg frying in fresh butter (p. 134). Major — — de Coverley disappears when Yossarian moves the bomb-line during The Great Big Siege of Bologna which, as we have seen, is some time before Yossarian allegedly meets Milo. Clevinger wonders how Milo can buy eggs at seven cents in Malta and sell them at a profit on Pianosa for five cents (p. 67), yet Clevinger is dead two and one half weeks before Milo supposedly starts his empire (p. 170). At the time of 70 missions, just after Thanksgiving, we find that Milo has been overseas for eleven months (p. 363). Yet it is stated that "Minderbinder . . . was not apparently even on Pianosa, at the time of Avignon and Snowden's death,"[9] which occurred about the middle of the summer. Milo is mentioned in connection with the Great Loyalty Oath Campaign (p. 104) which was broken up by Major — — de Coverley; therefore, it must have taken place before Bologna. Milo secretly feeds both Captain Flume and Major Major when they go into hiding, which is long before the period of 45 missions. We find that "April had been the best month of all for Milo" (p. 246). His mess hall ventures are going strong in the spring yet he is not supposed to have been made mess officer until the summer. If we add all these "chronological impossibilities" to the three already noted, there seems to be little doubt that Milo *was* around long before the time of 45 missions.

That it cannot be shown for certain that Milo was just beginning his career at the time of 45 missions, plus the fact that Heller clearly shows us that Milo's fortunes were booming long before this time, demonstrates quite amply that any theory which posits two juxtaposed time schemes developed to further the sense of absurdity is false. On the contrary, I believe a time scheme for the novel is possible in which all events follow quite logically one upon the other. With one or two minor exceptions, chronological paradoxes are quite rare in *Catch-22*. The following is a summary of the events of the novel in what I believe to be their proper chronological order.

Yossarian talks to Wintergreen at Lowry Field, Colorado (p. 105). We learn that sometime after this, Wintergreen strikes a waterpipe while digging holes as punishment for going A.W.O.L. The water is rumoured to be oil, and Chief White Halfoat is kicked off the base and eventually ends up on Pianosa as a replacement for Lt. Coombs who was killed in Kraft's plane when it was shot down during the second bomb-run over Ferrara. We also learn that Milo bombs the squadron seven months after Wintergreen strikes water.

Yossarian is a private at Lowry Field (p. 175). He discovers the hospital as a sanctuary when he enters it to escape calisthenics. Here he first learns to fake a liver condition. He spends ten days in the hospital, then fourteen more under quarantine with the soldier who saw everything twice. Yossarian imitates this soldier's symptoms for one more day but quits when the man dies. Before he leaves the hospital Yossarian must take the place of Guiseppi, the dying soldier, whose parents have come to visit him (pp. 180–184). This hospital stay coincides with Thanksgiving, and Yossarian resolves to spend all his Thanksgivings in a hospital.

One full year later we find Yossarian taking officer training in California under Lieutenant Scheisskopf (p. 67–70) and spending Thanksgiving in bed with Scheisskopf's wife, arguing about God. We learn of Scheisskopf's passion for parades (p. 70) and Clevinger's experiences with the "Action Board" (pp. 74–80).

Yossarian, Appleby, and Kraft fly from Puerto Rico to Pianosa and become involved in The Splendid Atabrine Insurrection (p. 105). Yossarian first refused to take his malaria pill in Puerto Rico and ten days later, Appleby, immediately upon arrival on Pianosa, tries to report Yossarian to Major Major, only to find that the Major is in hiding.

Yossarian begins flying missions under Colonel Nevers. When he has flown 17 missions Yossarian enters the hospital with a case of clap.

> Hungry Joe had finished flying his first twenty-five missions during the week of the Salerno beachhead, when Yossarian was laid up in the hospital with a burst of clap he had caught on a low-level mission over a Wac in bushes on a supply flight to Marrakech. Yossarian did his best to catch up with Hungry Joe and almost did, flying six missions in six days, but his twenty-

third mission was to Arezzo, where Colonel Nevers was killed,
and that was as close as he had ever been able to come to going
home. The next day Colonel Cathcart was there, brimming with
tough pride in his new outfit and celebrating his assumption
of command by raising the number of missions required from
twenty-five to thirty. Hungry Joe unpacked his bags and rewrote
the happy letters home. (p. 53)

Much important chronological information is to be gleaned from this paragraph. Yossarian and Hungry Joe seem to begin flying at approximately the
same time under Colonel Nevers when the required number of missions was
25. Yossarian has a total of 17 missions when he enters the hospital; Hungry
Joe, who continues flying, reaches 25 during this time. Discharged from
the hospital, Yossarian flies six more missions in six days for a total of 23
when Colonel Nevers is killed. Colonel Cathcart takes over and raises the
required number to 30.

One of the first acts of Colonel Cathcart upon taking command is to
volunteer the group for Ferrara, where ". . . his men had flown nine missions
. . . in six days and the bridge was not demolished until the tenth mission
on the seventh day, when Yossarian killed Kraft and his crew by taking his
flight of six planes over the target a second time" (p. 135). A great many
problems with time surround these Ferrara missions. We know that they
occurred after Yossarian had 23 missions because they were ordered by Colonel Cathcart who assumed command at that time (p. 53). We also know
that they occurred before the First Mission to Bologna which would have
been Yossarian's 32nd mission had he not aborted it. ("By the time of the
mission to Bologna, Yossarian was brave enough not to go over the target
even once . . ." p. 39). It is obvious that Yossarian did not fly all the missions
to Ferrara as there were ten flights in all and Yossarian could have flown a
maximum of eight (24–31 inclusive). This would mean that the final successful mission to Ferrara was Yossarian's 31st, though if he flew less than
his possible maximum of eight, then it might have been his 30th or 29th.
The squadron was first poisoned by Corporal Snark during the Ferrara missions (p. 19), an event Milo has not heard of so he could not have been on
Pianosa at this time (p. 63). When Corporal Snark poisons the squadron
again luring The Great Big Siege of Bologna (p. 123), Milo is already mess
officer during The Siege. This, however, conflicts with Corporal Snark's
remark to Yossarian, that Milo was made mess officer while Yossarian was
"in the hospital this last time" (p. 60). This is plainly not the hospital visit
at 17 missions necessitated by the clap, nor is it the hospital visit at 32 missions which occurred *after* Bologna. As far as we can determine there is no
hospital visit in between. Were it not for this remark by Corporal Snark,

we would assume that Milo had joined the squadron shortly after the Ferrara missions, and the chronology would follow plausibly. Similarly, were it not for the single reference (p. 19) made by Yossarian to the food first being poisoned during Ferrara, we might assume the poisoning occurred very early, even before Yossarian got the clap. This would allow Milo to have been made mess officer while Yossarian was "in the hospital this last time." Indeed, when Yossarian refers later to the first poisoning, he says to Milo: "every man in the squadron was sick. Missions were cancelled" (p. 63). This does not sound like Ferrara where ten missions were flown in seven days. It is difficult to see how any missions were cancelled when ten were flown in a single week.

There is a definite conflict in time as regards this whole business of Yossarian's releases from the hospital, the first food poisoning, Milo's promotion to mess officer, and the Ferrara missions. It is, of course, impossible to say for certain whether Heller deliberately included this conflict in the novel whether it was an oversight. There seems to be no artistic demand for the two conflicting statements of Yossarian, or for Corporal Snark's reference to Milo's promotion, so the whole matter might be interpreted as a slight slip in plotting. After all, the book was written and re-written, old episodes dropped and new episodes inserted over a seven-year period, and this business of the food poisoning during Ferrara may be an example of an event which has been changed or should have been changed during the book's final editing. Another example of this may be the puzzling statement by Yossarian after Ferrara when he suggests that Colonel Cathcart give him a medal because, "You gave one to Hungry Joe when he cracked up that airplane by mistake" (p. 137). As the only mention of Hungry Joe crashing a plane, this may be a reference to an event which Heller decided at some period in his editing to leave out, and the statement of Yossarian's is all that remains.

Major Major's retreat from the world also presents some problems in chronology. When Yossarian and Appleby arrive Pianosa from Puerto Rico, Appleby's first action is to report Yossarian to Major Major because he will not take his Atabrine tablets (p. 105). Major Major, however, is in hiding and Appleby cannot see him because, as Sergeant Towser tells him, "Major Major never sees anyone in his office while he's in his office." This contradicts the account of Major Major's actions preparatory to his going into seclusion. Major Major drops out of sight some time after he is appointed Squadron Commander by Colonel Cathcart; however, Colonel Cathcart does not take over the squadron until Colonel Nevers dies at the time when Yossarian has completed 23 missions. It is, therefore, impossible for Major Major to have already gone into hiding when Yossarian and Appleby first arrive on Pianosa. This inconsistency may be merely a detail which escaped Heller's notice, but I am inclined to view it as an inability on his part to resist placing the priggish and officious Appleby in a position where he can be humiliated by Sergeant Towser.

The next series of events occur during The Great Big Siege of Bologna which is central to the novel. The long, nerve-eroding wait for the dreaded flight to Bologna is important to the character development and motivation of Yossarian. He has lost his bravery over Ferrara and thus feels more keenly the sense of doom which pervades the base. A number of events occur during The Siege. Yossarian moves the bomb-line (p. 118), which causes Major de Coverley to fly to Florence and disappear (p. 114) and enables General Peckem to get a medal because he "was the only officer with sufficient initiative to ask for it" (p. 119). Chief White Halfoat first decides die of pneumonia at this time, (p. 126). Corporal Snark prolongs the wait by poisoning the fliers again (p. 123). Hungry Joe goes to pieces and tries to kill Havermeyer and a day later has a fist fight with Huple's cat (p. 128). Milo, Orr, and Yossarian fly to Cairo, and Milo corners the cotton market (p. 224). In order to pay for all the cotton which begins piling in the warehouses, Milo is forced to take contracts from both sides to bomb and defend the bridge at Orvieto, and later takes a second contract from the Germans to bomb his own squadron. Yossarian sees Wintergreen about Milo's Egyptian cotton (p. 120). Yossarian has a fight with Colonel Korn over the Lepage glue gun (p. 123). Orr is holidaying in Rome during The Siege and during the actual mission is on a rest leave after he ditched his plane over Genoa (p. 141). It never specifically mentioned how long The Great Big Siege of Bologna lasts. As time in the novel is measured only in terms of the number of missions flown, the length of periods when missions are not being flown is impossible to determine. I believe Heller is deliberately vague in his treatment of The Siege in order to avoid the necessity of being specific about the order and chronology of all the events which occur during this time.

Yossarian aborts the mission to Bologna by tearing out the wires in his intercom (p. 139). Bologna proves to be a milk-run (p. 143). The second run to Bologna encounters heavy flak, and Yossarian is reduced to a quivering hulk by Aarfy, who won't get out of the hatch way and keeps prodding Yossarian in the ribs (pp. 145–150). This was Yossarian's 32nd mission.

Yossarian runs to Rome and finds Lucianna (p. 144), then loses her (p. 161). When he returns to base he finds that the required number of missions has been raised.

> "Forty missions," Hungry Joe announced readily in a voice lyrical with relief and elation. "The colonel raised them again."
> Yossarian was stunned. "But I've got thirty-two, goddammit! Three more and I would have been through."

> Hungry Joe shrugged, indifferently. "The colonel wants forty missions," he repeated.
>
> Yossarian shoved him out of the way and ran right into the hospital. (p. 163)

Yossarian stays in the hospital for ten days, comes out and flies six more missions for a total of 38, then runs right back into the hospital when Colonel Cathcart raises the required number to forty-five. A number of important events occur during these six missions between hospital visits: the Avignon mission on which Snowden is killed is flown (He is alive in Rome [p. 162] but dead by this second hospital visit at 38 missions [p. 165]); Clevinger disappears (p. 170); Yossarian receives his medal for the Ferrara mission (p. 210) and sits naked in the tree watching Snowden's funeral (pp. 257–258).

During the hospital visit at 38 missions Yossarian first meets the Chaplain (p. 7), and also the soldier in white. The whole business of forging Washington Irving's signature and the subsequent investigations of the C.I.D. begin at this point. Yossarian and his friends are eventually driven out of the hospital by the friendly Texan, and Orr tells Yossarian about his apple cheeks and the whore who kept hitting him over the head (pp. 22–24). Yossarian flies six more missions and Colonel Cathcart raises the required number to 50.

> "Fifty missions," Doc Daneeka told him, shaking his head. "The colonel wants fifty missions."
>
> "But I've only got forty-four!" . . .
>
> "Fifty missions," he repeated, still shaking his head. "The colonel wants fifty missions."

Yossarian flies four more for a total of 48 but the Colonel raises the required number to 55.

> Yossarian slumped with disappointment. "Then I really do have to fly the fifty missions, don't I?" he grieved.
>
> "The fifty-five," Doc Daneeka corrected him.
>
> "The fifty-five missions the colonel now wants all of you to fly."
> (p. 58)

Yossarian goes to see Major Major about grounding him when he has 51 missions. Major Major offers him an opportunity to fly only milk-runs, but Yossarian turns him down (p. 101). After seeing Major Major, Yossarian goes to Doc Daneeka to be grounded. Doc Daneeka refuses to help and advises Yossarian to fly the remaining four missions so that he will be in a stronger position when he refuses to fly any more. Yossarian decides to fly the remaining missions, but before he reaches 55 Colonel Cathcart raises the number to 60 (p. 187). The season is now late August (p. 196). At this time, Dobbs comes to Yossarian's tent with a plan to kill Colonel Cathcart (p. 222), and the Chaplain reports to the Colonel about the prayers before missions which the Colonel hopes will get his picture in *The Saturday Evening Post,* and leaves with a plum tomato (p. 187).

Yossarian is wounded in the groin on the weekly milk-run over Parma and is hospitalized (p. 284). While Yossarian is in the hospital, Orr makes his last practice crash-landing off the coast of Marseilles during the second mission to Avignon (p. 301). In the hospital Yossarian has his experiences with Major Sanderson, the psychiatrist (pp. 285–293). He is visited by Dobbs who again tries to enlist his help in killing Colonel Cathcart (p. 295). A. Fortiori gets Yossarian's medical discharge while he and Dunbar are returned to combat (p. 299).

When Yossarian comes out of the hospital, the required number of missions is still 60. He tries to enlist Dobbs's help in killing Colonel Cathcart, because he has scheduled another mission to Bologna, but Dobbs now has completed his 60 missions and refuses (p. 309). Orr finishes his stove and asks Yossarian to fly with him on the mission to Bologna. Yossarian refuses and Orr disappears on that flight (p. 310).

After Orr's disappearance, Yossarian almost kills McWatt when McWatt flies too low returning from a practice mission (p. 326). During this time Yossarian begins taking Nurse Duckett to the beach. Just after McWatt frightens Yossarian by flying too low on a practice mission, he flies low over the raft at the beach and chops Kid Sampson in half and then flies himself into a mountain (pp. 330–333). Colonel Cathcart is so upset by the death of McWatt and Kid Sampson that he raises the number of missions to 65 (p. 333). When he hears that Doc Daneeka is also "dead," he raises the number to 70 (p. 334). "Yo Yo's" room-mates move in within forty-eight hours of McWatt's and Kid Sampson's deaths (p. 340). Yossarian runs to Rome and rescues Nately's whore from the generals (pp. 345–352).

Thanksgiving night Sergeant Knight shoots up the camp and Yossarian breaks Nately's nose, sending him to the hospital (p. 254). Yossarian, Dunbar, Hungry Joe, and the Chaplain check in as patients to visit him (p. 353). The soldier in white returns, pandemonium breaks out, and Dunbar "is disappeared" (p. 360).

Yossarian and Nately both finish their 70 missions (p. 367). Nately is afraid that he will be sent home, and thereby lose his whore, if he does not volunteer to fly more than 70 missions (p. 361). Colonel Cathcart wants to raise the required number to 80, but he is afraid the men won't fly any more (p. 367). He figures that if he "can get just one of the regular officers to fly more, the rest will probably follow" (p. 367). Milo tells him about Nately and Colonel Cathcart is overjoyed.

> "But Nately will fly more!" Colonel Cathcart declared, and he brought his hands together in a resounding clap of victory. "Yes, Nately will fly more. And this time I'm really going to jump the missions, right up to eighty, and really knock General Dreedle's eye out. And this is a good way to get that lousy rat Yossarian back into combat where he might get killed." (p. 367)

The next day, Yossarian cannot find Nately in time to persuade him not to fly and thus present a solid opposition to the increased number of missions. They all fly the mission to Spezia and Dobbs and Nately are killed (p. 369). This is Yossarian's 71st and last mission. From this point on, Yossarian refuses to fly any more missions, and the climactic chapters which follow are plainly chronological and need not be summarized at this point.

After spending such a great deal of time proving (what in any other novel would be taken for granted) that the chronological structure of *Catch-22* is indeed possible, one must face the question as to why Heller spent so much effort in obfuscation. The answer is, I believe, twofold. The most obvious is the effect created by treating all events as equally present. The intent is to confuse the reader's sense of order and to upset his basic assumptions regarding proper form and structure. The unorthodox treatment of time in *Catch-22* is both parallel to, and prepares the reader for, the unorthodox treatment of the subject matter. It is only fitting that a novel which deals with an apparently absurd and confused world should be written in an apparently absurd and confused style.

The second reason for Heller's obfuscation concerns itself mainly with numerous events occurring during The Great Big Siege of Bologna. By being vague (or even obtuse) as to the length of The Siege, Heller is able to deal with a large amount of humorous material, from a satiric treatment of a loyalty crusade to jokes about a Lepage glue gun, without the necessity of trying to locate events specifically in time. Heller does not need to develop an impossible time scheme to create a sense of absurdity and confusion in his novel; he achieves this effect better by obscuring and twisting a chronological structure which is both plausible and logical.

NOTES

1. Joseph Heller, *Catch-22* (New York, 1961). All Subsequent references are to this edition.
2. Jan Solomon, "The Structure of Joseph Heller's *Catch-22*," *Critique*, IX, ii (1967): pp. 46–57.

3. Solomon, pp. 47–48.

4. It should be noted that time in the novel is regulated by the number of missions flown by Yossarian and by the number of missions required by Colonel Cathcart. Yossarian never quite reaches the required number; each time he comes close the limit is raised by another five missions. Thus, during the hospital visit described in the opening chapter, Yossarian has completed 38 missions (p. 165) and the official number of required missions is forty. By the time he leaves the hospital and returns to fly his remaining two missions, however, the limit has been raised to forty-five.

5. Solomon, p. 47.

6. Solomon, p. 55.

7. Solomon, pp. 54–55.

8. Solomon, p. 52.

9. Solomon, p. 56.

RICHARD LEHAN AND JERRY PATCH

Catch-22: *The Making of a Novel*

The are two sources of the absurd in modern literature: one is the pro-lapsed world of (say) Camus and Sartre—Oran in *La Peste* or the concentration camp in *Les Chemins de la Liberté*—where the plague or military surrender, has led to a world without a center, where one has been cut off from an old way of life. In this fragmented world, one must construct himself once again, find new meaning, a new routine, a new system of moral and social values, a new way of measuring everything, including social status. Until there is once again a way of life which one can take for granted, every situation is unique and the individual lives estranged from everyone else, in an absurd and grotesque world.

The other source of the absurd is exactly the opposite kind of world—not the prolapsed world of Camus and Sartre but the overstructured and bureaucratic world of Kafka, where one does not exist if he does not have in I.D. card. This is the world of Heller's *Catch-22* (1961), where one is dead if his 201-file says he is dead, even if he is there to protest that the file is wrong.

Both worlds are sources of the absurd because they destroy meaning—the first destroys all preëstablished social and moral dictums so that the individual becomes a kind of hopeless wanderer in a foreign land; the second destroys the validity of sensory data and of human communication by reducing all meaning to tons of official forms and to a chain of command

Critical Essays on Catch-22, ed. James Nagel (Encino, Cal.: Dickenson, 1974): p. 44, from *Minnesota Review*, 7 (1967): pp. 238–244. © 1967 Minnesota Review.

that passes all responsibility up and then back down, until someone like ex-P.F.C. Wintergreen decides what should happen by forwarding some letters and destroying others. The two sources of absurdity—the chaos of the war and the mad system of bureaucracy—exist side by side in *Catch-22,* but the system for Heller is even more absurd than the war—a fact Captain Yossarian, Heller's main character, discovers one night in Rome when lieutenant Nately rapes an Italian girl and then with impunity throws her out a window while Yossarian is arrested for being on leave without a pass.

While it reveals the dark underside of life, while it is at times amusing, *Catch-22*—inchoate and incohesive, cracking in places under its own weight—is not entirely successful. Heller is best at depicting an upside-down world where one wins by losing and loses by winning. As an exercise in the absurd—the negation of a rational and meaningful world—not many novels can compete with *Catch-22.* Heller creates a sense of the grotesque and the incongruous—of *jamais vu,* that condition of mind which accepts the strange as familiar; and of *déjà vu,* that condition which accepts the familiar as strange. *Catch-22* presents a hallucinatory world which exists in reality but is one in which the mind refuses to believe that a naked man *is in fact* sitting in a tree; in which one can get into serious trouble by disobeying an order given by an officer who has disobeyed orders in giving that order; in which one has to be insane to be discharged from the Air Corps but in which the insane are willing to fight and thus have no desire to be discharged. The farfetched and ludicrous events in this novel sometimes contain truths that freeze the smile in horror. Captain Black's Loyalty Oath Crusade is ridiculous only because it is a slight exaggeration of the truth: the captain, demanding that the men sign the Oath before every meal, insists that Major Major, his hated rival, is a Communist because he has not signed the oath which the Captain refuses to let him sign. "'You never heard him denying it until we began accusing him, did you?'" Corporal Whitcomb's classic letter, signed by Colonel Cathcart, only slightly distorts the sincerity of "official" letters of condolence:

> Dear Mrs., Mr., Miss, or Mr. and Mrs. ....: Words cannot express the deep personal grief I experienced when your husband, son, father or brother was killed, wounded or reported missing in action.

Such passages in *Catch-22* go beyond comedy. As Heller puts it, "I wanted people to laugh and then look back in horror at what they were laughing at." Heller is less successful in *Catch-22* when, trying to use irony and paradox for purposes of caricature, he flies off into the realm of ludicrous fantasy: or when Milo Minderbinder, the mess officer and a capitalist's capitalist, bombs his own troops because the Germans, who pay their bills promptly, have so contracted; or when Captain Flume, the public relations officer, lives for months off berries and wild life deep in the forest, afraid of returning to headquarters because of Chief Halfoat, who has once threatened to kill him; when Major Major Major Major runs through a ditch at top speed and sneaks into his office through a back window and is available for conference only when he is not available; or when Captain Yossarian parachutes an Italian prostitute behind German lines because she is ubiquitous, continually appearing from nowhere and trying to kill him. Heller has overextended himself in these scenes and heavy-handedly destroyed the underlying truth by allowing them to become mere farce.

Catch-22 should have been scrupulously edited, whole sections removed, until we had one consciousness, Captain Yossarian's, breaking under the weight of the absurd; until we had, that is, a credible point of view, a consciousness that absorbed experience which was less than slapstick and adolescent fantasy. When Heller succeeds in *Catch-22,* and his success is sometimes considerable, he depicts Yossarian fighting the machine, Yossarian desiring to stay alive in an organization that finds him expendable, an organization that has lost the sense of humanity which Yossarian refuses to surrender.

Like Yossarian, Heller was a bombardier during the Second World War serving in the Twelfth Air Force stationed on the Island of Corsica, and many of the events in *Catch-22* reflect the logic (or the illogic) of Heller's firsthand experience with military bureaucracy. A great many of the events in the novel, however, have another source, at least according to Daniel R. Rosoff, a close friend to Heller for thirty-seven years. Mr. Rosoff has kindly shared with us his personal knowledge of Heller's early life and career—a knowledge that reveals that Heller incorporated a great many of his civilian experiences in *Catch-22,* but that he made these experiences more ridiculous by putting them in the context of war and in this way enhancing the sense of the absurd that he had acquired from his early life and reading.

Heller was born and raised in the Coney Island section of New York. His father died when he was four years of age, and his home was afterwards ruled by his possessive mother and sisters. From ten to nineteen years of age, Heller was a member of a neighborhood club, *ALTEO (All Loyal to Each Other),* whose members included Daniel Rosoff, Samuel Rolfe (producer-creator of *The Man from U.N.C.L.E.*), Harold J. Bloom (a television and motion-picture writer), and novelist George Mandel. Heller was the youngest of this group who still refer to themselves as "the Coney Island Renaissance."

During Heller's youth, *ALTEO* took the place of his dead father. When each of the club members took it upon himself to watch over one of the younger members, Rosoff became Heller's "brother." Rosoff confesses to having been both romantic and rebellious at that time—to having possessed the cynicism and the "black humor" so characteristic of the poor ghettoed Jews. Rosoff taught Heller how to "operate" as a member of a minority, and how to "scramble" during days when meals were not easy to obtain. Along with Rosoff and Mandel, Heller tried to write for money and, before entering the Air Corps, sold two stories. He told Rosoff that he "had found the formula," and in 1944 he went to Italy as a bombardier, believing that he would return to join *Esquire's* stable of writers in the manner of Irwin Shaw.

After the war, Heller married, and then found that he did not have the formula after all, that the editors of slick magazines would not buy his short stories. He and Rosoff wrote a play which attracted considerable interest, but which, "because of production limitations and difficulty in staging," was never produced. With nothing else to do, Heller studied at New York University on a scholarship and graduated with honors in 1948. He then took a Master's Degree at Columbia University and won a Fulbright scholarship to Oxford University. Upon returning from England in 1950, Heller went to Pennsylvania State University as an instructor in English, but he could take the academic life for no more than two years. In 1952, Mandel was living in Greenwich Village, but Heller was too busy to see anybody at this time, working from nine to five on *Time* and writing unsalable short stories during the evenings at home. Heller left *Time* in 1956 for *Look*, and in 1958 left *Look* for *McCall's*. In 1954, however, he began writing *Catch-22* that had been fermenting since 1947. Working five nights a week, writing three pages each night in red ink on yellow legal tablets, he kept at it for seven years.

According to Rosoff, much of the dialogue in *Catch-22* has exactly the quality of the conversations that Heller heard in his nine years with *ALTEO.* More important, Yossarian's encounter with the dying Snowden in *Catch-22* is drawn directly from Heller's own personal experience. Snowden, a young radio-gunner, suffers what Yossarian thinks is a severe leg wound. Yossarian treats and bandages the wound, tries to comfort Snowden. When, at Snowden's nod, Yossarian cuts away Snowden's flak suit, Snowden's entrails spill onto the plane's grated floor as Yossarian watches in horror. This is Snowden's secret and the secret of man—that man minus a soul is garbage. To escape from becoming garbage, Yossarian fights desperately to remain alive. The death of Snowden is narrated four times in the novel: each time Heller gives us more information, and at the end we know that Yossarian appears in the nude to receive his medal because he thinks that his uniform is still covered with Snowden's blood. Heller's repetitive method is intentional. "I wanted the feeling of simultaneous sweep," he maintains. "Snowden didn't just die once. He died before the novel began and he died all the way through it."

Heller also came by the character of Milo from personal experience, modeling him on a member of *ALTEO* called "Beansie," who now lives in California. Milo, whose religion is the principle of supply and demand, represents the economic aspect of war. Milo's great error in buying all of the Egyptian cotton crop and being unable to sell it is derived from one of Beansie's commercial misadventures. Beansie, because of the large lox-and-bagel breakfast trade in New York, devised a scheme to home-deliver lox, bagels, and coffee on a monthly basis. Heller, Mandel, and Sam Rolfe all aided him by stuffing advertisements of Beansie's service into New York mailboxes, and were all jailed for misuse of mail facilities. Beansie then found that he had no means of delivering the 40,000 odd bagels which he had purchased and stored in Mandel's second-story Village loft. As time passed, passersby were pelted with stale bagels during drunken reunions of *ALTEO*. Mandel moved, leaving over 30,000 bagels, the fate of which still remains a mystery.

After the Second World War Beansie bought a large surplus of Army color film and advertised its resale in photographic magazines. The success of this enterprise seemed assured because of the new interest in color film, which was in short supply. Beansie, however, was again embarrassed when the film turned out to be useful only for aerial photographs: it could not be used unless it was exposed at an altitude of 10,000 feet. Milo, like Beansie, sees the world in purely mercantilistic terms and is thus the only character in the novel who remains unafraid of Major de Coverly. To Milo, de Coverly is merely another customer.

It is Heller's closest friend, George Mandel, who had the greatest influence on *Catch-22*. The character of Yossarian is modelled on both Heller and Mandel. The physical description of Yossarian matches Mandel, and Yossarian's attempt to make a "separate peace, " as well as his strange appearance at Snowden's funeral, is reminiscent of Mandel's behavior as a soldier. Mandel, a thorough-going nihilist served as an infantryman in the European theater of the Second World War (the setting of his novel, *The Wax Boom*) and was severely wounded in the head. Today, Mandel lives only two blocks from Heller in Manhattan, and they often collaborate on screenplays. Mandel is an associate editor for Random House and the author of three novels, *Flee the Angry Strangers* and *The Breakwater* in addition to *The Wax Boom*.

An important influence on both the early careers of Mandel and Heller was Louis-Ferdinand Céline (Destouches). Heller discovered Celine's novel, *Death on the Installment Plan* (1938), while he was in Europe during the war. He later read *Journey to the End of the Night* (1934), and was reading *Guignol's Band* (1944) while working on *Catch-22*. *Guignol's Band* is an absurdist novel, a wildly irrational and nonsensical series of interior monologues woven into an equally irrational and almost nonexistent plot. Cascade, the main character, trapped by the insanity of his wartime world, attempts to reenlist in the army but is rejected because he receives a pension of 2,000 francs a year and is therefore considered disabled. The reason for his failure—he is rejected, not because he is unable to perform his army duties, but because some bureaucrat has decreed that all pensioners are unfit—exemplifies the kind of illogic which permeates *Catch-22*. The source of the absurd in both Celine and Heller is the bureaucracy which negates common sense and frustrates individual action.

Celine's *Guignol's Band* and Heller's *Catch-22*, however, differ greatly in tone and method. There is at best an affinity of mind between these two novelists. A much more direct influence on Heller at this time was that of George Mandel himself, especially Mandel's *The Wax Boom* (1962), a novel written before but published after *Catch-22*. Heller, who read the manuscript of *The Wax Boom* as Mandel wrote it, was obviously impressed, particularly with the forceful way in which his closest friend had attacked the army as an institution.

Like *Catch-22*, *The Wax Boom* reveals the evil that can come from the chain of command. It shows how the army can be a senseless and inhuman institution where lives are jeopardized by incompetent or ambitious officers and where men are helpless to protect themselves in the face of the all-powerful system. The incompetency of Captain Stollman and Lieutenant Simmons threatens the lives of everyone in the Second Platoon. As in *Catch-22*, most of the men are either so crazy that they do not care what happens to them or (like Sergeant Riglioni, who is the "brother" of Captain Yossarian just as Mandel is the "brother" of Heller) or so impotent that they are unable to change their circumstances.

Dobbs in *Catch-22* thinks seriously of murdering Colonel Cathcart; Sergeant Riglioni, in *The Wax Boom*, of murdering Lieutenant Simmons. Like Yossarian, Riglioni has in awareness of *déjà vu:*

> Riglioni went through demolished rooms searching for Gingold. And the room he found him in seemed a room he had been in before; the moment itself seemed a repetition of one recently gone by.

As Captain Yossarian ministers to the badly injured airman, Snowden, who repeatedly murmurs, "'I'm cold,'" so Riglioni ministers to the badly wounded Gene Proctor, who repeatedly whispers, "'Pretty please.'"

Perhaps because there is a tremendous sense of necessity—an inexorable sense of fate—in *The Wax Boom*, it is a far grimmer novel than *Catch-22*. There can be no escape for Sergeant Riglioni, no way out, nowhere to go—not even Sweden. He can never escape the stupidity and the ambition of a Captain Stollman, and Mandel never effects a humorous relief of the tension as Heller does. Such humor as there is in *The Wax Boom* is, however, like that in *Catch-22*, stemming from the profane (posted inside a gun turret is a picture of Christ, inscribed "To Ken Atman, with admiration, Jesus") and the ridiculous:

> "Give your call sign."
> "Huh? Reliable."
> "No . . . you're Mayflower!" It was First Sergeant Muldoon at Troop. "This is Reliable."

At the end of *The Wax Boom* Riglioni throws down his rifle, turns in his sergeant's stripes, and refuses to lead his men into battle. In like manner Captain Yossarian in *Catch-22* refuses to fly further combat missions. Captain Stollman tries to bribe Riglioni by offering him the job of First Sergeant the same way Colonel Korn tries to bribe Yossarian by offering him a hero's trip back to the States. Riglioni refuses the bribe—and also refuses to fight—sitting mesmerized by the flicker of candlelight in a cellar, as the Germans attack the town, killing him and his men, except Gingold, who lives through the some kind of wound that Mandel suffered in combat.

Catch-22 ends on a more optimistic note: Captain Yossarian has, like sergeant Riglioni, made his separate peace, is now committed only to noncommitment, and is planning to run away to Sweden and the promise of better things. We are hardly expected to accept this resolution literally. All we are expected to accept is a certain attitude or quality of mind. Yossarian escapes from the system, triumphs in his escape, and has a sense of new-found promise. Riglioni is trapped by the system, defeated by it, and dies because (for Mandel) there is no way back.

Both novels go far beyond routine "bitter" complaints about army life. They depict what can happen when the system becomes more powerful than the individuals who compose it. Mandel and Heller see man as more than just a small part of a vast machine, more than just a remorseless and dehumanized product of an institution. Though they do not question the fact that the army is necessary, they are intent on revealing the evil that such an institution can engender. Such an approach makes the fact that the army is necessary all the more frightening. Neither Yossarian nor Riglioni is willing to compromise, to sell out to the system, to be bribed; but Heller—in a very vague way, to be sure—at least suggests the possibility of a life outside the system, even in war.

When Heller began writing *Catch-22* he did not have the present ending in mind. When the novel was nearly finished, he submitted it to Simon and Schuster, who enthusiastically bought it, gave him an advance, and set a deadline for its completion. When the deadline came, Heller had still not finished the novel. When the deadline had passed, Simon and Schuster demanded the final chapters. Heller, faced with the task of drawing together his sprawling materials, finally did so, but with an abrupt shift of gears. Sherman Wincelberg unwittingly puts his finger on an important point when, in a review for *The New Leader* (May 14, 1962), he comments on the ending of *Catch-22*:

> For the last 30–40 pages Heller seems abruptly to have been persuaded that even a novel is original as his would be better for some sort of a plot, preferably in chronological order. So he hastily furnishes one, involving his startled hero in one of those soul-searching conflicts between conscience and self-interest which used to be so popular on live TV. It is very well done and all but, in contrast to the rest of the book's splendid contempt for such niceties, I find it a little on the square side.

The ending of *Catch-22* is more effective in suggesting a hope than in offering a solution. Mr. Rosoff maintains that Heller could not have written a different ending, could not have concluded his novel on a note of helplessness: "Joe is an ultra-liberal," Rosoff told us, "active in many social causes connected with human and civil rights. This commitment is apparent from his activities. Look at his writings in *The Realist* in 1964."

Catch-22 took more than seven years to write and altogether thirteen years to evolve. Although Heller has devoted more time to writing screenplays as *Sex and the Single Girl* than to writing prose fiction, he completed five years after the publication of *Catch-22*, another novel, soon to be released, a section of which was published in the September, 1966 issue of *Esquire*. The setting is once again a highly structured institution—a gigantic corporation—which turns its employees into functionaries, where machines performing routine tasks. "We *are* those punched cards they pay us with," says Joe Slocum, the central character. "They have knocked holes in us to label and limit us, and we go through machines of out daily routines. Really, I ask myself every now and then is this the most I can get from the few years left in this one life of mine?" Heller's hero is asking a question that many other Americans have asked before him—Thoreau for one. Thoreau, however, refused to become a part of the machine, while Joe Slocum is well-oiled and in gear:

> I've got bad feet. I've got a jawbone that's deteriorating and someday soon I'm going to have to have all my teeth pulled. I've got an unhappy wife to support and three unhappy children to take care of. I've got eight people working for me who have problems and unhappy dependents of their own. I've got anxiety: I

repress hysteria. I've got wars on my mind and summer riots, peace movements and L.S.D. I've got old age to face. My boy, though still an innocent and unsuspecting child, is going to have to spend from two to six years of his life in the Army or Navy, and probably at war. I've got the decline of American culture and the guilt and ineptitude of the whole Government of the United States to carry around on my poor shoulders. And I find I'm being groomed for a better job.

And I find that I want it.

Joe Slocum is as ambitious as Colonel Korn; the machine, in fact, would not work without such ambitious men. Heller has once again shown—and this is one of the unnoticed merits of *Catch-22*—that in the very center of the American nightmare is the American dream.

JAMES L. McDONALD

I See Everything Twice!
The Structure of Joseph Heller's Catch-22

"I see everything twice!" today's college student scrawls on the last page of his bluebook to signify that he had a bad day. "You've got flies in your eyes," he mutters at the campus policeman or the dormitory prefect. "Where are the Snowdens of yesteryear?" he asks, referring to a friend who has flunked out, been drafted, or suddenly made the Dean's List after two years on probation.

The use of the quotations testifies to the impact *Catch-22* has made since its publication in paperback just over four years ago. Like *The Catcher in the Rye, Lord of the Flies,* and *A Separate Peace,* Joseph Heller's novel has become one of those books which college students take up as their own, from which they draw the slogans which are meaningful to them in relation to the established power structures they live under.

I suspect, however, that students admire *Catch-22* for the wrong reasons. Though the book is in tune with the restlessness and rebelliousness of the times, and though the "Catch Cult" rightly praises its black humor and its anarchic (even pacifist) tendencies, it is not merely a book which reflects and forms current college opinion, It is a novel, and it seems time to discuss it as a novel: to examine, in some detail, its formal values.

On a first reading, *Catch-22*—switching its focus from one character to another, whirling crazily through a hodgepodge of slapstick antics, bizarre

The University Review, Vol XXXIV, No. 3; (Spring 1968): pp. 175–180.

horrors, grotesque anecdotes, and aimless digressions—may well make the reader try to rub the flies out of his eyes and wonder where the Snowdens of yesteryear or any year fit in. But close analysis reveals that Heller is a highly sophisticated, conscious artist who carefully manipulates the diverse and seemingly divisive elements of the novel to achieve structural unity: that discernible pattern which gives the reader a firm sense of the time, place, and thematic relevance of each unit in the novel, so that he knows where he is at each point in relation to where he has been before.

Ironically, the reader's bewildered "I see everything twice!" provides the key to the relation of the parts to the whole, what Chaplain Tappman calls "Déjà vu": "For a few precarious seconds, the chaplain tingled with a weird, occult sensation of having experienced the identical situation before in some prior time or existence. He endeavored to trap and nourish the impression in order to predict, and perhaps even control, what incident would occur next, but the afflatus melted away unproductively, as he had known beforehand it would. Déjà vu. The subtle, recurring confusion between illusion and reality that was characteristic of paramnesia fascinated the chaplain, and he knew a number of things about it."[1]

This is a remarkably clear description of the method Heller employs. Obviously, he is not dealing with this "characteristic of paramnesia" scientifically; but he is using the phenomenon as the basis of the novel's structure. Out of the welter of digressions, flashbacks, and anecdotes, he constructs his narrative and contrives thematic patterns so that the reader has the experience of seeing everything twice—the sensation which the chaplain calls "Déjà vu."

"Déjà vu" is, first of all, an explanation of and a reason for Heller's narrative construction. An artificial chronology of the novel's action can be worked out: the action proper begins with Yossarian's training in Colorado; it proceeds through his combat missions over targets like Avignon and Bologna, and the death and disappearances of his comrades; it is marked by Milo Minderbinder's rise to power and the raising of the missions from forty to eighty; and it culminates in Yossarian's refusal to fly any more missions, his discovery of the real meaning of "Catch-22," and his desertion.

The actual narrative, however, is not chronological. Heller—like Proust, Joyce, Virginia Woolf, and Faulkner—is the heir of Henri Bergson: he does not view time as something dependent on and made relevant by the artificial orderings of the clock or the calendar; rather he regards it as something governed and made tangible by the consciousness of the individual, his situation, and his memory. The past operates in the present by forming the individual's apprehension of the present, coloring and outlining each significant moment.

Thus Heller begins the novel in the middle of things, just beyond the midpoint of Yossarian's career as a bombadier when, in the hospital after flying forty-four of the required fifty missions, he meets the chaplain. From this point on, the action alternates between what happened before the opening of the novel, and what happens after it. Heller interweaves past and present, the past action continually crowding into the present. A character or situation in the present is outlined; then, through free association with some aspect of the character or situation, an event from the past, in the form of an anecdote, a digression, or a flashback, sweeps into and obliterates the present. This event, in turn, frequently merges with or flashes off to still another event. The past event, however, is seldom related as one complete, coherent unit. Rather the reader learns of it partially, in disjointed fragments: he has the "sensation of having experienced the identical situation before," the desire to "trap and nourish the impression," and the frustration of seeing "the afflatus" melt "away unproductively." Only tentatively and gradually can he reconstruct it, place it in relation to other events in time, and understand its significance.

The story of Snowden's death exemplifies Heller's technique. In Chapter Four, the reader learns the bare facts, that "Snowden had been killed over Avignon when Dobbs went crazy in mid-air and seized the controls away from Huple" (35–36); but then the account shifts to the intrigues of Colonels Cathcart and Korn. In the following chapter the incident is recalled, and the reader learns that Dobbs had broken radio silence with a plea to help Snowden, who lay dying in the back of the plane; but then the incident is dropped. It is not taken up again until Chapter Twenty-One, where some of its significance is hinted at: during the story of how Yossarian stood naked to receive the Distinguished Flying Cross, Captain Wren explains that "A man was killed in his plane over Avignon last week and bled all over him . . . He swears he's never going to wear a uniform again." (232)

In the following chapter the reader discovers that "Yossarian lost his nerve on the mission to Avignon because Snowden lost his guts," hears Snowden's plaintive "I'm cold," and sees him "freezing to death in a yellow splash of sunlight near the new tail gunner lying stretched out on the floor . . . in a dead faint" (230–231); but again the account shifts, this time to the story of Dobbs's plan to murder Colonel Cathcart. In similar fashion, additional information about the death of Snowden is supplied in subsequent chapters. Not until the second-last chapter of the novel, however, is the whole story reconstructed. In the hospital, Yossarian—bathed in an "icy sweat" which reminds him of Snowden—recalls the entire event and remembers "Snowden's secret" that "Man was matter," that "the Spirit gone, man is garbage." (455, 450)

One can describe the novel's overall construction, then, as an interplay between present narrative and the cumulative repetition and gradual clarification of past actions. The interplay portrays, dramatically, the manner in which the characters apprehend their world, and shows the impact of the past on their present attitudes and actions. Each moment in the present flashes their minds back to fragmentary images of past events which influence their behavior so heavily. The reader's gradual and partial realization of the nature and significance of past events matches those "weird . . . sensations" which the chaplain characterizes as *Déjà vu*.

Déjà vu further provides the basis for the method Heller uses to contrive the thematic patterns of the novel. He manipulates the characters, events, and situations into elaborate parallels which, through comparison and contrast, clarify and illustrate the novel's central themes. He thereby gives the reader the sensation of seeing everything at least twice, of "having experienced the identical situation before" because it parallels other situations or is related to others thematically.

Heller carefully sets two worlds in opposition to each other: the world of those in power, and the world of their victims. Revolving the action around that "subtle, recurring confusion between illusion and reality" which the chaplain notes, he centers the themes of the novel on the question of human identity. By a series of parallels, he clarifies the concerns and attitudes of both groups. Those in power attempt to succeed within an artificial system by adhering to its ethics, which reduce human beings to abstractions, statistics. Their victims attempt to preserve their identities by rebelling against the system—either through parody, or outright defiance.

The official attitude of those in power is outlined very clearly by the doctor who persuades Yossarian to pose for the parents of the dead Giuseppe as their son:

> "They [the parents] didn't come to see me," Yossarian objected. "They came to see their son."
> "They'll have to take what they can get. As far as we're concerned, one dying boy is just as good as any other, or just as bad. To a scientist, all dying boys are equal." (187)

For "scientist" the reader might well substitute "bureaucrat" or "officer" (or "Scheisskopf," the name signifying the role of all officers), or simply "those in charge." This is the official attitude: those in charge view all human beings as "dying boys," statistics, means to an end. Employing the crews as their pawns, they wage a constant battle for position and glory. Heller illustrates the attitude by paralleling the motives and methods of the officials along the entire scale of army rank.

The novel is marked by a series of bids for power, which the reader sees again and again. At the highest level of rank is the struggle between Generals Dreedle and Peckem. Just below it is the rivalry between Colonels Cathcart and Korn, with Cathcart's ambitions epitomizing the irrationality and pedantry of those who attempt to rise in the system. Cathcart treats all crews— "dying boys"—alike: he raises their missions and volunteers the squadron for the most dangerous assignments, not to help win the war, but to attain glory and promotion. His letter of sympathy, in the jargon which marks all the official communiqués in the novel, typifies his attitude:

> *Dear Mrs., Mr., Miss, or Mr. and Mrs. Daneeka: Words cannot express the deep personal grief I experienced when your husband, son, father or brother was killed, wounded or reported missing in action.* (354)

On a lower level there are Captain Black's loyalty oath crusade and the plots of the C. I. D. men. Finally there are Gus and Wes, who treat all patients alike, painting their gums and toes purple and forcing laxatives down their throats, regardless of the ailment: Triumphant over them all, of course, is Milo Minderbinder, whose Enterprises virtually make him ruler of the world, who regards whole armies as means to his end, impartially contracting to bomb both the Allies and the Axis for the profit of the syndicate.

The victims of the officials are bewildered and virtually helpless. They live in a world which, in keeping with the attitudes and actions of the officials, is irrational and inexplicable. As the warrant officer with malaria complains, "'There just doesn't seem to be any logic to this system of rewards and punishment.'" (175)

There is no real logic within a system manipulated by those who have the right of "Catch-22" which says "'they have a right to do anything we can't stop them from doing.'" (416) Thus Major Major Major becomes, almost automatically, Major Major Major Major and, by official whim, is made squadron commander; the dutiful Major Metcalf is shipped to the Solomon Islands to bury bodies; Dunbar is "disappeared"; the patriotic Clevenger and the innocent Chaplain are ruthlessly interrogated; Chief White Halfoat is the victim of the government and the land-grabbers; Yossarian is arrested for being in Rome without a pass while Aarfy, the murderer, goes free.[2]

All the dying men are treated alike and all men—in war—are dying. The dying, the dead, have no real identity—only official status. Death and life are merely matters of official routine: the question is decided, not through recourse to reality, but by reference to official lists and records.

The parallel incidents involving the soldier in white, Mudd, and Doc Daneeka typify the predicament. It is impossible to tell whether the soldier in white is dying or dead: wrapped up in plaster and gauze like a mummy, he is no more than a helpless unidentifiable victim. Equally helpless are Mudd (whose name signifies his fate) and Doc Daneeka. Mudd, the dead man in Yossarian's tent, was killed in combat over Orvieto; but according to official army records he is alive because he never officially reported for duty. Doc Daneeka, in reality, is alive; but according to official lists he is dead because he was officially listed, though not really present, in the crew of the plane which

McWatt flew into the mountain. Heller explicitly links the three victims, indicating the deliberate parallelism he sets up.

Yossarian complains that "'Anybody might be in'" that case of plaster and gauze that is the soldier in white: "'For all we know, it might even be Mudd!'" (174) Later, Sergeant Towser laments that "now he had *two* dead men on his hands—Mudd . . . who wasn't even there, and Doc Daneeka . . . who most certainly was there and gave every indication of proving a still thornier administrative problem for him." (350)

The problem the victim faces in maintaining his identity centers most obviously on Major Major Major, whose identity is fixed by a perverse practical joke: "It was a harsh and stunning realization that was forced upon him at so tender an age, the realization that he was not, as he had always been led to believe, Caleb Major, but instead was some total stranger named Major Major Major about whom he knew absolutely nothing and about whom nobody else had ever heard before. What playmates he had withdrew from him and never returned, disposed, as they were, to distrust all strangers, especially one who had already deceived them by pretending to be someone they had known for years. Nobody would have anything to do with him." (87)

His identity determined by the official list—the birth certificate—Major Major Major is abandoned by all. He has no real identity of his own; his fellow officers suspect that he is Henry Fonda. He becomes the perpetual outcast, one whose very existence is dubious. Finally he retires into bizarre seclusion, completely withdrawn from the squadron: he can only be contacted in his office when he is not there; when he is there, no one is permitted to enter.

Major Major Major's actions reduce the official attitude to absurdity, parodying it by turning it upon itself. Throughout the novel, the victims—and Major Major Major must be numbered among the victims, even though he is a high-ranking officer—attempt to preserve themselves by adopting masks designed to thwart the official attitude, to take advantage of the I. B. M. mentality of those in charge. Both Major Major Major and Yossarian pose as Washington Irving when they carry out official duties. Major Major Major takes the pose further by signing himself as Irving Washington, John Milton, or Milton John on official documents. Yossarian, in order to remain safe and secure in the hospital, adopts the identities of Warrant Officer Homer Lumley, Giuseppe, and A. Fortiori.

These masks belong to a pattern of acts of rebellion against the system, some comic, others deadly serious. As the novel progresses, the victims, growing more and more aware of the menace of the system, carry gestures of rebellion to the point of outright defiance. Yossarian—with the chaplain the moral conscience of the novel—is most blatant in defiance of the system: his moaning during the Avignon briefing, and his query "'Where are the Snowdens of yesteryear?'"; his insistence that there is a dead man in his tent; his nakedness after the Avignon mission and during the presentation of the medal; his efforts to halt the Bologna mission by putting soap in the squadron's food and moving the bomb line; his repeated requests to be grounded, his final refusal to fly any more missions, and his desertion. The system, as such, cannot be lived with. It cannot be changed. It cannot be thwarted, beyond a certain point. The only way to overcome "Catch-22" is to run away from things—to commit an act of treason, desertion in the face of the enemy. All of the action and the events of the novel point to this conclusion.

Throughout *Catch-22*, then, Heller is using *Déjà vu* as the basis of the methods by which he achieves structural unity. Constructing a narrative interplay between the past and the present, contriving elaborate parallel repetitions of and variations on his central themes, he enables the reader to say, with Yossarian, "I see everything twice!" He creates the discernible, ordered pattern which is of the very essence of art.

NOTES

1. Joseph Heller, *Catch-22* (New York, 1962): p. 209. Subsequent references to this, the Dell edition, will appear in the text.
2. Of course there is the inevitable backfire, when Scheisskopf is inexplicably made a Lieutenant-General, ends up in charge of Special Services, and is thereby made Group Commander.

THOMAS ALLEN NELSON

Theme and Structure in Catch-22

Many early critics of Joseph Heller's *Catch-22* have damned it either outrightly or with faint praise, lashing out at the novel with such epithets as a "jabberwock of a work," "nightmarish," "mildly eccentric," "scrambled," "an emotional hodgepodge," and, according to Whitney Balliett's *New Yorker* review, a novel containing only "a debris of sour jokes, stage anger, dirty words, synthetic looniness, and the sort of antic behavior a child falls into when he knows he is losing our attention." Until recently, critics have tended to disparage the artistry of the novel on the grounds that it contains too many gratuitous features: repetitiousness, loose structure, unnecessary subterfuge.[1] Such criticisms of the novel's apparent structural and thematic incoherence are answered to some extent by Minna Doskow's interesting analysis of Yossarian's final flight ("The Night Journey in *Catch-22*," *TCL*, XII [January, 1967]). Doskow argues that the structure of *Catch-22* resembles the archetypal pattern of the classic epic or romance, and that the novel's resolution represents a symbolic journey to the underworld (in Yossarian's final trip to Rome), resulting in Yossarian's recognition of responsibility. Doskow, therefore, suggests a relationship between the theme of Yossarian's escaping *to* responsibility and the structure of the novel.[2] Instead, however, of a standard romantic structure of descent and ascent, I think, as Heller himself has suggested, that *Catch-22* has a cyclical pattern of action which

Renascence: Essays on Values in Literature, Vol. XXIII, No. 4 (Summer 1971): pp. 173–182.
© 1971 Marquette University.

complements the multifarious ideas and issues associated with the theme of responsibility ("An Impolite Interview with Joseph Heller," *The Realist* [November, 1962]).

Of crucial importance in critically estimating Heller's thematic mastery and specifically the theme of responsibility is an understanding of the world of *Catch-22*. How is it portrayed? What are its values, its concept of order, of right and wrong, of man's place in the universe? Notice, for instance, the manner in which Heller represents authority on the island of Pianosa, a setting which suggests a microcosm of the modern world and to which Heller attaches some symbolic meaning on the novel's title page: "The island of Pianosa lies in the Mediterranean Sea eight miles south of Elba. It is very small and obviously could not accommodate all of the actions described. Like the setting of this novel, the characters, too, are fictitious." Authority on this island seems ethereal, hermetic, and tyrannical. Authority embodies a "system," or Establishment, which is inimical to individual welfare, a system which Yossarian views as the ubiquitous "they." Yet, Yossarian, the empiricist and sometimes idealist, reasons that "they" do exist—"strangers he didn't know shot at him." Because this society appears as mysterious and chaotic to a sensibility such as Yossarian's, judgments of importance come not from exalted authority, but from individual experience. What appears to Yossarian as pestilential insanity, however, symbolizes an arena for action and achievement to those who incorrectly believe they exercise some control over the course of their fates. The men of power and responsibility—Peckem, Dreedle, Cathcart, and their legion—attempt to impose some sense of order on the chaos, but when ex-pfc Wintergreen and those who have access to the mimeograph machine make crucial decisions, when Scheisskopf, a fatuous ass who excells in the system, regiments order in parades, we realize that in this society ruthless cunning or accidents of IBM fortune make right, not concepts of just law, individual freedom, or moral responsibility. Order in the system achieves its epiphany in Scheisskopf's toy soldiers and in the universality of M&M Enterprises.

Heller, obviously appalled by the prospect of an Armageddon, examines what results when no rational and humane basis for life exists in a world which harbors a military arsenal capable of destroying civilization. In view of such a situation, a society in which purblind men pursue their own advancement at any cost becomes absurd, destructive, and totalitarian. Clevinger's idealism fails him because the people in whom he has too much faith betray his trust by their willingness to apply power and selfish ambition as bludgeons to justice.

Heller develops several themes which grow out of his depiction of a workld of irrational and absurd contradictions. *Catch-22* contains an appearance-reality theme, one common to works which deal with the disparity between a given society's consensus values and irresponsible practices. Major

Major's background taught him those humanistic values of freedom, compassion, and goodness common to Christianity and the American democratic tradition, when, in reality, his society subscribes to a competitive and callous devotion to oneupmanship. Individuals within Major Major's society demonstrate all the residue of the American Dream: they marry, have children, are successful and ambitious, and yet they are the progenitors of psychological tensions far beyond their comprehension or control. Major Major's fear of recognition and responsibility results from an insidious protestant ethic which preaches the sanctity of human life but which condones human slaughter in the name of philistine expansionism, patriotism, and prejudiced fear. Major Major's primary failing, from his society's viewpoint, is his lack of insensitivity to these moral contradictions. As a result, Major Major is universally disliked as a "flagrant nonconformist."

For every Major Major in the system stand multitudes like Colonel Cathcart. Cathcart combines a plethora of contradictions: "He was dashing and dejected, poised and chagrined . . . complacent and insecure, daring in the administrative stratagems he employed to bring himself to the attention of his superiors and craven in his concern that his schemes might all backfire." While Major Major will stop at nothing to annihilate his identity, Cathcart will do anything to create an identity which might ameliorate his stature within the system; all his aborted identities contribute only to his paranoia, infantilism, and moral vacuity. Because of an insatiable ambition to be a general—a laudatory aim in his society—Cathcart views reality through the distorting perspective of chauvinistic bombast and in consequence his action conforms to dogma and fantasy rather than to reality. He constantly turns to Colonel Korn for the assurance that consensus absolutes are inviolable ("Atheism is against the law, isn't it?") while, in reality, his fate depends upon an administrative Russian roulette and the capricious whims of his superiors.

The most crucial theme, therefore, which emerges from the depiction of such a social system concerns the inability to pin down moral responsibility in a world which summarily witnesses and perpetrates the devaluation of human life. Who—or what—is responsible? Acts are accomplished with a certain degree of efficiency: planes take off, drop bombs, destroy people and property, all of which requires some form of organization and decision-making. Major Major abdicates the responsibility of his office (one which he did not seek) yet "whatever he was supposed to get done as squadron commander apparently was getting done without any assistance from him." Is the responsible party Major —De Coverly, a man who passes the majority of his time pitching horseshoes, kidnapping Italian laborers, and renting apartments to soldiers? De Coverly displays remarkable ingenuity by being the first on hand to get his picture taken following a city's liberation and by being the one who casually undermines Captain Black's Great Loyalty Oath Crusade. For all his recognition, however,

Major De Coverly assumes no responsibility; this seeming enigma comes to represent nothing more than just another rapacious war profiteer.

In order to enlarge upon the theme of responsibility (or irresponsibility) within the system, Heller highlights the activities of Milo Minderbinder. Milo, not content with the operation of one mess hall, works for both the Germans and the Allies, revealing in the process the contradiction between patriotic rhetoric and the capitalistic search for expanding markets. Like De Coverly and other characters of position, Milo refuses to bear any responsibility for the deaths and misery which his enterprises may inadvertently cause. Mudd, the man who ever was, dies over the bridge at Oriveto as a result of Milo's informing German antiaircraft of the American mission. Milo's rationale speaks for itself: "'I didn't him!' Milo kept replying passionately to Yossarian's angry protest. 'I wasn't even there that day, I tell you. Do you think I was down there on the ground firing an antiaircraft gun when the planes came over?'" That he did not actually pull the trigger, to Milo's thinking, exonerates him from any culpability in the death of Mudd, or later, in Snowden's death, whose pain could not be alleviated because Milo had removed the morphine from the first-aid kit, leaving only a note which testifies to an incredulous and malign innocence: "What's good for M&M Enterprises is good for the country."

If Heller depicts this world as a welter of evil, what, then, is his concept of man's relationship to the larger forces in the universe? Perhaps Yossarian's ruminations on death, hospital style, defines Heller's point:

> They didn't take it on the lam weirdly inside a cloud the way Clevinger had done. They didn't explode into blood and clotted matter. They didn't drown or get struck by lightning, mangled by machinery or crushed in landslides. They didn't get shot to death in hold-ups, strangled to death in rapes, stabbed to death in saloons, bludgeoned to death with axes by parents or children, or die summarily by some other act of God. Nobody choked to death. People bled to death like gentlemen in an operating room or expired without comment in an oxygen tent. There was none of that tricky now-you-see-me-now-you-don't business so much in vogue outside the hospital, none of that now-I-am-and-now-I-aint.

The *Weltanschauung* of Catch-22 chronicles a medieval world of suffering, misery, and death without a forgiving God as the trump card. In the place of God and redemption rises the system, defining life and death with a fusillade of charts, statistics, feathers in caps, and black eyes. If Nurse Cramer had read the thermometer correctly, the Man in White might have lived, if Colonel Cathcart had prayed less for tighter bomb patterns and more for human lives, great suffering might have been spared. The Warrant Officer's cynicism ("who gives a shit?") epitomizes the feelings of characters who have no faith in the possibilities of justice, whether human or divine: "Just for once I'd like to see all these things sort of straightened out, with each person getting exactly what he deserves. It might give me some confidence in this universe." This position rejects even experience, not just particular moral systems, believing that a morality based solely on experience produces an absurd determinism which contradicts itself from one day to the next.

The search for value in *Catch-22*—and such a positive element does exist in the novel—does not tread epistemological or ontological paths. What Heller initially stresses through those characters concerned with an ethical approach to experience—Yossarian, Orr, the Chaplain, characters with little position or power at stake—is their examination and rejection of consensus values which are no longer tenable (if they ever were). Those values tainted with self-aggrandizement, greed, or national gain in a world which could destroy itself, Heller—and a handful of his characters—considers infantile and self-righteous. Milo's free enterprise morality, Major Major's father's protestant ethic, Nately's patriotism and jingoism—all of these shibboleths—are no longer logical, moral, or practical. Yossarian, through individual protest, discovers an alternative to these values. When all possible corrective action is cut off and if ignoble conformity or rebellion are the only choices, then the recalcitrant individual must protest, even if flight becomes the only feasible manifestation of his dissent. Because the system defines reality through administrative machinations ("they can prepare as many official reports as they want and choose whichever ones they need"), Yossarian cannot stay and fight. Instead of merely representing a quixotic gesture, Yossarian's and Orr's flight stands as a positive renunciation of officialism and as an assertion of individual conscience.

Instead of being content with satiric nihilism, Heller promulgates a moral and ethical system which is basically humanistic and rational: man, a creature capable of reason, has a moral responsibility to oppose irrationality and inhumanity in his social and political institutions by demanding a rational code of ethics based on the needs of human beings living in a changing and potentially volatile world. The present system, he argues, with its outmoded approach to modern life, an approach which does not distinguish between means and ends, dehumanizes essential human relations. Man, when abstracted, impersonalized, and mechanized, loses the best features of his humanity: his desire to know truth, to create a rational and humane civilization, to realize and fulfill his need for love, to develop his capacity for creative endeavors. Instead, what the system offers as sexually ideal is characterized by the lurid paradise of flesh in the whorehouses of Rome, which assumes the guise of masculine fantasy. Or, in contrast to whorey pulchritude, Heller presents the indifference and frustration of the nurses. With Nurse Duckett, because no verbal or emotional rapport exists, Yossarian relishes the concrete sexual act: "He thirsted for life and reached out ravenously to grasp and hold Nurse Duckett's flesh."

This dehumanization process stands out in a medical motif which runs throughout the novel. Early in *Catch-22*, an unnamed colonel is examined, fingered, prodded, and dissected by a circle of specialists: "The colonel dwelt in a vortex of specialists who were still specializing in trying to determine what was troubling him. They hurled lights in his eyes to see if he could see, rammed needles into nerves to hear if he could feel. There was a urologist for his urine, a lymphologist for his lymph, an endocrinologist for his endocrines, a psychologist for his psyche, a dermatologist for his derma . . . ." Man, in a scientifically oriented society, can become only matter, a squalid object, like Mudd and the Man in White, without spirit or identity. Human beings, as illustrated by Aarfy's murdering of a servant, cease to be morally responsible agents and become garbage to be tossed out windows. And, to a scientist, "all dying boys are equal." This motif complements Heller's repetitious use of imagery which suggests death by obliteration and which culminates in Snowden's "secret": "It was easy to read the message in his entrails. Man was matter, that was Snowden's secret. Drop him out a window and he'll fall. Set fire to him and he'll burn. Bury him and he'll rot like other kinds of garbage. The spirit gone, man is garbage. That was Snowden's secret. Ripeness was all."

T o complement this complex interplay of ideas and motifs associated with the theme of responsibility, Heller constructs *Catch-22* through a series of what he calls, in an interview for *The Realist*, "recurring cycles." Events and characters which may be outrageously funny when first introduced acquire philosophical significance in the last part of the novel as the degeneration of values increases to alarming proportions. This structural device leads not to unnecessary repetition, as many have argued, but to an expansion of moral awareness in Yossarian and reader.

Chapters 1, 17, and 34 form such a cycle. One of several significant details in this cycle is the Man in White, who, when initially introduced, contributes to a prevailing sense of incredible absurdity: "A silent zinc pipe rose from the cement on his groin and was coupled to a slim rubber hose that carried waste from his kidneys and dripped it efficiently into a clear, stoppered jar on the floor. When the jar on the floor was full, the jar feeding his elbow was empty, and the two were simply switched quickly so that stuff could drip back into him." Yet, when Heller, in Chapter 17, returns to the same point in time, the Man in White, like human experience, takes on new dimensions as enlarged perspectives are applied. Now Heller characterizes him as a "stuffed and sterilized dummy," a figure symbolic of the lack of existence in the system. The events between these two chapters (2–16) lend credence to this interpretation by cataloguing such details as Cathcart's paranoia, Doc Daneeka's greed, the reduction of men to machines ("sightless, stupid, crippled things"), Hungry Joe's sexual frustration, Havermeyer's sadism, Kraft's parades, Black's Crusade, Aarfy's insensitivity, and a blatant devaluation of human life within the system. In Chapter 34, Dunbar cries "he's back" and properly allegorizes the Man in White's function in the novel: "He's hollow inside, like a chocolate soldier. They just took him away and left those bandages there." The Man in White symbolizes the ubiquitous, unknown, indeterminate non-entity who is so much a part of the system—and our society—and who, without his powers of sensibility and reason, represents simply another organism which takes matter, absorbs it, and excretes it or uses it up.

Significant in these recurring scenes is the setting of the hospital. In all three of these chapters, the hospital serves as a safe asylum from the outside world for Yossarian and Dunbar. Whereas in Chapter 1 we might view Yossarian as a profane and irresponsible malingerer, by Chapters 17 and 18 his "liver ailment" increases in thematic importance. When Yossarian realizes that the Soldier Who Saw Everything Twice is faking, he reverts to illusion for the purpose of survival; the hospital furnishes Yossarian the illusion of safety where, at least, death is more predictable and less messy than on the outside. Throughout most of the novel, Yossarian searches not so much for truth or moral responsibility, but for a bower of bliss. By Chapter 34, the hospital no longer represents a place of sanity (Dunbar is "disappeared") and, in Yossarian's last hospital stay (Chapter 41), Colonel Korn hovers over him while a team of doctors debate whether to cut him to pieces or not. Yossarian realizes that these illusions are not satisfactory—the system can still get to him in the hospital and in the whorehouses of Rome. Yossarian's final flight, unlike his earlier ones, symbolizes not one of illusory escape, but one of protest. Sweden represents an objective to move toward—and one fraught with danger—in order to change an intolerable situation.

In the final eight chapters of *Catch-22* (35–42), Heller completes and ties together a multitude of cyclical patterns which he so carefully establishes in the earlier parts of the novel. In Chapter 35, the development of Milo's role in the novel reaches its climax. At the nadir point of his development, Milo's ambitions seem harmless and even laudatory. In Chapter 7, Milo wants to serve the best food possible, a seemingly admirable adjunct to his belief in the free enterprise system. Yet, as Milo's political power extends as a result of his economic coups (Chapter 22, "Milo the Mayor"), Heller indicates how apparently harmless ambitions can shape values and attitudes which make men insensitive to human suffering. At Snowden's funeral (Chapter 24), Milo's concern for finding a market for his Egyptian cotton creates an impenetrable barrier between himself and Yossarian's despair. Snowden's death, like the travails of humanity in general, means nothing to Milo, while, to Yossarian, it represents a revelation of some kind. While Yossarian yearns for some understanding of human misery, Milo searches for loopholes and legal outs. Whereas Yossarian attempts to interpret life ("it's the tree of life"), Milo remains the literalist ("no, it's a chestnut tree"). And, finally, there emerges Milo the Militant (Chapter 35) who thrives, as does private enterprise, on war and its rhetoric. The novel's last reference to Milo (Chapter 42) implies that others—like Cathcart and Wintergreen—who could not lick him decided to join him. By this time, Yossarian has nothing to urn to for help but the inspiration of Orr's escape.

Chapter 36 ("The Cellar") brings two thematically crucial cycles into better perspective. When, in Chapter 1, Yossarian ends one of his censored letters with "I yearn for you tragically, A. T. Tappman, Chaplain, U.S. Army," he implicates the Chaplain in his Washington Irving deception. Similarly, throughout the novel, Yossarian and the Chaplain are linked together by their mutual quest for some light on the nature of reality (the Chaplain, characteristically, sees his search in terms of a religious quest) and through their sensitivity to human suffering. Like Yossarian, the Chaplain has his illusions—the "naked man" in the tree (Yossarian) as mystical revelation, the mysterious Flume as prophet of the woods (Chapter 25). These "mystical experiences" stimulate a renewed hope in the Chaplain but they are only valuable as indications of his inevitable rejection of private mysticism for rational humanism. The Chaplain's tie with Yossarian enlarges as the novel progresses and returns to particular motifs: the Washington Irving game, the naked man in the tree, and even his faking Wisconsin shingles (Chapter 34) bind the Chaplain's fate with that of Yossarian's. "The Cellar" allegorizes the theme that men are bound together irrevocably through their actions and that in apparently innocent and childish acts of rebellion, such as Yossarian's signing letters Washington Irving and A. T. Tappman, the moral responsibilities which one man has toward another can be breached. Ironically, the Chaplain, perhaps the most selfless man in the novel, feels guilt for crimes against the system which exist only in his disturbed imagination and in Cathcart's paranoia. The genuine miracle for the Chaplain occurs in Chapter 42 when he knows that Yossarian and Orr have escaped: he gains some courage and a sense of purpose in the knowledge that the system can be beaten—that "Catch-22" is fallible.

As Yossarian and the Chaplain gain knowledge, the system evolves into more phrenetic forms, so that by Chapter 37 Scheisskopf (now a general) symbolizes the absurdity and increasing degeneracy of a world without rational law, without justice, without its humanity. Through an administrative error (paper realities have replaced all other realities), Scheisskopf takes charge. Everyone—except those fortunate enough to escape—will march!

The sense of allegory which prevades the later chapters increases in Chapter 38, the chapter in which Nately's Whore attempts to kill Yossarian and in which Yossarian concerns himself with the fate of Kid Sister. Earlier in the novel, the whorehouse scenes furnished some excellent satire on the meaninglessness of war (the Old Man's debate with Nately in Chapter 23) and generally satirized masculine, sexual fantasies (Aarfy, for instance, bragging of never having "paid for it"). Nately's puerile attempts to metamorphose his whore into homogenized American nubility demonstrates how cultural myth overpowers reality. In Chapter 38, however, the "whores" can no longer be dealt with purely on the basis of our own masculine stereotypes—they develop into human beings who, like Snowden, are matter, who suffer pain, and who deserve better treatment. Yossarian assumes responsibility for Kid Sister because no one else does. Perhaps the fantastic sequences in which Nately's Whore attempts to kill Yossarian can be explained symbolically by the fact that she, being unschooled in the sophistry of the system, knows that someone must be responsible for Nately's death and Yossarian happens to be available. Thus, Yossarian, like Christ, assumes responsibility for those sins which others in the system refuse to acknowledge.

Not until Chapter 39 ("The Eternal City") does Heller attach a symbolic meaning to Rome other than as just another place for Yossarian to find respite from his fear of death. Like the hospital, Rome is not immune to the death, disease, and destruction which increases in the novel in direct proportion to Yossarian's enlarged awareness. Yossarian, as a compassionate knight-errant, views the ruins of Rome, from the whorehouse to the Colosseum, with a philosophical disgust not known to him earlier in the novel. Heller uses this setting as an allegory of an earlier civilization which, like ours, tolerated and perpetuated the exploitation and destruction of human life, except that now death is acted out on a grander scale and with a larger cast, so that Aarfy's unconcern for the death of one girl reduces all human life to insignificance: "I hardly think they're going to make too much fuss over one poor Italian servant girl when so many thousands of lives are being lost every day."

If anything, then, *Catch-22* is constructed meticulously, even, as Heller says in an interview for *The Realist*, "with a meticulous concern to give the appearance of a formless novel." The final three chapters (Chapters 40–42) complete the treatments of Snowden's death and his "secret" and Yossarian's final resolution to flee toward responsibility. At this point, a definite technique can be discussed and outlined: in the beginning of the novel, Heller treats people and incidents as though they were glimpses (Snowden's death, for example), and then he demonstrates that these actions and characters seen as glimpses at the first do have meaning and that they do come together; he stresses the point that people's acts are interrelated in an inescapable sort of way, that we are all bound by the same moral laws, and that all of us are linked to one another by the acts which we perform (or fail to perform); the novel's settings and situations do not necessarily represent America, but seemingly a monolithic world which closes off every conventional avenue of protest or corrective action and which, because it perpetuates many of the obsolete values of past generations, could easily reduce human civilization to a wasteland. Yet, to Yossarian, the answers seem so simple and so evident, but communication breaks down and a frightening sense of frustration prevails. Such frustration comes to the surface in a succession of scenes where characters are indifferent (they don't even care when they are poisoned by the soap in the potatoes), where people both physically and mentally cannot do anything, where, in short, human beings feel helpless in the face of total moral irresponsibility and insanity. With their will to resist gone, their moral courage sapped by fear, characters only have faith in the infallibility of "Catch-22," the god of the insane, an unwritten, unseen law which gives efficacy and decree to all the indifference and injustice in the novel. Like Yossarian, we know "Catch-22" does not exist—that human inequities require responsible human solutions—but does everyone else?

NOTES

1. See, for example, Richard G. Stern, "Bombers Away," *New York Times Book Review* (October 22, 1962): p. 50, who feels that the novel needs "craft and sensibility." An early review countering this mainstream of opinion is Robert Brustein, "The Logic of Survival in a Lunatic World," *The New Republic*, CXLV (November 13, 1961): p. 11, who discusses the "internal logic" of the novel.

2. See Sanford Pinsker, "Heller's *Catch-22:* The Protest of a *Peur Eternis*," *Critique*, VII (Winter, 1964–1965): pp. 150–162, who disagrees and argues that Yossarian is once again trying to escape *from* reality.

CLINTON S. BURHANS, JR.

Spindrift and the Sea: Structural Patterns and Unifying Elements in Catch-22

If my experience is at all representative, a particular and unusual danger lurks in the serious study of this work. Inevitably, there comes a time when, looking around at accumulations of notes, charts, and commentaries, you suddenly bust out laughing at yourself in an unexpected illumination of your own absurdity in taking the thing so seriously. In that strange flash of disorientation, you feel like one of Heller's characters, like maybe a bookkeeper for Milo Minderbinder.

Fortunately, this fit of sudden sanity dissolves, as it rightly should; for the comic anarchy which provokes it is only the surface of *Catch-22*, not its sustaining structure. Critics have consistently been challenged by the question of the work's structure and unity and with various and conflicting results. In the main, such discussions center around two viewpoints: some critics argue that the work is episodic and formless; others find it organized according to some particular principle or method.[1] Neither position, it seems to me, need necessarily, nor in fact does, exclude the other. The narrative surface is obviously episodic and apparently chaotic; but this surface formlessness is central to the novel's thematic experience, and it rises from strong and multi-level structural patterns and a variety of unifying devices.

Seeking these patterns and devices in *Catch-22* involves a long and often frustrating analysis, beginning with an elusive sense of underlying structure

Twentieth Century Literature, 19, pp. 239–250. © Hofstra University.

109

and unity and ending with that sense becoming conviction amidst an overwhelming mass of supporting information. Despite the constant episodic
zigzags which comprise *Catch-22's* narrative surface, the novel is built on a
central conflict, two sub-plots, and a host of motifs. What Heller has done
is to break up the logical and chronological development of these narrative
elements by taking bits and pieces of all three and mixing them together
with dashes of expository and rhetorical comment without regard to logical
or temporal or spatial connection. The result is an apparent—but only apparent—jumble of comment, character, and event consistent with contemporary
esthetic tendencies away from reason, time, and space as ordering categories.

Nevertheless, a basic narrative structure can be discovered holding the
novel subtly together. This structure can best be visualized as a kind of narrative tree, with the trunk comprised primarily of the main plot (Yossarian's
efforts to get off flying status either by achieving the required number of
missions or by having himself declared insane) and two sub-plots (the struggle between Peckem and Dreedle for command of the Wing, and Milo's
syndicate). Around this trunk grow in abundance two kinds of branches, arranged for visual convenience one on either side. Those on the left, whether
simple references or detailed episodes, are expository flashbacks made once
for informational purposes or repeated for thematic effect. Those on the
right are a different kind of flashback, one which I have not encountered
elsewhere. The best way to describe them, I think, is to call them foreshadowing flashbacks; that is, again whether simple reference or detailed episode,
most of them after the first add links in a chain of information drawn out
and completed at some length. Thereafter, references to these subjects become conventional flashbacks repeated for thematic effect. The result is the
paradox of suspense through flashbacks; and, I think, as this paradox suggests, an ingenious fusion of time planes into the simultaneity of existential
time, a fusion entirely consistent with what seems to me the fundamental
existential theme of the work.

Visualizing this narrative tree and looking down it, one discovers that
Heller has done something in each chapter to link it to the preceding chapter—a continuing action or condition, references to time or to historical
events, mention of the number of missions required or flown. Sometimes
these links are slight and tenuous, as in Chapters Six, Eight and Twenty-four;
they may appear at the beginning or be buried in the middle or only surface in
the end; still, they are usually there, and they do function, if only subliminally,
to tie the narrative together.

Amplifying this masked but functional narrative continuity, *Catch-22*
develops in a five-part alternating structure. The trunk of the narrative tree
bends twice, breaking its straight line into three sections and two substantial
bulges. The first part, through Chapter Ten, establishes and develops the nar-

rative present; that is, each chapter, however fragmented in time or place, event or character, does something to maintain and advance the narrative present and its problems established in the opening chapters. The second part flashes back to the Great Big Siege of Bologna in Chapters Eleven through Sixteen; and a third part returns to the narrative present as in the first part in Chapters Seventeen to Twenty-two. Another long flashback, this time to Milo Minderbinder's operations and to the origins and growth of his M & M Enterprises, forms a fragmentary but essentially sustained fourth part in Chapters Twenty-two through Twenty-four. A fifth part returns again to the narrative present in Chapter Twenty-five and remains there with increasingly less fragmentation to the end.

That these structural sections are neither arbitrary nor accidental is suggested by the clearly transitional chapters with which Heller surrounds the two major flashbacks. Chapter Ten ends by introducing the Great Big Siege of Bologna; and Chapter Seventeen opens shortly after the two Bologna missions by returning Yossarian to the hospital at the time of Chapter One and ends with Yossarian out of the hospital again and coming to Doc Daneeka a second time for aid after Major Major had refused to help him in Chapter Nine. Similarly, Chapter Twenty- two introduces the earlier trip to Cairo on which Milo had tried to corner Egyptian cotton; and Chapter Twenty-five refers both to the Chaplain's seeing a naked man in a tree at Snowden's funeral—the episode which ends Chapter Twenty-four—and to his continuing efforts in the narrative present to help Yossarian and the other men by trying to get the required number of missions reduced.

Despite *Catch-22's* many and sudden shifts in scene, episode, character, motif, and time, then, the narrative trunk makes it clear that Heller has distributed sufficient elements of continuity and transition to give the work a controlling structural design beneath its kaleidoscopic surface. However much this narrative surface may disguise it, *Catch-22* is built on a five-part alternating structure in which sections developing the central conflict and sub-plots in the narrative present (parts one, three, and five) alternate with long flashback sections providing additional background and exposition and also functioning to fuse the work's time planes (parts two and four).

Another glance down the narrative tree suggests a second structural pattern, a tonal structure. Beginning with the end of Chapter Twenty-nine and Chapter Thirty and culminating in Chapter Thirty-nine, the novel darkens measurably into almost insupportable horror. The crucial episode is the mission against the undefended mountain village, a totally unnecessary mission in which poor people unconnected with the war are to be killed without warning for publicity photos of tight bomb patterns. The tonal shift in this episode is clear and sharp. Earlier episodes focus on individual combatants as voluntary or involuntary participants in a familiar if horrifying and ridiculous game with ultimate consequences, like the descriptions of Yossarian's experiences on missions; or on perils and death remote in time, like the Ferrara mission; or on horrors contained within farcical situations, like Milo's bombing of the squadron. Such episodes reflect real horrors but to some degree, at least, cushion the reader against experiencing them, insulate their effects on him. Not so with the mission against the mountain village. It is immediate; it is probable; it is barren of justification; it is stark murder; it is unspeakable outrage; it is uncushioned horror. Even Dunbar, who has up to this point looked primarily after himself and sought only to lengthen his life span by taking no unnecessary risks whatever, rises in protest, denounces the mission, and risks court-martial by intentionally missing the village.

The tonal shift I am suggesting here is indicated in several other ways as well. Four of the novel's five basic structural sections and the beginning of the fifth precede the mission to the mountain village; no basic structural change follows it. Clearly, something different is going on in this final third of the novel from the structural alternation of the first two-thirds: something more focused, more concentrated, more intense. Similarly, most of the novel's riotous fragmentation of time, place, character, and event occurs in its first two-thirds: most of the flashbacks, for example, appear in these chapters. The ratio is around four or five to one, not only in number but also in the variety of their subjects, again suggesting a more intense focus in the novel's final third on the narrative present and its immediate problems. Finally, despite the long months of peril, neither Yossarian nor any of his friends, the central characters in the novel, die before the mission to the mountain village. But one by one they die or disappear thereafter, like lights going out in a gathering darkness.

A three-part tonal structure, then, seems evident. The first part, Chapters One through Twenty-nine, establishes the tone by which the novel is usually characterized: a predominantly and broadly humorous tone, a mixed tone in which fear and desperation are contained within and controlled by exploding jokes, gags, puns, parodies, and satiric attacks, the tone of a fireworks display in a thunderstorm. The second part, Chapters Twenty-nine through Thirty-nine, pivoting on the mission to the mountain village, shifts to a much different and more consistent tone, one of deepening despair whose growing darkness envelops the humor and turns it increasingly sick and savage. The third part, the last three chapters, shifts again to another mingled tone, one of resigned desperation broken by revelation and release.

Within these general structural patterns of organization and tone, Catch-22's central conflict develops in a conventional plot and sub-plot structure. The central conflict is, of course, Yossarian's struggle to survive the war either by flying the required number of missions or by getting himself removed from combat status. In each purpose, he finds himself constantly blocked: Col. Cathcart keeps raising the required number, and the military system functions by insuperable devices for keeping Yossarian on combat status. The resulting conflict develops in a generally classical pattern: exposition, initiation, complication, rising tension, crisis, and climax moving in the main chronologically and climactically within a welter of expository and foreshadowing flashbacks and providing points of departure for a host of related puns, jokes, parodies, and satiric attacks.

Catch-22 begins *in medias res* with Yossarian in full and close pursuit of the magic number: 45 missions are required, and he has flown 44. In Chapter Two, Col. Cathcart raises the number to 50 and in Chapter Six, when Yossarian has 48, to 55. In Chapters Nine and Seventeen, Yossarian has reached 51, but in Chapter Nineteen, the magic number rises to 60. By Chapter Twenty-eight, Yossarian is once more closing in; but Cathcart raises the ante again, to 65 in Chapter 30 and to 70 in Chapter 31. In Chapter Thirty-five, Cathcart raises to 80; and Yossarian, after reaching 71, decides in Chapter Thirty-eight to end this exercise in futility and fly no more.

Flashbacks provide additional information on Yossarian's efforts to gain this elusive military brass ring. Chapter Six returns to the previous Fall when 25 missions were required and Yossarian reached 23 by flying six missions in six days. At that point, Col. Cathcart became the new group commander and raised the number to 30 in celebration. By the time of the Orvieto mission the following Spring, 35 missions were required (Chapter Ten); and after the two Bologna missions, when Yossarian had 32, the number increased to 40 (Chapter Sixteen). In Chapter Seventeen, Yossarian reached 38, and Cathcart raised again to the 45 required in Chapter One.[2]

A similar pattern emerges from the second aspect of Yossarian's struggle to survive: his efforts to get off combat status. After leaving the hospital in Chapter One, he tries unsuccessfully to persuade Doc Daneeka to help him (Chapters Four and Five) and considers refusing to fly any more missions (Chapter Six). He decides to go to Major Major; and when he refuses to help (Chapters Seven and Nine), Yossarian tries Doe Daneeka again (Chapter Seventeen). He asks the Chaplain for help, and the Chaplain responds vigorously but without result (Chapters Nineteen, Twenty, Twenty-five). After Yossarian is wounded over Leghorn, the psychiatrist at the hospital certifies him insane but confuses him with another patient, who gets sent home instead of Yossarian; and he tries Doc Daneeka again (Chapter Twenty-Seven). In Chapter Thirty-eight, he refuses to fly any more missions; and after recognizing that he cannot go through with his deal with Cathcart and Korn (Chapters Forty and Forty-one), he deserts.

Here, too, flashbacks fill in important background material. In Chapter Ten, Yossarian decides not to fly the first Bologna mission; and in Chapter Fourteen, he aborts by forcing Kid Sampson to turn back. On the Avignon mission, he is smeared with Snowden's blood and viscera and refuses to wear a uniform again (Chapter Twenty-four). And a final flashback revealing the full import of Snowden's secret reveals as well the deepest motivation of Yossarian's struggles (Chapter Forty-one).

Like the structural and tonal patterns, then, this two-pronged central conflict functions coherently at the heart of *Catch-22*, though it is not always immediately or continuously available. In less detailed and more fragmentary form, two sub-plots work similarly within the apparent welter of the novel's surface. The lesser of these is the contest between Generals Peckem and Dreedle for command of the Wing. The background and opening moves of this contest are suggested in Chapter Three, and Peckem's aims and campaign appear in Chapters Twelve and Nineteen. General Dreedle's position and ultimate defeat are indicated in Chapter Twenty-one, and Scheisskopf joins Peckem and learns of his real war in Chapter Twenty-nine. In Chapter Thirty-six, Peckem replaces Dreedle, only to discover that his command is now under the broader jurisdiction of the newly promoted Scheisskopf (Chapters Thirty-seven and Forty).

A more fully developed sub-plot describes the rise of Milo Minderbinder from new mess officer to business manager of the whole war as head of M & M Enterprises. As with Yossarian, Milo's story begins *in medias res*. Chapters Two, Seven, and Nine reveal his extravagant and luxurious mess-hall operations in full bloom; and flashbacks in Chapters Ten, Twelve, and Thirteen explain how Milo became a mess officer and describe some of the operations of M & M Enterprises.[3] Syndicate operations and Milo's spreading influence and power appear in Chapters Nineteen, Twenty-one, and Twenty-two; and Chapter Twenty-four is a flashback to the beginnings of M & M Enterprises and its major operations. Chapters Twenty-eight, Thirty-five, Thirty-nine, Forty-one, and Forty-two reflect further glimpses of Milo's gourmet mess halls and his increasingly ubiquitous syndicate. In Chapter Forty-two, Col. Cathcart and ex-P.F.C. Wintergreen have joined Milo; and he is well on his way not only to controlling the war but also to owning the world by giving everyone a share in it.

As the narrative tree suggests, then, the episodic and fragmented narrative surface of *Catch-22* masks and is sustained by a complex and multi-dimensional structural design compounded of an alternating five-part basic structure, a three-part tonal structure, and a conventional plot and sub-plot structure. Moreover, this complex structural design is reinforced by several unifying devices: chronology, recurring characters, and a variety of motifs. The result is paradox: structure and unity sustaining and controlling episodic chaos.

However much the narrative surface may obscure it, the events of *Catch-22* are chronologically related. Heller refers to several specific dates and occasions and to historical events, and these can be supplemented by time references and cross-references in the text. We know, for example, that it is late August when the Chaplain talks to Col. Cathcart about lowering the missions from the new number of 60 (203, 283) and that this conversation occurs at least several weeks after Yossarian leaves the hospital at the beginning of the story. We also know, from a reference to his rest leaves in Rome (18), that Yossarian leaves the hospital and returns to his tent at least several weeks after the fall of Rome on June 6, 1944. We can thus infer that the narrative present at the beginning of the story is sometime in July, 1944. When Yossarian returns from the hospital at that time, he learns that Col. Cathcart has raised the required missions to 50; and a short time later, probably in middle or late July, he raises the number to 55. At this point, Yossarian recalls the death of Mudd "three months earlier" (111-12); therefore, since Mudd died on the Orvieto mission, we can date that mission as sometime in April, 1944.

By thus using firm dates and events as constant reference points and by cross-checking against them and against each other the main episodes of the novel, it is possible to organize an occasionally loose but generally reliable chronology for *Catch-22*:

1941	Yossarian in Army—qualifies for transfer to Air Cadet training
1941-1943	Yossarian an Air Cadet at Santa Ana, California, and Lowery Field, Colorado— Grand Conspiracy of Lowery Field
NOVEMBER 26, 1941	Yossarian in hospital at Lowery Field
NOVEMBER 26, 1942	Yossarian in hotel room with Mrs. Scheisskopf
1943	Yossarian goes overseas via Puerto Rico— Splendid Atabrine Insurrection
SEPTEMBER, 1943	Required missions at 25 Yossarian flies his 23rd, to Arezzo—Col. Nevers killed—time of Salerno beachhead— missions raised to 30
APRIL, 1944	Beginning of M & M Enterprises—Orvieto mission—death of Mudd

MAY, 1944	Required missions at 35
	Development of M & M Enterprises—Milo tries to corner Egyptian cotton
	Ferrara mission—deaths of Kraft and Coombs— first soap poisoning of mess
	Milo bombs squadron
	General Peckem schemes to take over combat command
	Great Big Siege of Bologna—second soap poisoning of mess—Yossarian's 32nd mission—missions raised to 40
	Yossarian goes into hospital
JUNE, 1944	Yossarian leaves hospital, flies six more missions—time of fall of Rome
	Yossarian and Orr on leave trip with Milo
	Avignon mission—death of Snowden
	Yossarian naked in tree at Snowden's funeral
	Yossarian naked at decoration for bravery in Ferrara mission
	Clevinger disappears in cloud
JULY, 1944	Missions raised to 45—Yossarian has 38, goes into hospital again—time of beginning of book
	Yossarian leaves hospital—missions raised to 50
AUGUST, 1944	Yossarian flies four more missions—missions raised to 55
	Yossarian flies 51st mission
	Yossarian tries to punch Col. Cathcart in Officer's Club
	Missions raised to 60; Paris liberated (August 25, 1944)
	General Peckem gaining in struggle with General Dreedle

SEPTEMBER, 1944	Yossarian wounded over Leghorn—goes into hospital again—Americans pushing into Germany, 8th Army takes Rimini, Gothic Line collapsing
	Yossarian returned to combat status—flies two more missions—second Avignon mission—Orr shot down again
	Third Bologna mission—Orr shot down and disappears
	Scheisskopf joins General Peckem's command
	Raid on small Italian mountain village—Germans above Florence Deaths of Kid Sampson and McWatt—missions raised to 65
OCTOBER, 1944	Missions raised to 70
	Yossarian gets new roommates—two months after invasion of Southern France (August 15, 1944)
NOVEMBER, 1944	Yossarian breaks Nately's nose on Thanksgiving Day—goes into hospital to see Nately—Dunbar to be disappeared
	Yossarian has 70 missions—Chief White Halfoat dies
DECEMBER, 1944	Missions raised to 80—Dobbs and Nately killed on La Spezia mission
	General Peckem becomes wing commander—under General Scheisskopf
	Yossarian has 71 missions, refuses to fly any more—Dunbar and Major Major disappear
	Yossarian knifed by Nately's whore—goes back into hospital
	Hungry Joe dies
	Col. Cathcart and Ex-P.F.C. Wintergreen partners in M & M Enterprises
	Yossarian deserts—Germans driving towards Antwerp in Battle of Bulge

Despite the general consistency of this chronology, Heller occasionally errs in computation. For one, it seems unlikely that Cathcart would increase the required number of missions only by ten in the seven or eight months between September, 1943, and May, 1944; and it seems even more unlikely that Yossarian would fly only nine missions in the same period—especially after flying six missions in six days in September. The relationship between the number required and the number Yossarian flies is consistent, but the totals are implausible. For another, Heller says at one point that Milo bombed the squadron "seven months" after the period in which Yossarian was an air cadet at Lowery Field in Colorado (109). But Milo formed his syndicate after April, 1944 (247), and Yossarian had already flown 23 missions seven months earlier in September, 1943 (54). Clearly, then, Heller is off here by a year or two. Again, Captain Black's Glorious Loyalty Oath Crusade is ended by Major — de Coverley when he returns to the squadron from Rome shortly after the fall of the city in June, 1944[5] (119–20). But Captain Black began his Crusade when Major Major was made squadron commander instead of him (116), and Major Major was already squadron commander when Yossarian joined the squadron some time before September, 1943 (109).

Such errors raise some interesting problems. To begin with, they are few and relatively insignificant when measured against the number of events and their generally consistent chronological relationship. Moreover, Heller occasionally makes almost offhand expository comments which indicate that he does have a clear chronology in mind. In describing Yossarian's and Hungry Joe's missions in September, 1943, for example, he concludes with the observation that shipping orders could have saved Hungry Joe "seven days earlier and five times since" (54). At that time, 25 missions were required; and Col. Cathcart, until late in the story, raises the ante by fives. "Five times" would put the number at 50—which is precisely the number required in the narrative present from which Heller is writing at this point.

It is tempting, therefore, to argue that Heller's errors are intentional, that he means them to disguise his general chronological consistency or to contribute to the fusing of time planes which, it seems to me, is an essential element in his thematic purposes. On the other hand and more likely, I believe, they could be the results of simple carelessness. Either way, such errors are insufficient to destroy the basic and generally consistent chronology or to prevent its functioning as a unifying element in the matrix of the story.

Another unifying element is Heller's use of recurring characters. Counting the characters in *Catch-22* poses the same problem as counting them in Chaucer's "Prologue": the sum depends on those you decide *not* to count. The full total of all the characters in *Catch-22* would number armies and hosts; but if the count is restricted to those who are named or otherwise individualized, the result is some eighty or ninety characters. And if the count is only of those whose recurrence is sufficient in number and in distribution to suggest a unifying effect, the total becomes a manageable but still significantly large twenty-six. Yossarian (40), Cathcart (30), Korn (25), Daneeka (22), Dunbar (22), Hungry Joe (21), McWatt (21), Milo (21), Nately (21), Black (19), Orr (18), Aarfy (17), Chaplain (16), Dreedle (16), Wintergreen (16), Nately's whore (15), Snowden (15), Major Major (14), Appleby (13), Danby (13), Halfoat (13), Peckem (13), Clevinger (12), Dobbs (12), Havermeyer (11), Duckett (10)—each recurs throughout the novel in the number of chapters indicated in the parentheses.

Another interesting and valuable way to assess Heller's use of recurring characters is to note how many of these twenty-six appear or are mentioned in each chapter. Two chapters (Six and Thirty) contain some mention or broader function of eighteen of these twenty-six characters, and only one chapter (Eighteen) has as few as one of them. The average is about fourteen per chapter; only three chapters contain less than five, and only fifteen chapters less than ten characters. Clearly, then, Heller uses recurring characters to further the paradox at the heart of his novel's structure: with so large a number of characters (supplemented by the other sixty or so recurring less frequently) in as many chapters, he can achieve a turbulent variety in any single chapter while evoking a subtle sense of unity between the chapters.[6]

Even more interesting and effective, it seems to me, is Heller's use of motifs as unifying elements. Two motif patterns function throughout *Catch-22*: general and climactic. By general motif I mean simply the conventional repetition of concept, theme, image, or event for thematic or stylistic or structural effect; and at least eight such general motifs recur in *Catch-22*: death (36), insanity (30), Yossarian and death (16), Yossarian and sex (14), disappearance (12), Yossarian and hospitals (11), Catch-22 (9) and Washington Irving signatures (7).

Here, again, as with the recurring characters, I have listed the motifs in the order of the number of chapters in which they are at least mentioned. Moreover, these motifs are distributed throughout the novel; and they reflect intriguing thematic suggestions. Supporting and illuminating the earlier discussion of the novel's central conflict, these motifs emphasize that death and insanity characterize the world of *Catch-22*, a closed-system world of sudden disappearance in which hospitals and bizarre behavior are Yossarian's only refuge, and sex and the life-force it represents his true rebellions.

More dramatic and much more complicated are the novel's climactic motifs, by which I mean essentially what I outlined earlier in discussing Heller's use of foreshadowing flashbacks—that is, a progressive repetition in which successive occurrences provide additional details up to a climactic point at which the motif is completed or its full significance revealed. At least six such climactic motifs recur in *Catch-22*: Nately and his whore (17), Avignon and the death of Snowden (14), Ferrara and the deaths of Kraft and Coombs (12), Orvieto and the death of Mudd (10), Orr's whore, stove, and ditching (9), and Milo's bombing of the squadron (7).

Clearly, these motifs are closely related thematically to the general motifs and with them to the central conflict: if the general motifs shade in the
conditions of the world in which Yossarian struggles to survive and the means
which he employs in his struggles, the climactic motifs highlight the principal events and persons through which he comes to know the real nature of
his world and his dire need to contend with it. Furthermore, these climactic
motifs function even more carefully and effectively than the general motifs
as unifying elements. Each one begins early in the novel; with one exception,
each develops through a wider range of chapters; and, again with one exception, each one ends its development in a late chapter. Like the general motifs,
then, these climactic motifs recur with sufficient frequency and distribution
to work as unifying elements; but they contribute even more valuably to this
end both in their function as foreshadowing flashbacks and also in the over-
lapping pattern of their development.

No one or two of these structural and unifying elements would do much
to support or control the apparent episodic chaos of *Catch-22*. But, taken together, the narrative links between chapters, the multi-dimensional structural
design, the disguised but generally consistent chronology, the recurring characters, and the two kinds of motifs form a surprising and impressive foundation of structure and unity beneath the shifting shapes and colors of the
novel's narrative surface.

Despite its occasional flaws, Heller's artistry in *Catch-22* is both more
effective and also more impressive than is sometimes granted. Moreover,
this artistry is thematically significant. Its combination of formal elements
working subtly within and sustaining an obvious surface formlessness argues
strongly that the novel's bombardment of jokes and its satiric barrage are
equally linked and that both derive from a shaping thematic concern at its
core. The sea, too, has its spindrift; but the spindrift is not the sea.

NOTES

1. John Aldridge sees *Catch-22* as an anti-novel, a parody on the novel form
("Contemporary Fiction and Mass Culture," *New Orleans Review*, I: 1, (Fall, 1968),
4–9); similarly, Constance Denniston sees it not as a novel but as an episodic and
formless mixture of genres—a romance-parody ("The American Romance-Parody:
A Study of Purdy's *Malcolm* and Heller's *Catch-22*," *Emporia State Research Studies*,
Vol. 14 (1965), pp. 42–49, 63–64); and Douglas Day considers it a grab-bag, an
anatomy in Northrup Frye's sense of the term ("*Catch-22*: A Manifesto for Anar-
chists," *Carolina Quarterly*, XV:3 (Summer, 1963), pp. 86–92). In contrast, G. B.
McHenry thinks *Catch-22* is constructed carefully on cinematic principles ("Significant Corn: *Catch-22*," *Critical Review*, Vol. 40 (1966), pp. 134–144); Jan Solomon
argues that behind its apparent chaos is a careful system of time sequences involving
two distinct and mutually contradictory chronologies ("The Structure of *Catch-22*,"
Critique: Studies in Modern Fiction, Vol. IX:2 (1967), pp. 46–57); James Mellard and

James L. McDonald each picks up Heller's use of *deja vu* in several incidents and makes it the structural principle of the whole work (Mellard, "*Catch-22:* Deja Vu and the Labyrinth of Memory," *Bucknell Review,* XVI:2 (May, 1968), pp. 29–44, and McDonald, "I See Everything Twice!: The Structure of Joseph Heller's *Catch-22,*" *University Review* (Kansas City), 34:3 (March, 1968), pp. 175–180); Gabriel Chanan points to an intricate molecular structure whose avenues of communication can reach out to any direction at any time ("The Plight of the Novelist," *Caim bridge Review,* Vol. 89: 2170 (April 26, 1968), pp. 399–401); and Minna Doskow finds in *Catch-22* a close reworking of the conflict and development of the archetypal classical hero ("The Night Journey in *Catch-22,*" *Twentieth Century Literature,* XII:4 (January, 1967), pp. 186–193).

2. Heller seems to have miscounted here. After leaving the hospital when he has 32 missions and 40 are required, Yossarian flies six more missions and reaches 38. Col. Cathcart then raises the number to 45, and Yossarian goes back into the hospital. This is the number required when he is in the hospital at the beginning of the book; and the day he gets out of the hospital, he learns from Doc Daneeka (at the end of Chapter Two) that the number has been raised to 50. Yossarian is outraged because, as he tells Doc Daneeka, he has 44. But if he had 38 when he went into the hospital, how could he have 44 when he came out—unless, of course he flew six missions while he was in the hospital! Or perhaps Yossarian came out of the hospital, flew six more missions, and went back in during the time 45 missions were required without Heller saying anything about it. It seems more likely that Heller, in completing his long Bologna flashback, either carelessly or intentionally forgot the 44 number he had had Yossarian state at the end of Chapter Two.

3. Heller's chronology is way off here. Major — de Coverley makes Milo the squadron mess officer after the Major returns from his triumphal entry into Rome in early June, 1944 (pp. 138–139). When Yossarian gets out of the hospital in July, Milo's mess-hall operation has grown gourmet in quality and international in scope (21, 62, 66), and he is thinking about forming his syndicate (68). But in Chapter Twenty-four, M & M Enterprises is already world-wide and flourishing in April.

4. After quotations and other references, I have put in parentheses page numbers from the Dell edition (New York, 1962).

5. This reflects another error in Heller's chronology. At the beginning of Chapter Twenty-six, Heller writes that if Yossarian "had not moved the bomb line during the Big Siege of Bologna, Major — de Coverley might still be around to save him . . ." (294). But the bomb-line moving and Major—de Coverley's consequent trip to Florence (135) were sometime in May; and the Jovean old Major had entered Rome with the liberating forces in June and been hit in the eye with a rose, had later arranged leave apartments in the city, and then had returned, ending the Loyalty Oath Crusade. If he disappeared and was thus unable to save Yossarian from being wounded in September, it must have been after June, not after May.

6. Gabriel Chanan makes what seems to me a brilliant and provocative observation about this aspect of Heller's dense net of characters. It gives us, Chanan suggests, a way to conceive that non-chronological aspect of our lives which exists laterally in a web of interrelationships not dependent on time or consequence (see note one above for documentation).

JOSEPH HELLER

A Special Message to Subscribers, Catch-22

Catch-22 was started in 1953, when I was thirty, and finished in 1961. It was my first novel. During this time I held jobs involving advertising or promotion writing, and I worked on the novel evenings and weekends and on my short annual vacations. The Second World War was already eight years past when I began, and my participation in that was limited to just ten months overseas. Had I wanted to write a realistic novel of World War II, I would have been handicapped by a lack of knowledge.

Much of the content of *Catch-22* and all of the spirit derive from civilian experience in this country in the years following the war. Readers among you my own age with long memories will recognize an abundance of chronological inaccuracies: loyalty oaths, blacklists, Major Major's father, Milo Minderbinder's platitudes, the allusion to the Alger Hiss charges in the microfilm concealed in the Chaplain's tomato—all belong to postwar history. These anachronisms were deliberate. People over the years have called my attention to other inconsistencies: that helicopters were not then used in air-sea rescue attempts; that IBM had no computers; that there are three, rather than two, missions to Bologna; that the rate of acceleration of a falling body is thirty-two feet per second. These errors were unconscious. But I have been lucky in my accidents and most have supplemented an effort to depict in bizarre and comic fashion familiar events that recur simultaneously in the present and the past.

Catch-22, Franklin Library Edition (Washington, D.C.: Franklin Mint, 1978)

These are people who refuse to believe that *Catch-22* was written *before* the Vietnam war. And recently a woman insisted to me that the conversations in Colonel Cathcart's office could only have been suggested by the Watergate tapes. Some of you now may think I tool my title from the popular phrase for the double-bind dilemmas imposed on us so often by bureaucratic chaos and inconsistency. But the title was invented for the novel in order to fill a descriptive need for a kind of experience with which I wished to deal in my fiction. Countless news events since 1961 have been described as catch-22 situations by the journalists and editors reporting them, and the term has acquired its widely understood meaning.

As I've said, I've been lucky.

J.H.
New York, N.Y. 1978

JAMES NAGEL

The Catch-22 *Note Cards*

One of the most intriguing aspects of the composition history of Joseph Heller's *Catch-22* is the existence of a large number of detailed note cards on which the author planned the structure of the novel before writing and analyzed its contents after the first completed draft. These note cards are lined, 5 X 8" Kardex cards of a type used by the Remington Rand office Heller worked in during the composition of the novel. The most important of these is a group of more than thirty cards, written in Heller's hand and headed "CHAPTER CARDS (outlines for chapters before they were written.)"[1] Given what Heller has said in a letter about the period of composition of the novel,[2] the date of these cards would be sometime around 1953, at which point, of course, the novel was still entitled "Catch-18."

Perhaps the most striking feature of these cards, especially in light of the frequent charges that the novel is "unstructured," "disorganized," or even "chaotic," is the detail of the planning stage of composition.[3] Not only are the main events in each chapter suggested, but characters are named and described, relationships among events are indicated, and key sentences are drafted. These cards correspond only roughly to what are now the forty-two chapters of *Catch-22*, but they are fascinating in their revelation of the acceptance and rejection of ideas and of the total growth of the novel. For example, a typical card, one now located about twelfth from the begin-

Critical Essays on Joseph Heller (Boston: Hall, 1984): pp. 51–61.

ning,[4] treats the characters and events for what was evidently considered to be a single chapter:[5]

1. Cathcart's background & ambition. Puzzled by ——— de Coverley.

2. Hasn't a chance of becoming a general. Ex-corporal Winter green, who evaluates his work, also wants to be a general.

3. For another, there already was a general, Dreedle.

4. [Arrow up] Tries to have Chaplain say prayer at briefing.[Arrow up]

5. Description of General Dreedle. His Nurse.

6.   Dreedle's quarrel with Moodis [sic].

7. Snowden's secret revealed in argument with Davis.

8. Dreedle brings girl to briefing.

9. Groaning. Dreedle orders Korf shot.

10. That was the mission in which Yossarian lost his balls.

The section of the published novel which relates to the items listed now comprises much of chapter 19, "Colonel Cathcart," and chapter 21, "General Dreedle," with chapter 20, "Corporal Whitcomb," almost entirely unrelated to these matters, interspersed between them. Thus the ten items on the card were developed into roughly twenty-one pages of the novel.[6]

The business of Colonel Cathcart's background and ambition now begins in chapter 19 with a description of Cathcart as a "slick, successful, slipshod, unhappy man of thirty-six who lumbered when he walked and wanted to be a general" (p. 185). The descriptive and background attention to Cathcart covers a bit over two pages and then gives way to what is listed on the card as Item 4, "Tries to have Chaplain say prayer at briefing." This sentence had directional arrows pointing up, and, indeed, it was moved into second position in the manuscript. It relates logically to Cathcart's ambition: "Colonel Cathcart wanted to be a general so desperately he was willing to try anything, even religion . . ." (p. 187). The idea is developed carefully: Cathcart is impressed by a photograph in *The Saturday Evening Post* of a colonel who has his chaplain conduct prayers before each mission. Cathcart's sudden interest in religion is related to his ambition: "Maybe if we say prayers, they'll put my picture in *The Saturday Evening Post*" (p. 188). The humor of the situation progresses as Cathcart's thinking develops:

"Now, I want to give a lot of thought to the kind of prayers we're going to say. . . . I don't want any of this Kingdom of God or Valley of Death stuff. That's all too negative. What are you making such a sour face for?"

"I'm sorry, sir," the chaplain stammered. "I happened to be thinking of the Twenty-third Psalm just as you said that."

"How does that one go?"

"That's the one you were just referring to, sir. 'The Lord is my shepherd I—'"

"That's the one I was just referring to. It's out. What else have you got?" (p. 189).

It leads ultimately to the Cathcart's admission, "I'd like to keep away from the subject of religion altogether if we can," and to the true object of his thinking: "Why can't we all pray for something good, like a tighter bomb pattern?" (p. 190). But the plan for prayer is abandoned when the chaplain reveals that the enlisted men do not have a separate God, as Cathcart had assumed, and that excluding them from prayer meetings might antagonize God and result in even looser bomb patterns. Cathcart concludes "The hell with it, then" (p. 193). Thus the first item on the card, about Cathcart, and the elevated item regarding prayer, grew to comprise the entire content of chapter 19. The secondary notions of each of these items were moved: Cathcart's puzzlement at ——de Coverley was delayed to chapter 21, and revelation that Milo is now the mess officer was placed earlier, in chapter 13, when Major——de Coverley promotes him out of a desire for fresh eggs.

The remaining items on the card were saved to become chapter 21, "General Dreedle." This chapter pursues two main concerns: obstructions to Cathcart's promotion to general, one of which is General Dreedle, and to General Dreedle himself. In the novel, the chapter is about equally divided between these two topics. The balance is enriching: the ambitious Colonel trying to get promoted is contrasted to the entrenched General trying to preserve what he has. Cathcart's problems here are precisely those that Heller listed as items two and three:

Actually, Colonel Cathcart did not have a chance in hell of becoming a general. For one thing, there was ex-P.F.C. Wintergreen, who also wanted to be a general and who always distorted, destroyed, rejected or misdirected any correspondence by, for or about Colonel Cathcart that might do him credit. For another, there already was a general, General Dreedle, who knew that General Peckem was after his job but did not know how to stop him (p. 212).

Wintergreen has, of course, been demoted from "ex-corporal" in the notes to "ex-P.F.C." in the novel. General Peckem, called P. P. Peckenhammer throughout the note cards, has been added as a further complication.

The business of General Dreedle, items five through nine, now occupies the last half of the chapter (pp. 212–220) with only minor alterations from the notes. "Moodis" is changed to "Moodus"; in the incident of the "groaning" at the staff meeting, Dreedle orders Major Danby shot, not Korn (p. 218). Two items are not treated: the business of Snowden's secret was saved for the conclusion of the novel (p. 430), a wise decision in that the Snowden incident is the major *déjà vu* scene and it becomes climactic of that device placed at the end. And, further, Snowden's secret, that man is matter, emphasizes the theme of mortality just when Yossarian is most concerned with death and survival.

The second matter not treated, relating to Yossairan's castration, is itself a startling revelation but one Heller later rejected in manuscript revision. The incident of Yossarian's wound was ultimately moved to chapter 26: Aarfy, known as "Aarky" throughout the notes, gets lost on the mission to Ferrara and, before McWatt can seize control of the plane, flies back into the flak and the plane is hit. Yossarian's wound is, in fact, in his thigh, but his first analysis follows the suggestion of the note card:

> He was unable to move. Then he realized he was sopping wet. He looked down at his crotch with a sinking, sick sensation. A wild crimson blot was crawling upward rapidly along his shirt front like an enormous sea monster rising to devour him. He was hit! . . . A second solid jolt struck the plane. Yossarian shuddered with revulsion at the queer sight of his wound and screamed at Aarfy for help.
>
> "I lost my balls! Aarfy, I lost my balls! . . . I said I lost my balls! Can't you hear me? I'm wounded in the groin!" (pp. 283–284),

Yossarian's mistake reveals, perhaps, a normal fear and an understandable confusion; it also unites the sexual theme with the dangers of war and, especially, to the destructive insensitivity of Aarfy. Yossarian's wound also serves the plot in getting him back into the hospital where the themes of absurdity, bureaucracy, and insanity are explored: Nurse Cramer insists to Yossarian that "it certainly is not your leg! . . . That leg belongs to the U. S. government" (p. 286); Dunbar moves a temperature card to become A. Fortiori (p. 285); Major Sanderson mistakes Yossarian for A. Fortiori and then pronounces him a manic-depressive because he is depressed by misery, ignorance, violence, greed, and crime (pp. 297–298).

Another note card of particular interest is one entitled "Night of Horrors" in the notes, and in the manuscript chapter derived from it, but "The

Eternal City" in the published novel. The note card contains seven entries, the first four of which concern matters not eventually made part of the chapter. These have to do with the discovery of penicillin by "Aarky." The discovery by Yossarian that the old man in the whorehouse is dead, and that the girls have been driven out of the apartment by the vagaries of "Catch-18," is thus the result of his search for a cure. He has come to the apartment in Rome to see Aarky. The villain in this episode turns out to be Milo, as Item 7 explains: "Milo is exposed as the source of penicillen, [*sic*] tricking both Aarky & Yossarian, and as the man who infected the girl to create a demand for his new wonder drug. Yossarian breaks with him." This concept, finally rejected, of course, would have been an interesting but perhaps unnecessary further development of Milo's corruption.

This idea, and all but one of the other suggestions of the card, were finally abandoned or subordinated to what appears as note 5: "Yossarian walks through the streets of Rome witnessing various horrors, among them the maid, who has been thrown from the window by Aarky." It is this concept which ultimately becomes the heart of "The Eternal City": Yossarian discovers that the apartment is in shambles, that the girls have been driven out, that the old man is dead. In the novel, of course, Milo is not pushing penicillin; instead, he initially agrees to assist Yossarian in finding Nately's whore's kid sister, but in the "grip of a blind fixation," he abandons Yossarian when he hears of a scheme to smuggle illegal tobacco (p. 402). This leads to Yossarian's "Night of Horrors," his surrealistic walk through Rome at night in which greed, violence, corruption, insanity, and death bombard his consciousness from all sides.[7] Aarfy has raped Michaela and thrown her out the window, and Yossarian is arrested for being AWOL.

The development of this note from initial conception to the finished novel is demonstrated by the manuscript draft of the chapter. "Night of Horrors" in manuscript is labelled "11B" and covers fifty pages. It is essentially what is now known as "The Eternal City" (pp. 396–410). Of the alterations from manuscript to final publication, most are minor, single-word revisions. In the first paragraph, for example, the description of Milo "with pious lips pursed primly" became "with pious lips pursed." That he speaks to Yossarian in "wounded, ecclesiastical tones," became simply "ecclesiastical tones." Only a few other such revisions are worthy of mention. In the manuscript, Yossarian, on his walk through Rome, comes upon a "man" on the ground in convulsions. The novel was revised so that Yossarian now discovers an "Allied soldier." The implication of this revision would extend the universality of human suffering, which Yossarian is discovering in this chapter, to military men not in combat but within the civilian world. The "military" as an organization is the perpetrator of the violence in the novel: the soldiers as individuals share in being its victims. That the individual is an "Allied soldier" rather than an "American" is consistent with a pattern of revision in this chapter. In another passage, Yossarian, in the manuscript, comes upon a "crying American sergeant" in a doorway; in the novel the man is simply a "crying soldier" (p. 406). Another point revealed in these revisions, one of particular interest to biographical scholarship, is that the island on which Yossarian is based, called Pianosa throughout the novel, is clearly identified as Corsica throughout the manuscript. Heller, of course, spent most of his active duty on this island.

Beyond these simple revisions there are only a few other passages of substantial alteration. Yossarian's discovery of Nately's whore's apartment in shambles originally, as note card item 6 suggested, contained the information of the death of the old man. The deleted passage read: "The old man had died of a stroke a few days earlier—once again he had marched with the majority—and the only one there was the old woman." In the novel, the news of the death of the old man is delayed two pages and the cause is made somewhat obscure: "'Something broke in here,'" the old woman says, pointing to her head. "'One minute he was living, one minute he was dead.'" (p. 399). It is now possible that "Catch-22" has contributed to his death.[8] On the other hand, somewhat more emphasis is given in the manuscript to Yossarian's outrage at "Catch-18," the justification offered for the raid on the apartment, a matter reduced in the novel to only a few sentences (p. 398). The "stout woman with warts and two chins" (p. 402) Yossarian passes as he leaves the police headquarters in the novel does not appear in the manuscript. Her addition would seem to signify an intensification of the grotesquerie of the scene and an implication that she may be involved with the police commissioner who has just chased Yossarian out of his office.

In the novel, "at the Ministry of Public Affairs on the next block, a drunken lady was backed up against one of the fluted Corinthian columns by a drunken young soldier . . ." (p. 404). This passage is a considerable improvement over the manuscript version: "at the Ministry of Public Affairs, a drunken girl ~~had been~~ was backed up against one of the fluted Corinthian columns by a drunken soldier trying to insinuate his you-know-what into her and-how. . . ." Another wise alteration a few pages later was the deletion of a moralizing narrative intrusion into the action asserting that "Justice was a blind-folded brute with a club, a pimp with a knife." This interpretive remark was deleted[9] and is simply implicit in the events rather than stated by the narrator. In other matters, Aarfy's justification for killing Michaela after raping her is, in the novel, that "'I couldn't very well let her go around saying bad things about us, could I?'" (p. 408). In the manuscript, the "us" was originally "an American officer," and another sentence followed: "that would ~~be bad~~ have been bad propaganda for our country." These are changes of a certain amount of substance, but, in general, what a comparison of this note card with the manuscript and novel reveals is that the substance of the chapter does indeed follow the note suggestions and that what Heller wrote in his first draft is remarkably close to what was ultimately published.

There are numerous other note cards as intriguing and significant as these two and several individual ideas that were developed or abandoned after their first conception in the notes. One important point that must be stressed, however, is that the heart of *Catch-22*, the basic plot and character formulations, the underlying conflicts and themes, were all devised at the initial stage of note card composition. That Snowden will be killed on the mission to Avignon, that in response Yossarian will parade in the nude and sit naked in a tree during the funeral, are all established on a card entitled "Ferrara." The kind of minor detail that Heller frequently changed is the suggestion on this card that when Yossarian is awarded his medal, still standing naked in formation, "Dreedle orders a zoot suit for him." Another such revision concerns what is finally in chapter 30, "Dunbar" (pp. 324–333), but is called "McAdam" in the notes.[10] The two most dramatic events of the chapter are here suggested: McAdam dives low over the beach, slicing Kid Sampson in half, and then commits suicide. The note card indicates and indefinite "man" as the victim and also suggests that "McAdam kills himself & Daneeker," which, of course, was revised, but the focus of the chapter is all there. This card, incidentally, also contains a fascinating suggestion: "Nurse Cramer's family tree traced back to include all known villains in History. She completes the line by being a registered Republican who doesn't drink, smoke, fornicate, or lust consciously & [is] guiltless of similar crimes."

Other random points of interest throughout these cards deserve comment. There are two suggestions that Yossarian and Dunbar are going to write a war novel in parody of Hemingway but that they are having problems getting their "Jew" to conform and they lack a "radical" to make the plan complete.[11] An entry for chapter 40, "Catch-22," entitled "Catch-18" in the notes, reads "in the morning, Cathcart sends for Yossarian and offers him his deal. Big brother has been watching Yossarian." The concluding phrase makes explicit an underlying thematic allusion to George Orwell's *1984*, one now more subtly beneath the action of the novel. The same card contains the suggestion that Nately's whore will stab Yossarian as he leaves Cathcart's office, which occurs in the novel, and that she will shout "ole" as she plunges the knife in, which does not.

The note for the final chapter, "Yossarian," contains not only plot suggestions but some interpretive remarks as well. There is a good deal of interest in Yossarian's mortality: "Yossarian is dying, true, but he has about 35 years to live." Another provocative entry, one rejected, is that "Among other things, he really does have chronic liver trouble. Condition is malignant & would have killed him if it had not been discovered." But perhaps the most important comments on the card are those relating to the thematic significance of Yossarian's refusal of Cathcart's deal. In the note card, Yossarian is to discuss the ethics of the deal, and his alternatives, with an English deserter: "Easiest would be to go home or fly more missions. Hardest would be for him to fight for identity without sacrificing moral responsibility." The following entry reads "He chooses the last, after all dangers are pointed out to him."

In the novel, the English deserter has been replaced by Major Danby, who, since he does not appear in the preliminary notes, would seem to be a late invention. The conception of the "fight for identity" has been slightly altered: Yossarian says, "'I've been fighting all along to save my country. Now I'm going to fight a little to save myself. The country's not in danger any more, but I am'" (p. 435). The "identity" motif has been submerged into the "survival" theme, one centered on Yossarian's physical and moral survival. Thus Yossarian can now claim: "'I'm not running away from my responsibilities. I'm running to them'" (p. 440). In thematic terms, this change is perhaps the most important discovery to emerge from a study of the preliminary note cards.

But the preliminary cards comprise less than half of all the cards there are. There are other groups of note cards detailing the activities of each of the characters in the novel, its structure and chronology, and the themes of sex and "Catch-18." There are even a group of cards which provide a page by page analysis of several chapters, listing items in much the manner of the preliminary notes but keyed to the page numbers of the manuscript. These cards are headed "Chapter Cards (Analysis of Chapters After They Were Written) [.]" A typical card is the one for the first chapter:

[MS pp.]	[*Catch-22* pp.]
p. 3.—Catch-18 leads Y. to censor letters with Washington Irving's name. CID man arrives	[p. 8.]
p. 4.—The Texan, Dunbar, and the warrant officer	[p. 9.]
p. 5.—Soldier in White	[p. 10.]
p. 7.—Nurse Cramer discovers that the Soldier in White is dead	[p. 10.]
p. 7.—Chaplain visits Yossarian.	[p. 11.]
p. 10.—Chaplain mentions Nately	[p. 12.]
p. 15.—Texan drives out everybody but CID man	[p. 15.]

These cards all contain this level of detail and demonstrate Heller's close scrutiny of his manuscript. One item of interest throughout these entries is the concern for the number of missions required relative to the number Yossarian has flown. Two points are clearly stressed: that Yossarian is working against a progressive requirement which advances at about the same rate he completes missions; that the novel does not proceed chronologically and thus the number of required missions is a key to the historical sequence of events.

The entries indicate the important elements of the chapters and many of these are familiar: T. S. Eliot business, Yossarian's willingness to be "the victim of anything but circumstance," the Loyalty Oath Crusade. Other items were revised in manuscript: Corsica was, at the last moment, changed to Pianosa; the death of Mudd (p. 107) has, in these notes, something to do with $E=MC^2$; P. P. Peckem is still called Peckenhammer; and chapter 12, published as "Bologna," is here entitled "Sgt. Knight." One card, labeled "Plans For Revision," suggests some of the changes to be made.

Heller has apparently decided, for example, to "build up" the role of Nately and to concentrate on his love for the whore. After the entry "Whores," Heller wrote: "Nately's whore mentioned more, together with her apartment & old Folks." There are also other plans: to increase the references to the Soldier in White, presumably to deepen the *déjà vu* effect; to concentrate on "Aark," soon to be "Aarfy," and to stress his interest in Nately, his getting lost on missions, and his righteousness ("world is full of the girls he wouldn't prod"). As even these few entries suggest, Heller's revision and planning at this stage of the composition of *Catch-22* were serious and meticulous, the depth of which is easily revealed by several related groups of cards.

There is a card, for example, entitled "Combat Targets" on which the key events of each of the major missions are listed, the most significant of which is the mission to Avignon when "Dobbs goes crazy & Snowden is killed." Another important card lists, in chronological order, each of the main events in Yossarian's career, from "Feigns illness at Lowery Field" to "Accepts Englishman's terms. Runs off with penicillan [*sic*] and gun, whore behind him with knife," a suggestion contained in the preliminary notes and continued here, but eliminated in final manuscript. For the most part, however, the events here suggested are those of the novel, with a few intriguing exceptions: the notation "Treats Snowden (Loses Balls, wrong wound: no morphine)" is certainly one of them. This entry is followed two cards later with "Wounded in legs when Aarky gets lost (Doesn't lose Balls)" which suggests that at least one important plot revision resulted from this outlining process. There is still a concern with syphilis and penicillin, as the entries "Wants to help kid sister with Syphillis [*sic*]" and "Daneeka gives advice only," as well as the final entry would indicate.

Another card analyzes the sex theme in the novel with entries relating to caring for the kid sister, Doc Daneeka's experience with the newlyweds and capricious copulation among nearly everyone. Two cards relate to the "Catch-18" concept, one of them suggesting a Catch-18 "Action Board." These two list various events which apparently fall within the bureaucratic enigma of Catch-18, from "Anyone who wants to be grounded can't be crazy" to "Black's Loyalty Oath Crusade is like Catch-18" to "Drive whores out in compliance with Catch-18."

Most of the notes, however, deal with character analysis, a matter Heller explored with great depth and perception. These cards detail the essential personality and role of each character, indicating both chapter and manuscript page number for each item mentioned. The most extensive scrutiny is given to Yossarian, of course. Here, in chapter by chapter account, are recorded Yossarian's activities and psychological and moral development, from his Assyrian heritage to his symptoms of paranoia, an item followed by the notation: "All he can do to maintain balance." Indeed, these entries stress the "insanity" theme very heavily. Heller records, "Insanity began with Dead Man. Stark naked after Snowden . . ." a matter treated in chapter 9. The following entry contains the comment "Stubbs thinks he's the only sane man left," an issue which now concludes chapter 10 when Dr. Stubbs says, "that crazy bastard may be the only sane one left" (p. 109).

Virtually every character in the novel of any significance is covered by Heller in these entries. One card, for example, traces Dunbar's role in the first twelve chapters and shows how he affects Yossarian: they are in the hospital together, Dunbar tells Yossarian there is no God, and he conspires with Nately to get Yossarian out of the officer's club. Another set of cards explores Nately's activities with emphasis on his "sheltered childhood and wealthy parents" and his love for the whore. Several of these entries are intriguing, especially "Becomes a Family man," and the concluding four notations: "Finishes missions," "Volunteer's [sic] for Halfoat's job," "Agrees to fly 75 missions," and "Killed."

In similar fashion the Chaplain, Milo, Doc Daneeka, Clevinger, Orr, Hungry Joe, Aarfy, McAdam (McWatt), Cathcart, and the rest are given scrupulous attention. Some groups of characters are covered together implying that they may play a single role: so it is with the Majors and, interestingly, with the whores. Nurses Duckett, Cramer, and Hanniball are covered on a single card, as are other pairs of characters: Bleistein and Wintergreen, General Peckenhammer (P. P. Peckem) and General Dreedle, and the Old Folks (a group listed as the old man, old woman, officer's maid, and the enlisted men's maid), although the old man and the old woman are also given scrutiny on a separate card. Another entry covers the Aides (Cargill, Korn, and Moodus) and still another, which lists Whitcomb, Danby, and Stubbs, is labelled simply "Others, Grp." In fact, there are so many cards, so scrupulously thorough, that presumably when Heller got to the end of the analysis and headed a card "Others, Misc." the only significant character left was Scheisskopf.

What emerges from an exploration of these note cards is not so much a new interpretation of the novel as a record of a creative process at work, one which appears, finally, almost entirely at odds with the portrait constructed by the earliest negative reviews of *Catch-22*. What were then frequent charges of faulty construction, illogical structures, chaotic events, must now be measured against the author's record of detailed, meticulous planning and analysis of his novel at each stage of composition. As these notes indicate, the creative impulse behind the novel was not a single conception but one which grew and altered slightly with reflection and revision. The names of many characters were changed; others were subordinated (such as the old woman) or emphasized (Milo). The central motivation of some key scenes was revised, as it was in "The Eternal City." That such changes were made in the course of composition is, of course, in no way remarkable; rather, what is striking is that so much of the novel was planned in advance on note cards and preserved intact throughout the composition. The fact that it was, however, leaves a valuable and fascinating record of the development of one of the most complex, and one of the finest, modern American novels.

Notes

1. These note cards, and all Heller manuscripts referred to, are on file in the Special Collections Division of Brandeis University Library. I am indebted to Joseph Heller for allowing me access to these materials and for reading this essay in manuscript and making many valuable suggestions. I would also like to acknowledge the generous assistance of Mr. Victor Berch, Brandeis University Library, in reviewing these manuscripts. Heller's comments on the note cards are variously in blue, red, and black ink, with occasional pencil notations.

2. Joseph Heller to James Nagel, 13 March 1974, p. 2. A copy of this letter is on file at Brandeis University Library.

3. See, for example, the following reviews of *Catch-22*: J. C. Pine, *Library Journal*, 86 (1961), 3805; William Hogan, "*Catch-22*: A Sleeper That's Catching On," *San Francisco Chronicle*, 3 May 1962, p. 39; Spencer Klaw, "Airman's Wacky War," *New York Herald Tribune Books*, 15 Oct. 1961, p. 8; Richard G. Stern, "Bombers Away," *New York Times Book Review*, 22 Oct. 1961, p. 50; Whitney Balliet, *New Yorker*, 37, 9 Dec. 1961, p. 247; *Daedalus* (Winter 1963), pp. 155–165.

4. It is now difficult to determine the precise order of the cards and even, in some cases, whether a given card was written before or after the initial draft. All references to numbers and groups of cards are therefore based on my own judgment and on the manner in which the cards are now grouped.

5. This card has ten numbered entries, split vertically after the seventh.

6. All references are to Joseph Heller, *Catch-22* (New York: Simon and Schuster, 1961). The pages referred to are basically pp. 185–192, 206–220. Subsequent references to this edition will be given within the text.

7. For a provocative discussion of this scene, see Minna Doskow, "The Night Journey in *Catch-22*," *Twentieth Century Literature*, 12 (1967): pp. 186–193. Rpt. in James Nagel, ed., *Critical Essays on* CATCH-22 (Encino: Dickenson Publishing Co., 1974): pp. 155–163.

8. I have explored the role of the old man, and his relationship to Yossarian, in "Yossarian, the Old Man, and the Ending of *Catch-22*," *Critical Essays on* CATCH-22, pp. 164–174.

9. From what is now p. 407.

10. The name "McAdam," of course, was eventually changed to "McWatt."

11. Two manuscript paragraphs developed from these suggestions were published in my essay "Two Brief Manuscript Sketches: Heller's *Catch-22*," *MFS*, 20 (1974): pp. 221–224. The manuscript seems to suggest that these paragraphs represent a serious attempt at a war novel by Heller rather than a parody written by his characters, as is clear in the note cards. Heller's comment to this point is contained in a letter on file at Brandeis University Library.

JOSEPH HELLER

Preface to Catch-22

In 1961, *The New York Times* was a newspaper with eight columns. And on November 11 of that year, one day after the official publication date of *Catch-22*, the page with the book review carried an unusual advertisement that ran from top to bottom and was five columns wide. To the eye the effect was stupendous. The book review that day, of a work by somebody else, was squeezed aside to the fold of the page, as were the crossword puzzle and all else. The ad had this caption: WHAT'S THE CATCH? And displayed at the top in silhouette was the comic cartoon of a uniformed figure in flight, glancing off to the side at some unspecified danger with an expression of panic.

It was an announcement ad for *Catch-22*. Interwoven with the text were mentions of praise from twenty-one individuals and groups of some public standing, most connected to literature and the publishing world, who had received the novel before publication and had already reviewed it or commented about it favourably.

Within days after publication, there was a review in *The Nation* by Nelson Algren (a client of my own literary agent, who had urged him to read it), who wrote of *Catch-22* that it 'was the best novel to come out of anywhere in

Catch-22, Vintage Books Edition (New York: Simon & Schuster, 1994). © 1994, Joseph Heller.

years'. And there was a review by Studs Terkel in a Chicago daily newspaper that recommended it about as highly.

So much attention to the work at publication was in large part the result of the industrious zeal and appreciation of my literary agent, Candida Donadio, and my editor, Robert Gottlieb, and I embrace the opportunity afforded now to dedicate this new edition to both of them, as colleagues and allies with talents that were of immeasurable value.

The work was not reviewed in the *Times* on publication. However, it was reviewed in the *Herald Tribune* by Maurice Dolbier, and Mr. Dolbier said of it: 'A wild, moving, shocking, hilarious, raging, exhilarating, giant roller-coaster of a book'.

That the reviewer for the *Herald Tribune* came to review at all this war novel by someone unknown was almost entirely the product of coincidence. S. J. Perelman, much better known and the subject of an interview by Mr Dolbier, was publishing his own book at just about that time. His publisher was Simon & Schuster, mine too, and the editor in charge of his work there was also the same, Bob Gottlieb. In answer to a question put to him by Dolbier about his own reading, Mr Perelman replied that he was very much engrossed in a novel pressed upon him by his editor, a novel called *Catch-22*. Returning to his office, Mr Dolbier later confessed to me, he found the book already in a pile with others he had decided he would not have time to study as prospects to write about. Had it not been for Gottlieb, there would have been no Perelman, and had it not been for Perelman, there would have been no review by Dolbier.

And had it not been for Dolbier, there might not have been the *Times*. Two weeks afterward, and probably only because of Mr Dolbier, the book was described with approbation in the daily *Times* by the reviewer Orville Prescott, who predicted it would not be forgotten by those who could take it and called it: 'A dazzling performance that will outrage nearly as many readers as it delights'.

The rest, one might say is history, but it is a history easily misconstrued. The novel won no prizes and was not on any bestseller list.

And, as Mr Prescott foresaw, for just about every good report, there seemed to appear one that was negative. Looking back at this novel after twenty-five years, John Aldridge, to my mind the most perceptive and persistent commentator of American literature over the decades, lauded Robert Brustein for his superbly intelligent review in *The New Republic*, which contained 'essential arguments that much of the later criticism has done little to improve on', and Mr Aldridge recognised that many in the early audience of *Catch-22* 'liked the book for just the reasons that caused others to hate it'.

The disparagements were frequently venomous. In the *Sunday Times*, in a notice in back so slender that the only people seeing it were those awaiting it, the reviewer (a novelist who also by chance was a client of my own agent, Candida) decided that the 'novel gasps for want of craft and sensibility', 'is repetitious and monotonous', 'fails', 'is an emotional hodgepodge', and was no novel; and in the esteemed *The New Yorker*, the reviewer, a staff writer who normally writes about jazz, compared the book unfavourably with a novel of similar setting by Mitchell Goodman and decided that *Catch-22* 'doesn't even seem to have been written; instead, it gives the impression of having been shouted onto paper', 'what remains is a debris of sour jokes', and that in the end Heller 'wallows in his own laughter and finally drowns in it'. (I am tempted now to drown in laughter as I jot this down.)

I do not recall that the novel was included in the several hundred books in the Christmas roundup of recommended reading of the *Times* that year or in the several hundred others picked out in the spring for summer reading.

But in late summer of 1962, Raymond Walters, on the bestseller page of the *Sunday Times*, which then carried regularly the column 'In and Out of Books', reported that the underground book New Yorkers seemed to be talking about most was *Catch-22*. (The novel probably was more heavily advertised than any other that year, but it was still underground). Not that much later, *Newsweek* carried a story to the same effect in a space more than a page wide. And late that same summer, I was invited to my first television interview. The program was the *Today* show, then a variety show as much as anything else. The interim host was John Chancellor. Mr Chancellor had recently returned from his newsman's post in the Kremlin, and he had agreed to accept the position on condition that he interview only those people he himself chose to.

After the show, in a bar close by the studio in which I found myself drinking martinis at an earlier hour than ever in my life, he handed me a packet of stickers he'd had printed privately. They read: YOSSARIAN LIVES. And he confided he'd been pasting these stickers secretly on the walls of the corridors and in the executive rest rooms of the NBC building.

Then came September and the paperback edition and with it, finally, an expansion in popular appeal that seemed to take the publishers, Dell, by surprise, despite elaborate promotion and distribution strategies. It seemed for a while that the people there could not fully bring themselves to believe the sales figures and that they would never catch up.

Paperback publishers print in the hundreds of thousands. For this, after an initial release of 300,000 copies, they went back to press five more times between September and the end of the year, twice each in October and December, and by the end of 1963, there were eleven printings. In England, under the auspices of the enterprising young editor, there Tom Maschler, it was that way from the start. Bestseller lists were new and rudimentary then, but *Catch-22* was quickly at the head of them.

For me the history of *Catch-22* begins back in 1953, when I started writing it. In 1953, I was employed as a copywriter at a small advertising agency in New York, after two years as an instructor in English composition at Pennsylvania State University, which was then a college. Early on, in anxious need of an approving opinion, I sent the opening chapter off to the literary agents I had managed to obtain after publishing a few short stories in magazines, in *Esquire* and *The Atlantic*. The agents were not impressed, but a young assistant there, Ms Candida Donadio, was, and she secured permission to submit that chapter to a few publications that regularly published excerpts from 'novels in progress'.

In 1955 the chapter appeared in a paperback quarterly *New World Writing* (an anthology that also contained, under a pseudonym, an extract from another novel in progress—Jack Kerouac's *On the Road*). There came complimentary letters of interest from a few editors at established book publishers, and I was encouraged to continue with a work I now saw realistically was going to take me a good many years longer than I at first had guessed.

In 1957, when I had about 270 pages in typescript, I was employed at *Time* magazine, writing advertising-sales presentations by day when not furtively putting thoughts down on paper for my work on the novel at home that evening. And Candida Donadio was establishing herself as a preeminent agent in her own right, with a list of American authors as clients as impressive as any. We agreed it made sense to submit the partial manuscript to some publishers, mainly to obtain a practical idea of the potential for publication of the novel we both thought so much of. She was drawn toward a new young editor she knew of at Simon & Schuster, one she thought might prove more receptive to innovation than most. His name was Robert Gottlieb, and she was right.

While Gottlieb busied himself with those pages, I, with a four-week summer vacation from bountiful *Time* magazine, began rewriting them. Gottlieb and I met for lunch, mainly for him to gauge my temperament and ascertain how amenable I would be as an author to work with. After I listened to him allude with tact to certain broad suggestions he thought he eventually might be compelled to make, I handed him my new pages with the boastful response that I had already taken care of nearly all of them.

He surprised me with concern that I might take exception to working with someone so young—he was twenty-six, I think, and I was thirty-four. I was more greatly surprised to learn from him later that both he and his closest colleague at Simon & Schuster, Nina Bourne, were intimidated at first by an air of suspicion I projected that I did not know I even possessed. I have not been suspicious of him since, and I doubt very much that Gottlieb, who went on to become the head of Alfred A. Knopf and then the editor of *The New Yorker* magazine, has ever again been intimidated by anybody.

And what I still remember most agreeably about him is that he did not ask for an outline or once seek for even a hint of where this one-third of a novel he'd seen was going to go. The contract I received called for an advance of fifteen hundred dollars, half on signing, which I did not need, and the remainder on completion and acceptance.

Probably, I was his first novelist, but not his first to be published; other authors with completed manuscripts came to him in the three more years I needed to finish mine. Probably, I was Candida's earliest client too. Both were as delighted as I was with the eventual success of *Catch-22,* and the three of us have been revelling in our recollections of the experience ever since.

On February 28, 1962, the journalist Richard Starnes published a column of unrestrained praise in his newspaper, *The New York World-Telegram,* that opened with these words: 'Yossarian will, I think, live a very long time'.

His tribute was unexpected, because Mr Starnes was a newspaperman in the hard-boiled mode whose customary beat was local politics, and the *World-Telegram* was widely regarded as generally conservative.

To this day I am grateful to Mr Starnes for his unqualified and unsolicited approval and bless him for the accuracy of his prediction. Yossarian has indeed lived a long time. Mr Starnes has passed on. Many people mentioned in that first advertisement have died, and most of the rest of us are on the way.

But Yossarian is alive when the novel ends. Because of the motion picture, even close readers of the novel have a final, lasting image of him at sea, paddling toward freedom in a yellow inflated lifeboat. In the book he doesn't get that far; but he is not captured and he isn't dead. At the end of the successor volume I've just completed, *Closing Time* (that fleeing cartoon figure is again on the book jacket of the American edition, but wearing a businessman's chapeau and moving with a cane), he is again still alive, more than forty years older but definitely still there. 'Everyone has got to go,' his physician friend in that novel reminds him with emphasis, 'Everyone!' But should I ever write another sequel, he would still be around at the end.

Sooner or later, I must concede, Yossarian, now seventy, will have to pass away too. But it won't be by my hand.

JOSEPH HELLER, 1994
East Hampton, New York

DAVID STREITFELD

Catch-23: *With the New Sequel to His Postwar Classic, Is Joseph Heller Cashing In or Cashing Out?*

It was 33 years ago, but Joseph Heller still hasn't forgotten how *The New York Times Book Review* wounded him and his first novel. Then, as now, the *Times*'s endorsement was crucial for literary fiction, which was too bad for Heller: The review, he heard several weeks before it appeared, was negative. So much for his labor of seven years, the enthusiasm of his editor and agent, the 7,500 copies that had been hopefully sent to bookstores. "The effect on me, and my then wife, my two young children, was absolutely depressing," the writer recalls. "Waiting for that review to come out, I didn't think any of us would ever smile again."

On October 22, it finally appeared, three miserable paragraphs tucked back on page 50. Among the jabs: "gasps for want of craft and sensibility . . . much too long . . . repetitive and monotonous . . . it fails . . . an emotional hodgepodge." Two other novels reviewed on the same page, the comedic *Loo Loo's Legacy* and the tale of a young gynecologist, *The Halliday Affair*, got better notices.

But Heller had the last laugh. His book, of course, was *Catch-22*, which would survive Richard G. Stern's cavalier dismissal to sell more than 10 million copies and emerge as the most influential novel of the postwar age. For many readers, *Catch-22* quickly became a touchstone—an anticipation, explanation, and confirmation of the anti-military and anti-government sentiments that blossomed during the Vietnam years. Its very title, developed by Heller in a

New York Journal, Vol. 27, Issue 36 (September 12, 1994): pp. 100–105. © 1994 David Streitfeld.

passage that he wrote with little premeditation, quickly became an everyday expression for an absurdly paradoxical and problematic situation. Novelists tend to expect a lot from their books—a spacious ego goes with the territory—but in this case, even the most self-worshiping writer couldn't have wished for more.

Heller wasn't as lucky in 1988 with his fifth novel, a sarcastic mediation on Rembrandt, Aristotle, and history called *Picture This*. He had hopes, he says, it might be another *Catch*, that it would "capture the intellectual imagination." (There's a fine example of the authorial ego at work.) Then came the daily *Times* review by Walter Goodman, who complained there was "precious little adventure or mystery here, and the comedy comes and goes. . . . The opinions are not particularly fresh or elegantly delivered. . . . Sophomoric."

That review, too, "had a devastating effect on me," says the 71-year-old Heller. "It made no reference to the book as a novel, just attacked it in a very sneering way. Even at my advanced age, with money for the book guaranteed, it was an awful situation. It does not make anyone happy to have something he's worked on, and for which he has high hopes, be dismissed or attacked publicly."

Then, just two weeks ago, the *Times* was at it again, running a Q&A with Heller in the *Book Review*. Whatever the intention of this odd little piece, the effect was to ridicule the writer even before his new book—*Closing Time: The Sequel to 'Catch-22'*—was in stores. This was made clear in Barbara Gelb's introduction, where she detailed her supposed friendship with Heller by talking about how unpleasant he is: "For 20 years now, I have managed to overlook his frequent sulkiness, his gluttonous table manners and his tendency to growl No before he even knows what the question is." For good measure, she said that when she profiled him in 1979, when her husband, Arthur, was the deputy managing editor of the *Times*, "he did his best to appear winsome. . . . But the minute he knew the article was safely locked up, the winning ways all but vanished."

With that anecdote—something Heller emphatically denies, incidentally—the *Times* made sure everyone who interviews the writer during the next two months will make his or her article a little more critical, in order not to seem to be falling for his charm.

Readers, too, will make their opinions known. Some will undoubtedly feel Heller has desecrated the memory of the first book; others may admire the attempt but fault the execution; and there may be some—who knows?—who like the sequel more.

It's not entirely unusual for a serious writer to produce, after many years, a sequel to an acclaimed earlier work. John Updike followed up *Rabbit, Run* with *Rabbit Redux* and then extended the one-a-decade trick with two more volumes. Thomas Berger tracked the adventures of his boisterous hero Carl Reinhart in four novels written over twenty years. But never has a writer done a sequel to something that scored so big in so many ways the first time around. Why tempt fate by inviting invidious comparisons?

Closing Time, now being shipped to bookstores by Simon & Schuster, takes the Air Force crew last seen in Italy during the latter part of World War II—Yossarian, who doesn't want to fly any more missions for the very rational reason that he might get killed; the scheming mess sergeant Milo Minderbinder; the unctuous Chaplain Tappman—and plunks them down in the contemporary world. They're old men now, putting their affairs in order, reminiscing about their glory days (the crucial scene in *Catch-22*, the death of the gunner Snowden, is flashed back to several times), getting ready to die.

There's little plot as such, but plenty of action. Milo is now a defense contractor, and Yossarian is a consultant. They're trying to sell the military a faster-than-light bomber, which provides the opportunity for some humor: "You can bomb someone before you even decide to do it. Decide it today, it's done yesterday!" the bomber looks like a flying wing. "And what does a flying wing look like?" You guessed it: "Other flying wings." The vice-president, clearly patterned after Dan Quayle, wants only to play video games. "I can't appoint a chief justice until I'm the President, and he can't swear me in until I appoint him," he explains brightly. "Isn't that a Catch-22?"

Whatever its merits, *Closing Time* is no simple pastiche or rehash of the earlier book. In fact, the novel is probably too ambitious, a complex stew of transposed autobiography and meta-fiction. Among the minor characters are "Joey" Heller and Kurt Vonnegut, and a character stumbles for a few pages into the climactic episode of that other famous antiwar novel *Slaughterhouse-Five*. ("We've gotten to be good friends," says the real Vonnegut. "That's one reason I haven't read the book. I don't want to have an opinion on it.")

Sitting next to the pool at his East Hampton house, Heller is immensely proud of his new work. "It turned out to be a perfect novel with a perfect title for me at this stage of my life and career. There's a feeling here of collecting everything I know, everything I've experienced, everything I dread experiencing in the future, and putting it into the context of a unified work."

The house, complete with adjoining cottage, is relatively modest by Hamptons standards—there's nothing to distinguish it from the dwelling of, say, a retired mid-level public-relations executive. Heller's second wife, Valerie, is upstairs dressing for a party the couple will attend this afternoon. Menawhile, he plays fetch with the dog and explains himself.

It may seem inevitable in retrospect, but for more than twenty years the notion of a sequel to *Catch-22* was merely a joke. "Hey, what are you going to write next?" his longtime editor, Bob Gottlieb of Knopf, would ask. "*Catch-23?*" Heller would laugh. "We never discussed it as a serious possibility," Gottlieb says.

A publisher known more for its ability to churn out commercial bestsellers than for creating lasting works of literature changed Heller's mind. Phyllis Grann, head of Putnam Publishing Group, announced a two-book contract with Heller in 1987 for *Picture This* and a sequel to *Catch-22*, the whole package worth in the neighborhood of $4 million. "I got less than I asked for and more than I deserve," the writer said at the time.

Before this, he had never made a huge amount of money and, indeed, seems to have been less interested in doing so than many other writers. Oh, sure, as a tyro long ago he dreamed of making "hundreds of thousands of dollars, living in the south of France, and going skiing with Irwin Shaw in Switzerland. "But even his one out-of-the-park home run, those 10 million copies of *Catch-22*, didn't yield a huge payday.

"It sold 2 million paperback copies, I think, within a year. But the cover price was 75 cents and the royalty was then about 6 percent, which was split with the hardcover publisher. So you're talking about a couple of pennies per copy for me."

When the Mike Nichols movie was released in 1970, adding another boost to the book's sales. "I remember getting a check for $68,000, which is the most money I had ever seen."

By the eighties, however, the up-front cash available to certain writers had grown enormously. For Grann, the prospect of tapping into 10 million fond, cultish memories must have been irresistible. (She declined to be interviewed for this article.) For Heller, on the other hand, the commitment was casual. "I had no idea what the book would be," he says, "or even if I would really write it."

But as he was working on *Picture This,* he had a dream involving his mother. As soon as he woke up, he thought of a sentence: "In the middle of his second week in the hospital, Yossarian began dreaming of his mother, and he knew he was going to die." This was the same way his novels always began: One or two sentences, followed by laborious accretion, would result in a complete work. For *Catch-22,* the sentences were rhapsodic: "It was love at first sight. The first time he saw the chaplain, Someone fell madly in love with him." ("Someone" later acquired a name: John Yossarian.) For *Something Happened,* Heller's rather good 1974 novel of stultifying corporate life, they were laconic: "In the office in which I work there are four people of whom I am afraid. Each of these four people is afraid of five people."

When Heller gets these sentences, he says, he is compelled to follow through. "Novelists like myself, we don't get many ideas. I never had more than one idea at a time." While he felt "huge trepidation" in trying to top himself, that was also part of the project's appeal. He wanted to "write the sequel without being accurately accused of emulating *Catch-22* or of duplicating it, and yet have it be a continuation as a work of literature."

To get started, he reread *Catch-22* for the first time in 30 years. He was impressed. "I thought, it's a wonderful book, a little bit overwritten with adjectives and adverbs, but dazzling in the quality of imagination. I was also surprised by the literary vocabulary. I don't have that now. I don't recall ever having it."

Still—the authorial ego now working overtime—he figured he could pull off a sequel. Then *Picture This* was published, receiving the savaging in the daily *Times* that Heller remembers so well. The Sunday *Times Book Review* wasn't much better ("sometimes reaches such extremes that the chief effect is incoherence").

The book fizzled—selling so poorly, Heller says, that for the first time in his career he didn't earn out his advance. Like a bride who wakes up the morning after an impulsive marriage, Phyllis Grann began to wonder what she had committed herself to.

So did Heller. Although the official reason given at the time was that "Heller decided he was not prepared to begin writing," as the *Times* cooperatively put it, the real problem was that $4-million contract, the vast majority of which was apportioned for the sequel. "You run into this challenge with a large advance of writing a book that will be popular to a mass audience," the writer says: "*Catch-22* was something of a fluke."

By mutual agreement, the contract was dissolved in 1989. Heller's off-again, on-again agent, Candida Donadio, sought out other publishers. One of them was Simon & Schuster. "I was told, 'You can have this for $1.2-million,'" remembers one source. "A few days later, it was down to $800,000. The price was going south in a hurry." Simon & Schuster has always been proud of the fact that it was the original publisher of *Catch-22,* so the idea went all the way to chairman Dick Snyder's office. The answer was a firm no: Heller's talent was exhausted.

He continued writing, and Donadio says she got two good offers. But the writer turned them down, saying he now wanted more money. Donadio, who had first started representing the novelist in the fifties, was thrown overboard, and ICM's Amanda Urban (younger, more aggressive, less devotedly arty) was hired. She persuaded Simon & Schuster in early 1991 to take on the book after all. Michael Korda, who became its editor, says he eagerly snapped it up. "My feeling when it was being offered around—and I expressed it very strongly to Dick [Snyder], who felt even more strongly than I did—was that it was inappropriate for the sequel to *Catch-22* to be published anywhere else," says Korda, adding that the original book "was a major moment in Simon & Schuster's postwar history."

So why did the publisher reject *Closing Time* the first time around? Korda says he hadn't heard about that and finds the whole notion "highly improbable." He also rejects speculation that the deal was in any sense a payback for Urban, who had just been burned by Simon & Schuster's last-minute cancellation of her client Bret Easton Ellis's misogynist slasher tale *American Psycho*. "That never occurred to me," Korda says. "I wasn't involved in *American Psycho*."

In any case, says Heller, "the advance was very, very modest. I felt much better that way." (Reports place it at around $750,000.) He says he's already earned back the money through foreign sales to fifteen countries ranging from Norway to Taiwan, Italy to Brazil. And Heather Schroder, ICM's director of foreign rights, confirms it: "The publishers who had been with him previously all bought this book, a real sign of enthusiasm. We didn't have to go looking."

The official U.S. publication date is October 10, the thirty-third anniversary of the publication of *Catch-22*. A multi-city tour is planned. Most authors dread these, but Heller is actually looking forward to his. "I'm a narcissist and an exhibitionist," he says lightly, "It's good being the center of attention, having people make a fuss over me. And I love the good food, the good hotels."

He was in such good spirits he was not only calculating that *Closing Time* would be on the best-seller list—with an announced first printing of 200,000 copies, it's obviously a strong possibility—but also hoping that the hardcover reissue Simon & Schuster is doing of *Catch-22* "will finally make it" to the list as well. That would require a miracle.

But then, Heller had received nothing but good news when we first talked in mid-July. "There's no indication of any hostility toward it, or any dissatisfaction. I'm more secure with this book [than any of his previous books] and more complaisant." Even then, though, there were distant clouds.

I'm keeping my distance from the publisher," he said. "I'm wondering why I haven't been told of a book-club sale, wondering what [the woman in charge of selling rights] is going to do with the paperback. I'm in a state of curiosity of suspense, but I'm not going to let it become acute."

As it turns out, the Book-of-the-Month Club declined to make an offer for *Closing Time*, even though it would have included the rights to *Catch-22* as well. "There wasn't a tremendous amount of enthusiasm for it here, "says editor-in-chief Tracy Brown. The Literary Guild picked up the books and is offering them as an alternate. "By it's very nature, *Closing Time* would have a problem as a main selection," says editorial director Arlene Friedman. "It doesn't have the broader appeal it would need for our membership, which is predominantly female. But we think a lot of people are going to want to see what Joe Heller has done."

As for Hollywood, Urban concedes that a movie sale is "going to be hard." She points out that, among other things, the film would require a largely elderly male cast. There's been a good audio sale, but the paperback auction will wait until after publication. *Vanity Fair* canceled its profile.

Much more disturbingly, the prepublication reviews are in. *Publishers Weekly,* in its August 1 issue, expressed "keen disappointment," saying there was "far too much sophomoric doodling. . . . Despite flashes of the old wit and fire, this is a tired, dispirited and dispiriting novel." *Kirkus* was even more brutal, saying that *Closing Time* was "the long-unawaited sequel to an American classic. . . . In an act of absurdity worthy of *Catch-22,* Heller has written a sequel to a novel that needed no sequel. It advised readers to "pretend the sequel never happened."

Says Penny Kaganoff, *Kirkus*'s merciless editor-in-chief, "There comes a time when an author just can't write anymore. That's the time to close the computer down. There's no embarrassment in resting on your laurels. If someone wanted to do him a favor, they would have stopped him. But when you get to a certain level [of stardom], no one tells you anything."

Candida Donadio, who has remained close to Heller even though she ultimately didn't agent *Closing Time,* says, "From the very beginning, I always had worries, nerves, about an attack. They could possibly shit on it. 'This isn't Yossarian; this isn't the book I loved so much.' But then I thought genuine Heller lovers would make the adjustment." If the reviews continue to be this bad, she says, "I suspect he may not choose to write again."

This is no way for any writer to cap a career. With Heller, it's particularly painful. If it were Philip Roth, no one would mind his getting creamed, just to see the smirk wiped off his face. But Heller is a nice guy, at least for a writer. For instance, when he gets letters from people whose loved ones suffer from Guillain-Barré, the neurological syndrome that nearly ended his life a decade ago, he sends them a copy of his book on the subject, *No Laughing Matter.* His career has been an honorable one. He has never, at least until now, directly or egregiously exploited the fact that he wrote such a popular and influential book. His biggest mistake was writing his best novel first, but that happens to all too many novelists.

B︎ob Gottlieb, the editor of *Catch-22,* notes that "the visceral response" in the prepublication reviews "would be utterly different" if *Closing Time* had had some minor surgery—changing the names of the characters, removing the references to its predecessor. If, in other words, it weren't a sequel.

"What I sense most in those reviews is a personal rebuke," says Gottlieb. "If you have a lifelong love affair with a book, you're likely to want a sequel to be, in essence, the same book. But *Closing Time* couldn't possibly be the same—the events are 50 years later; Joe is an older man writing about a different time. He isn't capable of writing about a different time. He isn't capably of simply writing the same book again. So of course there's bound to be a disappointment to those who want *Catch-23*."

His own view of *Closing Time:* "I was very impressed with large parts, less impressed with other parts, but I certainly thought it a valid and worthy book." Would Gottlieb have counseled Heller not to write it? "Serious writers should do what they feel they should do," the editor says. "You can't prescribe for them."

In this case, that's true of readers as well. There's a large group out there who will either buy *Closing Time* out of love for the original or avoid it for precisely that reason. "It can work either way," says Gottlieb. "People can resist the idea of a sequel to a book that is very meaningful to them, or they may feel they must read it. A perfect example of the latter is the unspeakable *Scarlett*," the sequel to *Gone With the Wind* that was ridiculed by reviewers but avidly consumed by readers.

The editor refuses to make predictions: "It's a very dicey business—there's no question. Joe is running a risk by doing this."

Bob Wietrak, a director of merchandising at the Barnes & Noble bookstore chain, likewise straddles the fence: "There's a lot of interest and anticipation in *Closing Time*. We've positioned it as a best-seller, but we will see and react. If the reviews aren't good, that will affect it."

As Heller waits, and worries, he can look at the bright side. At least that $4-million advance isn't hanging over his head. Do authors feel horrible if they get a huge advance for a novel and then the book sells only four copies?

The writer pauses, "I would say authors feel bad even without a big advance if their book sells only four copies."

When Joseph Heller said that, he was smiling.

CHRISTOPHER BUCKLEY

Götterdämmerung-22

Sequels, it's been said more than once, are not necessarily equals. Doubtless Joseph Heller and his publisher, Michael Korda, made a bet over how many irksome reviewers would scramble to be the first to reach for that chestnut as publication approached for "Closing Time" (Simon & Schuster; $24), which its cover unmistakably proclaims to be "The Sequel to 'Catch-22.'" To call yourself the sequel to one of the most important books of the twentieth century is to lead with a chin the size of Jay Leno's. But then the *New York Review of Books* called "Something Happened" (1974), Heller's novel about a corporate tool who accidentally smothers his son, a failed sequel to "Catch-22," so the poor man is damned if he does and damned if he doesn't. At any rate, it needs quickly to be said that there is some awfully good stuff in the sequel to "Catch-22." Over all—well, as Sonny Liston's manager used to say, "You know, Sonny has a lot of good points. It's his bad points that aren't so good."

I say "quickly" because of the piling on that has been under way now for over a month. In August, Barbara Gelb, playing the role of Mme. Defarge, told readers of the *Times Book Review* about Heller's "frequent sulkiness," "gluttonous table manners," and evanescent amiability. More recently, David Streitfeld contributed a piece to *New York,* quoting various literary insiders, including Heller's good friend Kurt Vonnegut, who said that he

The New Yorker, Vol. 70 (Oct 10, 1994): pp. 104–109. © 1994 Conde Nast.

hadn't read the book, even though he's in it (makes for easier dinner-party seating in the Hamptons); the usual sources within Bookville on how Putnam backed out of its contract with Heller after his novel "Picture This" bombed; another source saying that the asking price for "Closing Time" went into free fall before Dick Snyder, then chairman of Simon & Schuster, reportedly turned it down and Michael Korda, on the principle that S. & S., as the original publisher of "Catch-22," ought to publish the sequel, pushed for it and got it at a sort of bargain-basement price; and Korda himself, denying that his decision to publish "Closing Time" was a payback to Heller's agent, Amanda Urban, for S. & S.'s having finked out of publishing Bret Easton Ellis's unfortunate yuppie serial-murder book, "American Psycho." How would you like to be a seventy-one-year-old certified American literary heavyweight, only to have your latest work be rumored to owe its publication to a Bret Easton Ellis-mollification clause? What praise there was for "Closing Time"—from Robert Gottlieb, the editor of "Catch-22"—was somewhat faint.

So, Joe—glad you wrote "The Sequel to 'Catch-22'"? To such inquiries Heller has patiently replied that birds gotta sing, girls gotta dance, and writers gotta write. The criticism of Heller may be in part a form of backhanded compliment to "Catch-22," which for most readers is Heller's masterpiece. It's as if people were annoyed with him for messing with characters they've come to regard over the years as their own. But if all that "Closing Time" accomplishes is to make people go back and reread "Catch-22," then it will have done something worthwhile. Contemplating "Catch-22" in 1994, as we proceed with God knows what in our occupation of one Caribbean island, makes you wonder if it isn't more relevant now than it was when it came out—in October, 1961, six months after our spectacular decision *not* to try to occupy tile, island immediately to the left.

"Catch-22" wasn't generally hailed as a masterpiece when it came out. It never hit the *Times* best-seller list. Simon & Schuster says in its publicity material for "Closing Time," though, that "Catch-22" has sold ten million copies "in the United States alone." During the year following its publication, it did sell a respectable forty thousand copies in hardcover. There was a lot of competition: Leon Uris's "Mila 18," which forced a despondent Heller to change his title from "Catch-18" to "Catch-22"; Harold Robbins' "The Carpetbaggers"; Robert Heinlein's "Stranger in a Strange Land"; J. D. Salinger's "Franny and Zooey"; and Ken Kesey's "One Flew Over the Cuckoo's Nest." Most of those forty thousand copies sold in the New York area, and to make the List you have to sell in Peoria, too.

It was probably because of the reviews that Peoria wasn't buying. As Streitfeld noted, the *Times* panned it in three paragraphs on page 50. Poking about the library, I found a few other reviews:

Mr. Heller's talents for comedy are so considerable that one gets irritated when he keeps pressing. . . . There is a difference, after all, between milking a joke . . . and stretching it out till you kill it.
—*The Atlantic*

Heller's talent is impressive, but it also is undisciplined, sometimes luring him into bogs of boring repetition.
—*Time*

Monotonous.
—*San Francisco Chronicle*

Several extremely funny passages . . . . But the book as a whole is less effective than it might be.
—Granville Hicks, in *The Saturday Review*

He wallows in his own laughter, and finally drowns in it. What remains is a debris of sour jokes, stage anger, dirty words, synthetic looniness, and the sort of antic behavior the children fall into when they know they are losing our attention.
—Whitney Balliett, in *The New Yorker*

The Nation, predictably, did like it. "This novel is not merely the best American novel to come out of World War II," Nelson Algren wrote. "It is the best American novel that has come out of anywhere in years." And Robert Brustein, of *The New Republic*, was beside himself: "Joseph Heller is one of the most extraordinary talents now among us. He has Mailer's combustible radicalism without his passion for violence and self-glorification . . . and he has Salinger's wit without his coquettish self-consciousness."

All told, it seems miraculous that the book went on to sell nine million nine hundred and sixty thousand copies in softcover, and that the title went on to enter the language in a way that no other book title has. How often have you uttered the phrase, usually after a run-in with the Department of Motor Vehicles? Thirteen years after its publication, Nixon's attorney James St. Clair used it while manfully arguing his client's sinking case before the Supreme Court, explaining that you can impeach a President only if you have evidence that he committed a crime, and you can't collect criminal evidence against a President. One of the justices, Heller observed with amusement in a 1975 interview with *Playboy*, placed himself in the role of Yossarian, telling Mr. St. Clair, "Wait a minute, you lose me there."

"Catch-22" would almost certainly never have entered the language, or even come out in paperback, if an interviewer for the *New York Herald*

Tribune, which had done its part to insure the book's demise, hadn't chanced to ask S. J. Perelman if he'd read any good books lately. He replied, "'Catch-22.'" The rest is history, and prologue to "Closing Time."

For all its flaws, "Closing Time" is a summing up by one of the last of the great writers of the Second World War generation. James Jones and Irwin Shaw are dead, Kurt Vonnegut seems to have had his say, and, with Norman Mailer off in Minsk channelling the ghost of Lee Harvey Oswald and doing P.R. for Madonna in *Esquire,* it appears Heller still owns the field that in 1961 became preeminently his. The opening sentence of "Closing Time"—quite a switch from "Catch-22"'s breezy "It was love at first sight"—is elegiac. The novel's protagonist, an aging veteran named Sammy Singer, who was not a character in the prequel, begins, "When people our age speak of the war, it is not of Vietnam but of the one that broke out more than half a century ago and swept in almost all the world."

Though many of the best parts of the book are about Sammy's—and his buddies'—experience of the war, "Closing Time" isn't "about" the Second World War. It's Heller's "The Best Years of Our Lives." It's about the End, the Apocalypse—whether by Alzheimer's or stroke or cancer or by New York City bus terminal. It's about growing up in Coney Island before the war. Large chunks are devoted to *où sont les bumper cars d'antan* evocations of the Steeplechase amusement park there, the old neighborhood, and how everything changed after the war. It's sort of Proustian, with bagels instead of madeleines. "I suppose," Heller told Ms. Gelb, "this is the first time I've written seriously about Jewish characters." They're certainly more real than the *oy gevalt* caricatures he wrote about in "Good as Gold."

Sammy is a good man, who, after serving with Yossarian and the others in the "fighting" 256th Squadron on the island of Pianosa, off Elba, went on to become a promotional copywriter at *Time.* (Heller did the same.) The war really *did* change things: "In his work in the city Sammy found himself among Republicans for the first time." His life, like Prufrock's, has been measured out in coffee spoons of disappointment, along with some larger spoonfuls, in the form of his wife's death from cancer and his son's suicide. (Heller has named no fewer than three of the main characters' sons Michael, not an especially reader-friendly device.)

Sammy's relationship with Lew Rabinowitz, his old friend from Coney Island, is the emotional heart of the novel, and it has touching depth. Heller, up to his usual structural tricks, gives both Sammy and Lew a narrator's "I"; again, he can't be accused of making it easy, but then he never has ("Catch-22" has sixty characters). The chapters in Sammy's voice are the best parts of "Closing Time," perhaps because, despite Heller's asseverations to Ms. Gelb that "this is not autobiography," they read like autobiography, and of a very high order.

Sammy is not a funny man. There isn't much for him to be funny about, not at this point in the game: "I enjoy myself a lot, playing bridge, taking adult education courses and subscribing to concerts at Lincoln Center and the YMHA . . . doing my direct-mail consulting work for cancer relief. But I am only marking time. Unlike Yossarian, I expect nothing much new and good to happen to me again." No one in "Closing Time" has much to look forward to, except perhaps for some good morphine on the way out with the cancer. All the main characters are in their sixties and seventies. Heller has shaved ten years off Yossarian; what the hell, as McWatt used to say in "Catch-22" as he turned back to make another bomb run. Everyone is in and out of hospitals, hallucinating (another big help for the confused reader, who will suddenly find Yossarian conversing with Ulysses S. Grant), gradually deteriorating, and generally, as Sammy said, marking time. Back on Pianosa, Yossarian "had decided to live forever or die in the attempt." "Closing Time" is what he got for living forever.

Yossarian was the appealing Everyman-Sisyphus of "Catch-22," the one reasonably sane guy in the loony bin. He's lost a lot of that appeal in the fifty years since. For one thing, he has bought into the loony bin, as Milo Minderbinder's partner, and is now a wealthy businessman, twice divorced, worried about his son, and horny for his nurse.

For his part, Milo, a former mess sergeant who makes Gordon Gekko took like an amateur, has done well for himself as a—surprise—billionaire arms dealer. Our last glimpse of Milo had him abandoning a desperate Yossarian on the streets of Rome in order to run off so he could get in on the illegal tobacco market. He is his old, incorrigible self as he connives to get the United States military to buy his superstealthy bomber—called the Shh-hhh!—which flies faster than the speed of light. As he puts it, "you can bomb someone before you even decide to do it." His competition is one Harold—ahem—Strangelove, who's pushing his own version of a post-Stealth bomber. Milo has gone on to become exactly what his "Catch-22" class yearbook would have predicted for him: Most Likely to Prove Lenin Right.

Ex-Pfc. Wintergreen, who kept going AWOL in the old days, and ran the United States Air Force by his deft sabotaging of the paper flow through the squadron's mailroom, is back as well. He's still his foulmouthed self—all the more so since it's 1994, and "fuck" is just another punctuation mark. (I couldn't find a single "fuck" in "Catch-22." Heller substitutes "furgle," and the Italian whores beckon the boys with "Ficky-fick?" Of course, in 1961 Madonna was still the Mother of Christ.)

And this wouldn't be much of a sequel without Chaplain Tappman, the hapless Anabaptist padre ("It isn't necessary to call me Father"), whose duty it was to censor the squadron's mad home. (Lending a hand, Yossarian blacked out all the words except "a," "an," and "the" in one of his letters, and, in another, blacked out all but the greeting and wrote at the bottom, "I yearn for you tragically. A. T. Tappman, Chaplain, U. S. Army.") The Chaplain has since developed a rather peculiar malady: he urinates heavy water, the kind that's used to make nuclear bombs. The government, as indifferent and intractable as it was during the war, abducts him for obscure reasons of national security, and Yossarian, putting his shoulder to the Sisyphean rock once again, can't get a straight answer as to his whereabouts. The Catch-22 of the nineteen-nineties, it turns out, is the Freedom of Information Act—or, as Chaplain Tappman explains it, "a federal regulation obliging government agencies to release all information they had to anyone who made application for it, except information they had that they did not want to release." This will delight anyone who has ever filed an F.O.I.A. request with Big Brother Sam, only to get back, months later, a phonebook-size thicket of papers with all the words blacked out except "a," "an," and "the." This is classic Catch-22, with its Möbius-strip impenetrability—the logic and the excuse of the totalitarian mind-set.

The only problem is that the totalitarians running the show in "Closing Time" don't have the bite—or, ultimately, the menace—of the colonels in "Catch-22." Of course, there's no war going on in "Closing Time," other than the video games being played in the Oval Office. These totalitarian heavies start out ludicrous and end up ludicrous, even after they've triggered the missiles. Apocalypse is as Apocalypse does, and this one comes off as a Potemkin Armageddon, perhaps because by this time the reader has been force-marched through so many of Yossarian's hallucinations that you really can't tell what (the fuck) is going on, and whether the apocalypse is real or not. If it is a real one it's pretty feckless, with the horsemen riding on carrousel steeds. So what's to be afraid of? The real horrors of "Closing Time" lie elsewhere—in the quotidian, Leopold Bloom—like defeats and attritions.

Heller's Washington, D.C., where the carrousel horses are stabled, along with a perfect Dan Quaylean Vice-President, is funnier and more sophisticated than the one in "Good as Gold," but it's still not his most successful locus comicus. The crowning glory is Heller's depiction of the Port Authority Bus Terminal, on his home turf of New York. Anyone who has had the pleasure of passing through there will recognize this appalling agora of villainy as the genuine article. This is the book's ground zero, and the place toward which Yossarian is ineluctably drawn. (Go figure.) Amusingly, Heller told Ms. Gelb that he himself has set foot in Port Authority only once, and that was a long time ago, before it became the worm in the apple that it is today. He hired "a very good researcher" to supply him with the details, but, in spite of this, the setting did not lose anything Dickensian in the word-processing:

> There was scarcely a charmed body with enough living ace to be free of another body more dissipated and fetid tumbled against it. People squabbled. There were shouts, quarrels, stabbings, burns, sex, drugs, drinking, and breaking glass; by morning there were casualties and an accumulation of filth of all sorts save industrial waste. There was no water or toilet. Garbage was not collected until morning, when the locals roused and took themselves to the sinks and the toilets in the rest rooms in sanitary preparation for the day's work ahead and, despite posted bans, to bathe and do laundry in the washbasins. . . . The astringent smell of caustic disinfectant hung ineradicably it, the air like the carbolic harbinger of a remorseless decay.

Yuck! Or, as Yossarian ruminated while searching for Nately's whore's kid sister in the nocturnal squalor of Rome, "What a lousy earth!" He is drawn to Port Authority initially to rescue his son from arrest for turnstile jumping, and repeatedly afterward because of the intriguing, infernal (as in Dante) network of secret tunnels underneath it, and finally because Milo plans to hold his own son's extravagant wedding there, with the President as best man. Yossarian's wanderings below are scarcely less gruesome than his peregrinations through whorish Rome:

> "I'll do you for a nickel, mister," said a flat-chested girl . . . while a stout woman with a painted lids and rouged cheeks and dimpled faces of fat around the chubby knees exposed by her tight skirt looked on from ahead, laughing to herself.
> "I'll lick your balls," the woman proposed while Yossarian walked by, and rolled her eyes coquettishly. "We can do it in the emergency stairwell."
> Now he tensed with outrage. I am sixty-eight, he said to himself. What was there about him that gave these people the notion he had come to the terminal to be done or have his balls licked?

Only a pro like Heller could pull off such simultaneous horror and humor. This is the same affronted voice that kept asking in "Catch-22," with vanquishing naïveté, why everyone was trying to kill him. The gloriously vulgar wedding that eventually takes place in this unlikeliest of connubial bowers—thirty-five hundred guests, four thousand pounds of caviar, a million champagne tulips, a forty-four-foot-high wedding cake and Secret Service agents posing as rigidly as George Segal statues—is out of Nathanael West by way of Tom Wolfe.

It's hard, in the end, not to read "Closing Time" as a commentary on Catch-22." Heller's style has deepened and matured—to use a presumptuous word. He flew more than sixty bombings missions in the Second World War himself, and since writing "Catch-22" he has looked the Grim Reaper in the eye again, in the form of Guillain-Barré syndrome. He has paid full price for the gravitas on these pages, and the melancholy. The problem with gravitas, as anyone who's trudged through Russian wit, will tell you, is that it enables a fair bit of prolixity. Heller *is* prolix and he *is* repetitious. He goes back to the same wells too many times, and there isn't much in the way of a plot. But then, just as your patience is about to give out (let's be honest—just as you're about to put the book down), there will be a glimmery gem, often comic: "Mr. Tilyou always kept at hand a shiny new dime to give Mr. Rockefeller, who . . . came begging almost daily in his repentant struggle to collect back all those shiny new dimes he had handed away in a misguided effort to buy public affection, which he now understood he never had needed." There are enough of these to justify the price of admission to "Closing Time," and the occasional long standing in line for the rides. And, finally, there's this sort of startling realization: that Heller is at his best, which is as good as it gets, when he's *not* trying to be funny.

Toward the end of "Closing Time," with the cosmic gloaming setting in, the missiles warming in their silos, and the caterers preparing the wedding feast, you can hear the still, sad music of Heller's humanity as Yossarian wanders through the heart of darkness underneath Port Authority and learns that the ur-G.I. of the Second World War generation is gone:

> Kilroy was dead, McBride revealed. "I felt I should tell you."
>
> "I had a feeling he was," said Yossarian. "There are people my age who'll be sorry to hear that. Vietnam?"
>
> "Oh, no, no," McBride answered with surprise. "It was cancer."

It's Yossarian as Marlow, being told, "Mistah Kilroy—he dead"; this is Heller's requiem for his generation.

When Heller does try to be funny, he's Sonny Liston in full swing—and, if nothing else, it reminds you of the moment when postmodern absurdist comedy was born. Even the book's critics conceded that "Catch-22" had some of the funniest moments in fiction. Remember Chief White Halfoat, the swarthy Indian from Oklahoma, who, "for occult reasons of his own, had made up his mind to die of pneumonia"? And Captain Flume, who lived in mortal fear of Chief White Halfoat?

Captain Flume was obsessed with the idea that Chief White Halfoat would tiptoe up to his cot one night when he was sound asleep and slit his throat open for him from ear to ear. Captain Flume had obtained this idea from Chief White Halfoat himself, who did tiptoe up to his cot one night as he was dozing off, to hiss portentously that one night when he, Captain Flume, was sound asleep he, Chief White Halfoat, was going to slit his throat open from ear to ear. Captain Flume turned to ice, his eyes, flung open wide, staring directly up into Chief White Halfoat's glinting drunkenly only inches away.

"Why?" Captain Flume managed to croak finally.

"Why not?" was Chief White Halfoat's answer.

I was truly mystified to find Heller saying, in that old *Playboy* interview, "I wasn't aware that 'Catch-22' was a *funny* book until I heard someone laugh while reading it. The experience was pleasant but also unsettling. . . . I'm suspicious of comedy." Trying to resolve this koan, I wondered if Heller isn't a Janus figure of American fiction—one face to the darkness, staring it down, the other blinking into the sun. Something else he said in that interview steers you in this direction: "I'm inclined to be serious about most matters, yet jokes keep coming to my mind. This disturbs me." Why? "Because humor comes too easily, and I'm suspicious of things that come too easily."

There's much in "Closing Time" that can't have come easily. As the critics sharpen their knives and aim for the dotted lines marked "Cut here," it seems we can afford to celebrate "Catch-22"'s thirty-third anniversary by welcoming Yossarian, Sammy, Milo, Lew, Wintergreen, and Chaplain Tappmann, even as we take leave of them, and give credit to their creator, who has given us such consequential imperfections, and has dared not to leave well enough alone.

DAVID M. CRAIG

From Avignon to Catch-22

Rage, rage against the dying of the light.

—Dylan Thomas

Joseph Heller's experiences as a bombardier over Avignon during World War
II were catalytic to his career as a writer. In the experiences over Avignon,
Catch-22 begins. These experiences did not spark Heller's desire to be
an author, for that had burned unabated since childhood.[1] Nor did the
reaction the Avignon experiences occasioned occur quickly, regularly, or
consciously. Rather, Avignon provided in highly compressed form Heller's
essential subject—human mortality—and Avignon engaged his imagination in a way that this subject could eventually be given expression. No
Catch-22 reader is likely to forget the result, the Snowden death scene over
Avignon or the secret of Snowden's entrails: "Man was matter . . . Drop
him out a window and he'll fall. Set fire to him and he'll burn. Bury him
and he'll rot like other kinds of garbage" (429–430). While the evidence
for the importance of Avignon is unmistakable, many pieces of the story
are unknown or missing today. Heller's public accounts of these experiences come long after he has begun to feature Avignon in his writing, and,
predictably, these accounts partake of the persona of Joseph Heller, the
author of *Catch-22*.[2] The accounts are couched in jokes that distance the
experience from the man.

War, Literature & the Arts, 6.2 (Fall–Winter 1994): pp. 27–54.

Heller's early writing furnishes some of the links between his real-life experience and *Catch-22*, and these early fictional versions of Avignon illuminate the novel (and, for that matter, Heller's subsequent writing) as if by ultraviolet light, defamiliarizing the familiar. Avignon serves as the setting for two unpublished stories, "The Miracle of Danrossane" and "Crippled Phoenix," Heller's only short stories about the war.[3] Avignon also figures prominently in the planning material for *Catch-22*, most notably in an early draft of the Snowden death scene.[4] In this material, not in the published stories that preceded *Catch-22*, one first discovers Heller's masterplot, the core narrative that propels each of his novels. This masterplot—what I call the "dead child story"—consists of the same constellation of narrative elements: guilt, secret knowledge, bad faith, and the death of children (or, alternatively, of wounded innocents). The thrust and destination of this narrative is death, a death that serves, as does Snowden's in *Catch-22*, as the occasion for narrative clarification.[5] The narrative's import is as humanly simple and as humanly complex as mortality itself: humans are matter With this masterplot, Heller seeks to do what Tolstoy does in *The Death of Ivan Ilych*, to have character and reader alike experience the immanence and imminence of death. Like Ivan Ilych, we are apt to be resisting readers, able to acknowledge, as Ivan does, the rightness of the syllogistic reasoning that says "Caius (or Snowden) is a man; men are mortal"; but not wanting, as Ivan and Yossarian do not want, to apply this abstraction to ourselves. Heller's early writing about Avignon, then, allows exploration of the process by which he draws upon and gains control over personal experience and documents its "increasingly conscious transformation into writing" (Said 196).[6]

Each of the accounts of Avignon—"The Miracle of Danrossane," "Crippled Phoenix," the early manuscript, the published one, and, as I discuss elsewhere, "'Catch-22' Revisited"—has an aspect of meta-narration entailing a struggle of how to locate and voice the story. In "The. Miracle of Danrossane," the Avignon story—that is, the dead child story—is a secret known only by the local residents, and Heller's plot unfolds his American protagonist's efforts to find someone who will disclose the secret. In "Crippled Phoenix," the story resides within the principal characters themselves, in the guilty pasts of Dan Cramer, an American pilot, and Morain, a member of the French underground. The plots of both stories depend upon working out what can and cannot be told as well as what can and cannot be confronted. In an early manuscript version of the Snowden death scene, Yossarian endeavors to have the chaplain understand his own reactions to what happened over Avignon, not the event itself. Finally, in *Catch-22*, Yossarian endeavors to unlock the significance of Snowden's dying words and, in so doing, to plumb the meaning of death. As in the previous versions, Yossarian's understanding hinges upon telling the story of what happened, albeit to himself. In each story of Avignon, Heller makes the telling of the story as important as the having told, as if the repeated tellings will help the author himself understand what happened.

During the war, Heller flew two missions to Avignon. Before the Avignon missions, he had, by his own account, romanticized war: "I wanted action, not security. I wanted a sky full of dogfights, daredevils and billowing parachutes. I was twenty-one years old. I was dumb" ("Revisited" 51). Avignon shatters his romantic wishes, for as he remarks in "*'Catch-22'* Revisited": "There was the war, in Avignon, not in Rome or Ile Rousse or Poggibonsi or even Ferrara" (141).[7] On the August 8, 1944 mission to bomb a railroad bridge, Heller for the first time saw a plane shot down.[8] As a bombardier on one of the lead planes, which had been assigned to drop metallic paper to disrupt the radar for the anti-aircraft guns, Heller could look back on what was happening to the rest of the squadron. He saw a burning plane fall into an uncontrollable spin. Parachutes billowed and opened: he would later learn that three men had gotten out, while three others were killed in the crash. One of the three survivors was found by members of the Avignon underground, hidden and eventually smuggled back across enemy lines. This mission provides the basis for the "Crippled Phoenix" and, presumably, the inspiration for the survivor's guilt that its protagonist Dan Cramer experiences.

On August 15, 1944, Heller's squadron returned to Avignon to bomb another railroad bridge over the Rhone, and this mission would provide the model for the Snowden death scene. For both Heller and Yossarian, it was their 37th mission. In notes Heller made in 1966 about the mission, he records: "Man wounded in leg. Wohlstein and Moon killed" ("Chronology 2/13/66," Heller papers, Brandeis University). According to Heller, the details from the novel correspond

> . . . perhaps ninety percent to what I did experience. I did have a co-pilot go berserk and grab the controls. The earphones did pull out. I did think I was dying for what seemed like thirty minutes but was actually three-hundredths of a second. When I did plug my earphones in, there was a guy sobbing on the intercom, "Help the bombardier, but the gunner was only shot in the leg." (Heller, "Translating" 357)

In recounting the experience, Heller confines the correspondences between the actual and the novelistic Avignon missions to "physical details" and denies any similarity between Yossarian's emotional reactions and his own.[9]

Heller's own explanations as well as his fictional use of Avignon indicate that more than physical details are at play. Whether factual or fictional, each account that Heller gives of Avignon contains an Ur-plot that turns upon an intense experience of personal mortality. In answering interviewers' questions about his own experience, Heller repeatedly dwells on his sensation that he had died in the air above Avignon. He remembers pressing the talk button of his head set, hearing nothing, and thinking he was already dead. Heller stresses his sense of distorted time, of events that unfolded in microseconds seeming to last much longer.[10] His change of habits after this Avignon mission also testifies to the mission's effects; from then on, Heller carried a personal first-aid kit and vowed never to fly once his combat missions were over (a vow kept until 1960 when a 24-hour train ride convinced him to reassess the dangers of flying). The comic "*Catch-22* Revisited" retelling provides a perspective on Heller's reactions in that he makes himself, not the wounded airman, the victim. "I went to the hospital the next day. He looked fine. They had given him blood, and he was going to be all right. But I was in terrible shape, and I had twenty-three more missions to fly" ("Revisited" 142). Of course, the wound becomes mortal in *Catch-22,* or as Heller laconically describes the wound's change: "He was shot through the leg . . . But I added to it and had him shot in the middle" (Barnard 298).

"The Miracle of Danrossane" and "Crippled Phoenix" mark the artistic steps by which the wound gets relocated. Together with the early draft of the Snowden death scene and *Catch-22* itself, the stories offer a complex range of reactions to death: denial, confusion, immersion, and understanding. While all of these reactions figure in each work, one predominates in each, as if designating stages in Heller's thinking, from denial in "The Miracle of Danrossane" to understanding in *Catch-22*. As this progression indicates, the stories and manuscript draft of the death scene provided the vehicle by which Heller worked out his master plot, and determined that *death* could serve as thrust and destination for his narratives. In the stories, the journey toward this death is spatial and temporal, a visit to Avignon in "Danrossane" and a return to it in "Crippled Phoenix." In *Catch-22* and the novels that follow, the journey becomes psychological and emotional, one culminating in a death that surfaces, like Snowden's does, as if from the protagonist's subconscious.

"The Miracle of Danrossane," the slighter of the two unpublished war stories, recounts a correspondent's visit to the village outside Avignon where his father was born. This story's plot turns upon a father's denying his sons' deaths. The correspondent is intrigued by the name of the inn in which he stays, *L'Auberge des Sept Fils* [Inn of the Seven Sons]. While Durland, the innkeeper, will not talk about the name, the mayor tells the correspondent Durland's story. This telling provides the principal plot of Heller's story. Even though Durland had been a Nazi collaborator during the war, his seven sons had been killed by the Nazis as a reprisal for the death of two German soldiers. Durland himself bears responsibility for his sons' deaths because he neglected to protect them. The story is irony-laden: the Nazis' random selection of reprisal victims results in the deaths of Durland's sons (hence the darkly ironic title); although the Nazis think their selection random, one of Durland's sons has, in fact, been involved in killing the Nazi soldiers as revenge for the rape of a village girl by the soldiers; one of the actual killers goes free even though he volunteers to turn himself over to the Nazis and despite the mayor's informing on him. Durland himself never comes to terms with his sons' deaths; in fact, he tells the correspondent that his sons are out working in the fields.

In this earliest Avignon story, Heller announces the concerns that will characterize his subsequent accounts, as well as provide the principal concerns of his novels: guilt, secret knowledge, bad faith, and, most crucially, the death of children. "The Miracle of Danrossane's" underlying structure has the primitive, evocative force of a folk tale. A young man, who is looking symbolically for his father (and thus for his own origins), finds a surrogate whose act of paternal bad faith has caused his own sons' deaths. Refusing to acknowledge their deaths or his own complicity in them, this father lives "respectably" in a house memorializing the dead sons. When the correspondent discovers the father's secret, he returns home and, as artist, transforms the secret into story. Thus conceived, the story the reader has just read originates in guilty, concealed knowledge—a conception that aligns it with such myths as those of Prometheus and the Garden of Eden, myths which Heller explicitly draws upon in *Catch-22*. The architecture of "Danrossane," particularly the crucial element of the sons' deaths, is striking for the way that it anticipates the design of Heller's novels. Later characterizing this design, Heller says:

> Death is always present as a climactic event that never happens to the protagonist but affects him profoundly. I think I'm drawing unconsciously from experience for inspiration. The child, the dependent child or sacrificed child is always there. I would think that the death of my father when I was about five years old had much to do with that. There was almost no conversation about it . . . Indeed, the traumatized child denies death very successfully, and then sublimates it, which I think is the process that went on in me. But it leaves me very sensitive to the helplessness of children and the ease with which they can be destroyed or betrayed deliberately or otherwise.[11] (Flippo 60)

Whether one accepts Heller's psychological explanation for the phenomenon or not, one cannot escape the way in which death serves as climactic event and as catalyst for narrative clarification in his writing and does so from the onset of his career.

"Crippled Phoenix" marks another step on Heller's journey toward *Catch-22*. Guilt-caused confusion characterizes the story's account of death, and, like the novel, this story features a protagonist who has been wounded in the leg. As its title signifies, the life after the Avignon death is crippling; there is no phoenix-like resurrection. Evidently, Heller spent considerable time on the story, for there are three versions of it in the Brandeis collection and he tried placing it with different literary agents. Possessing clear affinities with *Catch-22*, as well as with *Something Happened*, "Crippled Phoenix" tells a double story of conscience: that of Dan Cramer, an American pilot who feels guilty for surviving the crash in which he was the only survivor, and of Morain, a French peasant who aided with Cramer's escape after the crash. Cramer has returned to Avignon to see Morain, to whom he feels grateful and about whom he feels guilty because Morain's son had been killed when a bombardier with one mission left to fly dropped his bombs too early. Cramer has an additional reason for guilt in that he has been unfaithful to his wife during a recent stay in London, and, even in bed with his wife in Avignon, he finds his mind wandering back to Luciana, a wartime liaison in Rome.[12]

More crucial to the action of the story, Cramer fails to come to terms with all this guilt. First, although Cramer goes to see Morain with the intention "of help[ing] him in some way," he cannot provide the support that Morain wants, for Morain suffers from his own wartime guilt. To Cramer, Morain confesses that he was afraid his daughter would be taken away to a Nazi work camp and so he forced her to become the mistress of a German official (which ruins her life and that of her child born of the relationship). Although Morain explicitly asks him to return to visit, Cramer, even after agreeing to, cannot bring himself to do so. Second, he fails to come to terms with his wife, although he shares some of the details with her about the wartime plane crash, which he alone survived. Convinced that his wife is too superficial to understand his feelings, especially about the war, he allows her to believe that their marital difficulties have been reconciled, all the while despising her.

Significantly, Cramer, who stands in Yossarian's position as participant in events of the past, cannot fully disclose his story to anyone; he thus remains isolated and tormented. In a symbolically resonant moment, Heller communicates the moral wilderness that Cramer has brought himself into because he is unable to confront his guilt; he also conveys the way in which Cramer has deliberately estranged himself from his wife.

> Suddenly, though, [Cramer] was frightened. The forest was immediately before them (his guide, his wife, and himself), and he realized that Katherine belonged only to the fringe of his emotions, on that their endless surface of amiability and routine, and that

everything might still be all right if he kept her there. But they were already between the trees.

This passage forecasts the role that Avignon will play in *Catch-22* (as well as anticipates Slocum's marriage in *Something Happened*). The passage locates the wilderness within the self, that wilderness which, as Conrad demonstrates in *Heart of Darkness,* is the territory of the modern condition. While the same elements—dead children, secret knowledge, guilt, and bad faith—constitute the story, Heller relocates them. In "Danrossane," Durland's history was part of public discourse, unknown only to the correspondent, the outsider. In "Crippled Phoenix," Cramer's and Morain's pasts are secret—in particular, the responsibility that each feels for a death. Each discloses his guilty past in the vain hope of confessional relief. However, both disclosures fail because the two men look to others to assuage their own inner guilt: Morain to Cramer when the injured party is his daughter and Cramer to his wife when he cannot accept his own actions. The guilty knowledge of what happened at Avignon isolates and estranges, at least until what happened there can be fully confronted and related. As the early manuscript version of the Snowden death scene powerfully suggests, this is what *Catch-22* is about.

An early draft of the Snowden scene documents Heller's evolving conception of Avignon and dramatizes the imperative for reporting what happened there. Snowden represents the death at a distance—Yossarian recounts the experience to the chaplain. Yet, this early version is raw and, in some ways, more emotionally charged than the novel. While the Snowden scene plays off the bloody hands scene in *Macbeth,* the literary allusion seems like a patina over what Heller will call in *God Knows* the "stink of mortality and reek of mankind" (107). In Heller's early rendering, Yossarian not only sees death, but also immerses himself in it.

> "Dirty hands," Yossarian said. "Yesterday they touched a dead man's flesh."

The chaplain attempts to comfort him, but Yossarian continues:

> "A dead man's private parts. I spoke to Doc Daneeker. Probably his lungs, his pancreas, his liver, his stomach, and some canned tomatoes that he had for breakfast. I hate canned tomatoes . . ."

The chaplain tries again.

> "But you don't understand. I enjoyed it. I actually enjoyed touching the graying flesh, the clotting blood. I actually enjoyed touching

his lungs, his pancreas, his liver, his stomach and some canned
tomatoes from his breakfast, even though I hate canned tomatoes.
I made excuses to myself to touch every shriveling shred."

The chaplain tries one final time to console Yossarian.

"But even that's not the worst of it. I rubbed blood all over myself.
And do you know why I rubbed blood all over myself? To impress
people. To impress those God damned Red Cross biddies with
the smiles and doughnuts . . . and by God, it impressed, even Doc
Daneeker, who broke down and gave me some codeine and told
me about Cathcart and a tour of duty." (Heller papers, Brandeis
University)

There are many noteworthy differences between this early version and the
published one. Snowden's mortal wound is open, displaying what Heller
will call in the novel "God's plenty" (429). Yossarian is compelled to touch
the viscera, then compelled to relate to the chaplain his enjoyment of doing
so. He has previously told Doc Daneeker about his experience. In *Catch-22*,
Yossarian tells no one, although his recollections have the quality of telling
the story to himself. Time works differently as well. In the manuscript, the
experience, only a day old, has the immediacy of the here and now, while in
the novel version, it emerges as if from Yossarian's subconsciousness. In *Catch-22*, the intensity of Yossarian's remembrance erupts into the present: "liver,
lungs, kidneys, ribs, stomach, and bits of . . . stewed tomatoes" (429). The
same message is embedded in both—*man is matter*—but in the manuscript,
Yossarian, and perhaps Heller, has not yet apprehended its significance.

The unpublished early version is, at once, more public and more private
than the Avignon of the *Catch-22*. The appropriation of the dirty hands
motif from *Macbeth* dissociates this version from Heller himself, connect-
ing it to a literary past rather than a personal one.[13] Also by having Yossarian report the story, Heller publicizes Avignon in a way that third-per-
son narration would not. This recounting of Avignon proclaims Yossarian's
guilty consciousness, whereas the novel displaces it into the tree-of-life
episode, in which Yossarian's nakedness reveals his guilt (likewise triggered
by Snowden's blood).[14] Simultaneously, this early version is more private,
more evocative of the Heller who experienced Avignon and of the author
who repeatedly sets key scenes there. The confessional quality of the incident, with Yossarian trying to make the chaplain understand what he has
done, directs attention to the personal reaction to the experience. Finally,
Yossarian's revelation that, on one level, he enjoyed the experience points to
the complexity of Heller's own experience over Avignon. This early version

illustrates the attraction of the horrifying—an attraction that Heller seems compelled to specify.

Significantly, before the idea for *Catch-22* came to him, Heller had virtually given up writing. Of the time between the short stories that he wrote in the forties and the novel which he began in 1953, Heller later said, "I wanted to write something that was very good and I had nothing good to write. So I wrote nothing" (Sam Merrill 68). Out of the silence—a silence that he partially filled with reading—came a new method of writing anti-realist and comic in orientation. Reading

> the comic novels of Evelyn Waugh and Celine's *Journey to the End of the Night* ... Nathanael West's *Miss Lonelyhearts,* and ... Nabokov's *Laughter in the Dark* particularly, I was comprehending for the first time that there were different ways to tell a story, and the methods these people used were much more compatible with my own technical ability ... with my own imagination. (Ruas 151)

The realization that there are many ways to tell a story is what Heller's evolving use of the Avignon experiences documents.[15] The discovery was long in coming, though, for he did not publish *Catch-22* until 1961, sixteen years after the publication of his first story. By this time, he was 38, the same age as two other late-blooming, first-time novelists, George Eliot and Willa Cather.

Heller's key discovery involves discourse, not story, the *how* of narrative rather than the *what*.[16] His Avignon short stories (as did most of his other short stories) had linear plots that unfolded on a single narrative level. In each, characters journeyed to Avignon (or nearby Danrossane) to learn something from the past. Heller's narrative method was straightforward, the plots proceeding until access was gained to characters who disclose crucial, secret knowledge from the past. In *Catch-22*, Heller makes discourse—the narrative act itself—part of the story as well as its means of transmission. The Avignon mission on which Snowden dies illustrates this. As is well-known, Heller's narrator distributes references to the mission throughout the novel; sometimes cryptically as in the first reference: "Where are the Snowdens of yesteryear?" (35); sometimes explicitly as in: "the way Snowden had frozen to death after spilling his secret to Yossarian in the back of the plane" (170). In effect, the narrator dissects the Avignon plot as if performing a narrative autopsy on Snowden. This dissection creates a much richer narrative progression than that of the Avignon stories, one that depends upon discourse (the vertical narrative axis) as well as upon story (the horizontal axis).[17] Three effects follow from this: first, the meaning of Snowden's secret depends upon the interplay among narrative levels and involves the contrast of tragic and comic perspectives; second, Heller uses the synthetic dimension of narrative to complicate the narrative progression so that the authorial reader must participate in the unraveling of Snowden's secret; and third, Heller can make the text the verbal embodiment of Snowden's secret, that is, mortality exists in the conjunction of mind and matter.[18]

Heller's first reference to Avignon typifies the way he takes advantage of the interplay among the narrative levels. Yossarian's question about the Snowdens of yesteryear has complementary roles in the novel's story and discourse, in each case providing the pathway to who Snowden is and what his secret entails. For Yossarian, the question speaks to both an actual and a linguistic quest; he wants to know "why so many people were trying so hard to kill him" (34). To gain the knowledge he seeks, Yossarian, like the protagonists of the Avignon stories, must unlock a secret from the past, a secret of which Snowden is the embodiment (potentially, this knowledge is already available to him because he has already ministered to the dying Snowden). But the question is also about language as well as about history, as becomes clear when Yossarian translates it into French: "*Où sont les Neigedens d'antan?*" [Where are the Snowdens of yesteryear?] (35). Heller underscores the seriousness of this linguistic dimension with the narrator's comment about Yossarian's willingness "to pursue [the corporal of whom he asked his question] through all the words of the world" (35). The narrator, of course, knows the answer to Yossarian's question, but instead of relating it, explains to the narrative audience why the question is so upsetting.[19] In doing so, the narrator also makes this query part of another narrative, that of the Fall. "Group Headquarters was alarmed, for there was no telling what people might find out once they were free to ask whatever questions they wanted to"—a concern for which Colonel Korn devises the ingenious solution of permitting only those people to ask questions who never asked any (35). At this moment, the story is simultaneously proceeding on different narrative planes, its comedy, in part, stemming from the resulting incongruity. Heller's discourse takes Yossarian's question to a higher level where Group Headquarters' response echoes the fears of the God from Genesis, who worries that Adam and Eve, possessing the knowledge of good and evil, may now be tempted to eat from the tree of life. The mythic echoes refigure Yossarian's Avignon experience as a fall into mortality and mortal knowledge, a point that Heller makes more forcefully in the subsequent tree-of-life scene.

The reference to "the secret Snowden had spilled to Yossarian" exemplifies the synthetic narrative progression of *Catch-22*, the progression implied by the novel's language. The episode advances the plot: for Yossarian, being in the hospital is better than flying over Avignon with Snowden dying (164). As the narrator formulates the matter, it is not just because the hospital is safer, protecting Yossarian from war, but also because people "couldn't dominate

Death inside the hospital, but they certainly made her behave" (164). Death has become a character and its plot is the Lisa Doolittle story: "They had taught her manners. They couldn't keep Death out, but while she was in she had to act like a lady" (164). With this conception, Yossarian and the narrator seek to control death. Of course, their plotting undoes them. In Heller's mordant, novel-long joke, death is no lady, although this metaphor does, for Heller, speak to its nature.[20] As with the many euphemisms for death, this reference makes dying seem familiar, comfortable, and acceptable.

As novelist, Heller knows better, representing death as violent, certain, and inevitable; and yet, he rages against its sway. In *Catch-22*, unlike his Avignon stories, he finds a form to express his outrage, the humor of the novel's discourse being its expression. His handling of "the secret Snowden had spilled to Yossarian" reference can illustrate this: his mixing comic and tragic perspectives; his verbal pyrotechnics, his delight in language as language; and his presentation of crucial narrative information (i.e. what exactly the secret entails) in a way that resists understanding. The passage itself iconically embodies Snowden's secret, the coded message encased by and hidden among the myriad external and internal threats to one's life.

> There were too many dangers for Yossarian to keep track of. There was Hitler, Mussolini, and Tojo, for example, and they were all out to kill him. There was Lieutenant Scheisskopf with his fanaticism for parades and there was the bloated colonel with his fat mustache and his fanaticism for retribution, and they wanted to kill him. There was Appleby, Havermeyer, Black and Korn . . . There were bartenders, bricklayers and bus conductors all over the world who wanted him dead, landlords and tenants, traitors and patriots, lynchers, leeches and lackeys, and they were all out to bump him off. *That was the secret Snowden had spilled to him on the mission to Avignon . . .*
> There were lymph glands that might do him in. There were kidneys, nerve sheaths and corpuscles. There were tumors of the brain. There was Hodgkin's disease, leukemia, amyotrophic lateral sclerosis. There were fertile red meadows of epithelial tissue to catch and coddle a cancer cell. There were diseases of the skin, diseases of the bone, diseases of the lung, diseases of the stomach diseases of the heart, blood and arteries . . . (170–171)

Heller is in high comic form here. Repetition, alliteration and pseudo-classification schemes, among other things, control the sequencing of details, and the details themselves multiply, even as I truncate them with ellipses, as if the details were cancer cells. The nonsense of this— "the many diseases . . . [of] a truly diseased mind"—has, of course, a deadly seriousness, although neither Yossarian, nor the narrative or authorial audiences can entirely understand this yet (171). It is easier to proclaim human mortality than to understand it, easier to catalog external and internal threats to one's life than to comprehend them. This is what *Catch-22* is about; this is what readers along with Yossarian must be educated to. As the "The Miracle of Danrossane," "Crippled Phoenix," and the early version of the Snowden death scene demonstrate, here is also the journey that Heller himself has made from Avignon to *Catch-22*.

The second Avignon mission serves further to educate Yossarian and the authorial audience, and Heller's handling of it illumines the way in which he has transmuted experience into art. The mission is largely non-narrated, because Yossarian does not fly on it, having been previously wounded in the leg over Leghorn. Nevertheless, the mission provides an essential gateway to apprehending Snowden's secret and to Sweden, where Yossarian can indeed "live forever or die in the attempt" (29). In his notes to the novel, Heller describes how Yossarian's squadron comes to return to Avignon, and this description highlights another interpretation of Snowden's death, that of the army bureaucracy. "In the Chaplain's presence, Colonel Cathcart volunteers the Group for another mission to Avignon: he is instituting the procedure of having form letters sent to the families of casualties, and he wants to obtain a large number of casualties quickly enough to be written up in the Christmas issue of the *Saturday Evening Post*" (Heller papers, Brandeis University). In fact, however, no one is killed on the mission, although Orr, Yossarian's bunkmate and guide to Sweden is shot down. Orr seizes the opportunity to test all the equipment and supplies on his life raft in preparation for his journey to Sweden. After the mission, Yossarian leaves the hospital only to learn that the number of mandatory flying missions has been raised once more. At this news, he agrees to enlist in Dobbs' plot to assassinate Colonel Cathcart. If Yossarian would instead listen to Orr, who wants Yossarian to fly with him, Yossarian would have taken the direct route to Sweden, for Orr is shot down on his next mission, only to resurface in Sweden at novel's end. However, Yossarian would have not learned what he needs to, nor would Heller's readers.

In narrative terms, this Avignon mission operates according to the principle of substitution. The premises of the Snowden scene are reversed, with Yossarian himself playing the part of injured airman. For example, when Yossarian is wounded in the leg, he immediately overestimates the seriousness of the wound, immediately believing it to be life-denying, albeit sexually so. "I have lost my balls! Aarfy, I lost my balls! . . . I said I lost my balls! Can't you hear me? I'm wounded in the groin!" (283–284). In Heller's notes to the novel, the wound was, in fact, intended as a castration, a conception that lends further evidence to the importance Avignon holds to Heller (Nagel, "The

Catch-22 Note Cards" 52–53). During the mission itself, Yossarian safely resides in the hospital recuperating, a proleptic version of the stay during which
he finally cracks Snowden's secret. The danger of the mission also constitutes
a substitution, the ambitious colonels who need casualties causing the real
peril, rather than the Germans. This Avignon episode underscores what Yossarian has yet to learn: the significance of the threat posed by living in society,
confirmed when Yossarian subsequently agrees to be the colonels' pal and to
say nice things about them. At novel's end, thinking about this deal, he allows himself to remember Snowden and for first time meditates on his own
experience over Avignon. Examining the entrails, albeit in memory, Yossarian
confronts what he has previously refused to acknowledge.

With the design of the Snowden death scene, Heller expects the authorial audience to return to Avignon with Yossarian, demanding that they too
inspect Snowden's exposed vital organs and understand the message those organs contain. The narrative approach is erratic, recapitulating the comi-tragic
rhythms of the novel as a whole.[21] Yossarian is in the hospital recovering
from the side wound that the knife-wielding Nately's whore inflicts on him.
Predictably, the danger that the wound occasions results from the doctors
who want to treat him by operating on his liver, not from treating the wound
itself.[22] Heller's method is comic, but his point is serious:

> "Where were you born?" [asks a fat, gruff colonel with a mustache.]
> "On a battlefield," [Yossarian] answers.
> "No, no. In what state were you born?"
> "In a state of innocence." (420)

The meaning and humor of this exchange depend upon the interplay
between discourse and story. The incongruity of meanings that results alerts
the authorial audience to what Yossarian must still learn. He does not yet
realize the deal that he has just accepted from Colonels Cathcart and Korn
to "[s]ay nice things about [them]" (416) is "a way to lose [him]self" (456). To
discover this and to learn Snowden's secret, Yossarian must first unravel the
message of the strange man who keeps repeating, 494 "we've got your pal,
buddy. We've got your pal" (422). At this point in the novel, Colonel Korn,
the chaplain, and Aarfy all fit the message, for each could be the pal: Korn
because he knows what the deal demands, Aarfy because he has been the
navigator on so many of Yossarian's "missions" and the chaplain because he
has indeed been Yossarian's friend. Instinctively, Yossarian realizes that each
of the obvious possibilities is wrong, and in "the sleepless bedridden nights
that take an eternity to dissolve into dawn" (426), he resolves the riddle. In
the perverse logic of riddles, Snowden "had never been his pal" but was "a
vaguely familiar kid who was badly wounded and freezing to death" (426).

If Snowden was only vaguely familiar in life, he will become, through the power of recollection, intimately known in death. In death, he is Yossarian's pal and catalyst for his essential discovery of self.[23]

The death scene is so frequently analyzed that it needs little further examination here. I want, however, briefly to consider a passage from earlier in the novel which sets up this inspection. Its progression is reminiscent of Heller's own artistic journey toward Avignon: slow, hesitant, made in uncertain steps. The passage speaks to the problem at the heart of *Catch-22*, that of locating the wound and telling its story.

> And Yossarian crawled slowly out of the nose and up on the top of the bomb bay and wriggled back into the rear section of the plane—passing the first-aid kit on the way that he had to return for—to treat Snowden for the wrong wound, the yawning, raw, melon-shaped hole as big as a football in the outside of his thigh, the unsevered, blood-soaked muscle fibers inside pulsating weirdly like blind things with lives of their own, the oval naked wound that was almost a foot long and made Yossarian moan in shock and sympathy the instant he spied it and nearly made him vomit. And the small, slight tail gunner was lying on the floor beside Snowden in a dead faint, his face as white as a handkerchief, so that Yossarian sprang forward with revulsion to help him first. (341)

Yossarian crawls back through the plane, as if moving back in time as well as in space. He mislocates the wound and even then cannot immediately bring himself to treat it, choosing instead to aid the tail gunner. The essential story, human mortality, is reified in Snowden's flesh. In his revulsion, Yossarian can better deal with the gunner's "dead faint" than with Snowden's living wound. The simile, "like blind things with lives of their own," renders mortality as a mysterious otherness, not just Snowden's but also, implicitly, Yossarian's own.

Eventually, Yossarian traces the wound with his fingers, just as he did in the manuscript version, and when he does, he unwittingly begins to explore his own mortality as well as Snowden's deadly wound. Yossarian finds "[t]he actual contact with the dead flesh . . . not nearly as repulsive as he had anticipated, and excuse to caress the wound with his fingers again and again to convince himself of his own courage" (428). The reworking of these details from the manuscript confirms their importance, but significantly shifts the emphasis and meaning of the scene. In the manuscript, Yossarian caresses the viscera, in the novel the fleshy leg wound. In the manuscript, Yossarian attempts to "impress" others with actions as if this will authenticate his courage, while in the novel he wants to ascertain his own courage. But, in both cases, he initially touches without understanding. In fact, after fingering and then treating Snowden's leg wound, Yossarian can assure him confidently, "You're going to be all right, kid . . . Everything is under control" (429). Of course, it isn't. What Yossarian needs to understand lies open before him, signified by the blood *"dripping . . . like snow melting on the eaves, but viscous and red, already thickening as it dropped"* (emphasis added, 427). For Heller, the mystery of mortality lies in human embodiment—in the flesh, not in the spirit. Life begins and ends with the body. With his hands inside Snowden's wound, Yossarian experiences this, feels what he does not yet understand. However, his physical grasp anticipates and makes possible apprehension of the message of Snowden's entrails.

In Yossarian's famous insight, Heller defines mortality as a fusion of mind and matter, Yossarian's conceptualization of man enduring even as Snowden's body dissolves into bloody inert matter. Reflecting upon Snowden's death, Yossarian comes to understand his own mortality. As Denis de Rougement observes, "Suffering and understanding are deeply connected; death and self-awareness are in league" (51). Heller insists that Yossarian trace the contours of Snowden's and thus his own mortality: "liver, lungs, kidneys, ribs, stomach, and bits of stewed tomatoes Snowden had eaten that day for lunch" (429). The prose is hard and violent, as hard and violent as Snowden's wounds; its violence partakes of the violence of Heller's experience of treating a wounded colleague. The viscera of humans tether them to the material world. The visera also take in the material world, digesting it like Snowden's stewed tomatoes. When the digestive process is viewed as Snowden's is, it becomes ugly and repulsive. But Heller believes these entrails also allow the viewer, as prophets have long believed, to detect the secrets of human existence: "Man was matter, that was Snowden's secret. Ripeness was all" (429–430).[24] Finally, Yossarian deciphers the message that has been available to him all along. The message identifies the two components of humanity: the material that inexorably leads to death, and the spiritual that Heller leaves deliberately ambiguous. In formulating the spiritual element, Heller omits the verb, so that the statement reads "the spirit gone." This formulation neither affirms nor denies the existence of spirit; it simply announces the concept. Without predication, the concept cannot be completed or brought to fulfillment. As deconstructionists would argue, the verb's absence only can be noted.

Heller's insistence that his authorial audience inspect Snowden's viscera also accomplishes quite a different end, what Bakhtin calls the "familiarization of the world through laughter" (23). "In this plane (the plane of laughter) one can disrespectfully walk around whole objects; therefore, the back and rear portions of an object (and also its innards, not normally accessible for viewing) assume special prominence" (23). Death, of course, is the object that Heller wants to inspect. By means of such elements as "the

Snowdens of yesteryear," the Death that behaves, and the litany of threats to Yossarian's life, Heller has taken his authorial audience on this kind of narrative walk in his peripatetic approach to Avignon. In the catalog of Snowden's vital organs, Yossarian, the narrator, and Heller act out the imperatives for Bakhtin's comic formula. Having already familiarized the reader with the elements of this catalog, especially the liver and the tomatoes, the beginning and ending of the catalog, Heller allows the reality of mortality to be known, familiarized in a laughter that ridicules. Death, as well as life, is stripped in Heller's catalog, his comic dismemberment destroying the power that death had when it was unknown.

In retracing some of Heller's steps to the Snowden death scene, one is reminded of the blacking factory sections of David Copperfield and how they have helped to explain so much of Charles Dickens's life and art. Like Dickens, Heller uses his art to digest personal shocks, to explain them to himself, and to give an intelligible picture of the world in which such things occur.[25] So too like Dickens, Heller is a great humorist, and the acuity of his social vision frequently has been missed, as was Dickens's, in the laughter his fiction occasions. This laughter offers an escape from social institutions whose grip on the individual seems as intractable as that of *Catch-22* on Yossarian. While providing the pathway and accommodation for Snowden's secret, this laughter is begotten by pain. Heller's early representations of Avignon instance this; there is no humor in "The Miracle of Danrossane" or "Crippled Phoenix." For Heller, the painful recognition of Snowden's secret generates anger, anger usually expressed by black humor and unleashed by the genius of his novelistic discourse. He rages against the dying of the light.[26]

NOTES

1. Since childhood, Heller wrote stories and submitted them for publication, sending them to places like the *New York Daily News*, *Liberty*, and *Collier's*. He also dreamed of becoming a dramatist and in high school aspired to writing comedies like those of Moss Hart and George S. Kaufmann.

2. Heller's interviews continually address the issue of correspondence between his life and fiction, with Heller giving a variety of answers, sometimes contradictorily so. For a representative selection of interviews treating his war experience, see: Heller, "Translating," *Gentlemen's Quarterly*, Sam Merrill, Weatherby, Barnard, and Flippo.

3. "The Miracle of Danrossane," "Crippled Phoenix" and all other unpublished material to which I refer are part of a collection of Heller's papers that Brandeis University Library holds. In addition to these stories, Heller also worked on a novel about the war as early as 1945, which involved a flier nearing the end of his required quota of bombing missions and thinking about the meaning of the war.

4. James Nagel has done the seminal work on the manuscript and other working papers for *Catch-22*, but much more study remains to be done. Nagel isolates interesting and important changes between Heller's early plans and published novel, arguing that this material documents the author's "meticulous planning and analysis of his novel at each state of composition" ("Note Cards" 404); see Nagel.

5. While the Snowden death scene in *Catch-22* provides the most memorable formulation of such a death, variants on this story reappear at the end of the rest of Heller's work. In the novels, the crucial death always occurs in the penultimate chapter, with the exception of *Good as Gold* in which the funeral occurs in the penultimate chapter. In *We Bombed in New Haven*, Captain Starkey must tell and retell each newly named version of his son that he will die on the next bombing mission. In the ending of *Something Happened*, Slocum finally calls back to memory the details of the accident in which he killed his son, the spurting blood and twisted arms and legs. But he resists the knowledge available in this recollection, concluding it instead with the plea, "Don't tell my wife" (562). In a reversal of the pattern, *Good as Gold* closes with Bruce Gold standing at his mother's grave hoping for a message that does not come. The death of another "child," his brother Sid, has brought him to the cemetery. *God Knows* concludes with King David yearning for a God who will understand and make understandable the grief he feels for his dead sons: "I feel nearer to God when I am deepest in anguish" (338). In *Picture This*, Heller revises one of history's most famous death scenes, that of Socrates, so that he dies with the retching and convulsions caused by ingesting hemlock. Finally, in *Closing Time*, Heller uses Kilroy's death to mourn the passing of the World War II generation, to parody the dead child story, and to cast a retrospective light upon *Catch-22* in general and Snowden's death in particular.

6. Said makes a larger point about the relationship between certain writers' careers and the texts produced by them that can usefully be applied to Heller and, by extension, to his authorial returns to Avignon: "the text is a multidimensional structure extending from the beginning to the end of the writer's career. A text is the source and aim of a man's desire to be an author, it is the form of his attempts, it contains the elements of his coherence, and in a whole range of complex and differing ways it incarnates the pressures upon the writer of his psychology, his time, his society. The unity between career and text, then, is a unity between an intelligible pattern of events and for the most part their increasingly conscious transformation into writing" (196).

7. Each of these sites has personal significance to Heller: Rome, which Heller visited shortly after it was liberated, afforded him his most memorable wartime leave (see Note 12); Il Rousse was an army rest camp on Corsica near where he was based; Poggibonsi was the destination for his first bombing mission, a mission on which he got bored and dropped his bombs too late; and Ferrara was the first mission on which Heller's squadron lost a plane.

8. There is a discrepancy in Heller's dating of this first Avignon mission; he lists it as August 8 in the "Chronology 2/13/66" and as August 3 in "'Catch-22' Revisited." In the "Chronology," Heller describes the mission as follows: "Rail Road bridge. Hirsch shot down, Burrhus, Yellon killed. First plane I saw shot down" (Heller papers, Brandeis University).

9. Notably, Robert Merrill, among others, agrees with Heller: "the fact that *Catch-22* appeared sixteen years after the end of World War II suggests that its author was not primarily interested in recapturing the intensity of his own experiences" (4).

10. See, for example, Sam Merrill 68 and Barnard 298.

11. In recounting a letter that his editor received from Bruno Bettelheim, Heller extends the implication of this narrative pattern, admitting in the case of *Something Happened* that the protagonist may be complicit in the child's death: "Now it could be that in terms of drawing on recesses of my mind, with which I'm not in touch, what Bruno Bettelheim said was there [i.e., the validity of a death in which a father deliberately kills his son]. I was not aware that I was aware of it" (Ruas 164).

12. Luciana apparently is an early version of the Luciana of *Catch-22*. As Cramer remembers her: "Luciana was best. Tall, young, and graceful, she was a novice at love, and he remembered her smile as she came to him, her ingenuous astonishment at the sudden force of her passion, and the fumbling manner." This early appearance of Luciana is also interesting for the light that it sheds on Heller's artistic recycling of personal experience. As he tells interviewer Sam Merrill, "[Yossarian's] encounter with Luciana, the Roman whore, corresponds exactly with an experience I had. He sleeps with her, she refuses money and suggests that he keep her address on a slip of paper . . . That's exactly what happened to me in Rome. Luciana was Yossarian's vision of a perfect relationship. That's why he saw her only once, and perhaps that's why I saw her only once. If he examined perfection too closely, imperfections would show up" (64). As *Catch-22* reveals though, the Luciana plot is more closely tied to Heller's core authorial concerns than his remarks about his own personal experience would indicate. In the novel, Luciana's "perfection" is already impaired, for she has been wounded in an air raid and wears a pink chemise to hide her sear even while making love with Yossarian. Yossarian, however, is fascinated by it, runs his hands over it, and insists that she relate its story. Later after he has torn up the slip of paper with her address on it, Yossarian's search for her leads him into symbolic encounters with death: death in his nightmares about the Bologna mission and proleptic death he looks for her in Snowden's room.

13. While the allusion to *Macbeth* dissociates the experience from Heller's own, it also represents a connection, for Heller studied Shakespeare at Oxford while on a Fulbright Fellowship between writing his Avignon stories and planning *Catch-22*. This study may well provide another pathway between Heller's personal experience and the novel. The planning material to *Catch-22* reveals the extensive role literary allusions played in Heller's conception of the novel, especially Shakespearean allusions. For studies of these allusions in *Catch-22*, see Larson, and Aubrey and McCarron.

14. The importance of these elements—death, blood, guilt, and touch—is confirmed by the way that Heller reworks them in *Something Happened*. In its climactic episode, Slocum responds to the "streams of blood spurting from holes in his [son's] face and head and pouring down over one hand from inside a sleeve" by clutching him to his chest and in the process accidentally suffocating him (562). Unlike Yossarian, Slocum resists recounting the event, instead refiguring it, as Heller's chapter title tells us, into how "My boy has stopped talking to me."

15. David Seed shows how war novels like James Jones's *From Here to Eternity* and Norman Mailer's *The Naked and the Dead* also contributed to Heller's evolving conception of *Catch-22*; see 23–33.

16. Extending structuralist thought, Seymour Chatman uses the distinction, story and discourse, to differentiate between narrative content and the means by which this content is transmitted.

17. Patrick O'Neill insightfully demonstrates the way in which humor in modern and postmodern texts depends upon privileging discourse over story. In particular, he is interested in what he calls entropic comedy, comedy that is aware of the fictionality of all discourse and "of the element of play" that is involved in the production of any meaning (23). O'Neill's discussion of *Catch-22* as an example of entropic satire is also valuable, although I disagree with his conclusion that the novel's discourse undercuts the implications of its story.

18. I borrow the notion of a synthetic element of narrative from James Phelan, although I am modifying his definition. Phelan explores the relationship between character and narrative progression, and he conceives of three aspects of character, which in turn contribute to narrative progression: thematic (as conveyer of narrative and authorial meaning), mimetic (as designation for a "person," albeit a textual one), and synthetic (as linguistic construct). I use the concept of synthetic component of narrative progression, without attaching it to character.

19. Peter Rabinowitz distinguishes between narrative and authorial audiences. The authorial audience is the ideal reader posited by an author, the reader who completely attends to authorial intentionality. By contrast, the narrative audience is the reader implied by the text itself, by its narrative and rhetorical structure; this reader participates in the illusion that the text is real, that it constitutes a world.

20. There are several ways in which Heller's imagination links death and women. In the short stories, women frequently occasion symbolic, if not literal deaths. For example, in the unpublished "The Death of the Dying Swan," when Sidney Cooper returns home, he gives up his quest for life and, in effect, accepts death: "He longed for people who were real, people who lived with honest passions and found vigorous pleasure in the mere event of existing, people for whom death came too soon" (Heller papers, Brandeis University). *Something Happened* and *Good as Gold* work variations on this pattern. But Heller also associates women with insensate death, that in which senility (the death of the mind) precedes physical demise. The most noteworthy example of this occurs when Slocum believes his mother's senility and death foretell his own: "I can see myself all mapped out inanimately in stages around that dining room table, from mute beginning (Derek) to mute, fatal, bovine end (Mother), passive and submissive as a cow, and even beyond through my missing father (Dad)" (401). Finally, Heller connects passion with death, as when he uses Yossarian's love-making with Nurse Duckett on the beach to set up the scene in which McWatt's plane hits Kid Sampson, thereby turning the ocean red with blood and severed limbs. Similarly, Yossarian's passion for Luciana leads to death, albeit via memory and dreams.

21. Heller's comic strategies depend upon continually negating or reversing expectations. Typically, Heller's scenes suddenly darken in mood, as he reveals that what the reader has just been laughing at begets violence, death, or the morally outrageous; or similarly, dark scenes beget comic ones, dramatically changing the character of the text. Thus, the comic and the tragic function both as figure and ground in much the way they do in an Escher drawing. They constitute a pattern in which the relationship between figure and ground constantly reverses itself, so that first one element then another assumes the foreground.

22. The threat to operate on Yossarian's liver extends a novel-long joke and set of allusions to the Prometheus myth. As in this instance, the effect is usually double-edged, occasioning laughter and signifying mortality. The motif culminates, of course, in the Snowden death scene when Yossarian inspects the wounded airman's

liver along with the other viscera. Heller uses tomatoes to a similar end, especially all the jokes about the chaplain's hot plum tomato. The stewed tomatoes that spill out of Snowden's stomach take part of their meaning from the tomato jokes that preceded them.

23. Heller reprises this conception in his conclusions to *God Knows* and *Closing Time*. In *God Knows*, the image of David's youthful self provides the catalyst for self-discovery. Lying on his deathbed, David serves as his own Snowden. In *Closing Time*, Yossarian and Sammy Singer, a narrator and Heller figure, talk about how Snowden, scarcely an acquaintance in life, becomes the closest of friends in death and the source for what they want to talk about for the rest of their lives.

24. This inspection accomplishes another kind of education as well, one that undercuts the typical military education and that reproduces the experience of combat veterans. As an aside, it bears attention that Heller satirically treats military education throughout *Catch-22;* for example, in such episodes as Lieutenant Scheisskopf's parades and the many briefing sessions. As described by John Keegan in his classic study *The Face of Battle,* the aim of such an education "is to reduce war to a set of rules and a system of procedures—and thereby to make orderly and rational what is essentially chaotic and instinctive. It is an aim analogous to that . . . pursued by medical schools in their fostering among their students a detached attitude to pain and distress in their patients, particularly victims of accidents" (20). Yossarian has long recognized the insanity of war, but he has not, even while treating the wounded Snowden, taken the next step of recognizing his complicity in this insanity. Nor has he yet comprehended the effects of a "military" education. As his subsequent actions demonstrate, his studied recollection of Snowden's death occasions these recognitions. The death scene also serves as a brilliant representation of the sensations of the combat veteran. Again to draw upon John Keegan, in battle the combatants experience a "sense of littleness, almost of nothingness, of their abandonment in a physical wilderness, dominated by vast impersonal forces, from which even the passage of time had been eliminated. The dimensions of the battlefield (in this instance the inside of combat aircraft) . . . reduced [the combatant's] subjective role, objectively vital though it was, to that of a mere victim" (322). Keegan's account closely parallels Yossarian's sensations in the Snowden scene and defines what Yossarian—and by extension the reader—must be reeducated to reject.

25. Edmund Wilson provides the classic formulation of the effects of childhood trauma on Dickens's subsequent career in "Dickens: The Two Scrooges." In part, I have adapted Wilson's argument to discuss the effects Avignon have on Heller's fiction and to draw my characterization of Dickens's comic art.

26. I have greatly benefited from the suggestions of Linda Van Buskirk, Randall Craig, Donald Purcell, John Serio, and Peter Freitag.

WORKS CITED

Aubrey, James R., and William E. McCarron. "More Shakespearean Echoes in *Catch-22.*" *American Notes & Queries*, 3 (January 1990): pp. 25–27.

Bakhtin, M. M., "Epic and Novel." *The Dialogic Imagination,* ed. Michael Holquist, trans. Carl Emerson and Michael Holquist. Austin: University of Texas, 1981.

Barnard, Ken. "Interview with Joseph Heller." A *Catch-22* Casebook, eds. Frederick Kiley and Walter McDonald. New York. Crowell, 1973: pp. 294–301.

Chatman, Seymour. *Story and Discourse*. Ithaca, NY: Cornell University Press, 1978.

Craig, David M., "Joseph Heller's Catch-22 Revisited" *War, Literature, and the Arts*. 1.2 (1989–90): pp. 33–43.

Flippo, Chet. "Checking in with Joseph Heller." *Rolling Stone*. 16 April 1981: pp. 50+.

Heller, Joseph. *Catch-22*. New York: Simon and Schuster, 1961.

——. *Catch-22* and After." *Gentleman's Quarterly*. March 1963: pp. 95 +.

——. "'*Catch-22*' Revisited." *Holiday*. April 1967: pp. 44 +.

——. "On Translating *Catch-22* into a Movie." A *Catch-22* casebook, eds. Frederick Kiley and Walter McDonald. New York: Crowell, 1973.

——. *Something Happened*. New York: Knopf, 1974.

——. *Good as Gold*. New York: Simon and Schuster, 1979.

——. *God Knows*. New York: Knopf, 1984.

——. *Picture This*. New York: Putnam, 1988.

——. *Closing Time*. New York: Simon and Shuster, 1994.

Keegan, John. *The Face of Battle*. New York: Viking, 1976.

Larson, Michael. "Shakespearean Echoes in *Catch-22*." *American Notes & Queries*. 17 (1979): pp. 76–78.

Merrill, Robert. *Joseph Heller*. Boston: Twayne, 1987.

Merrill, Sam. "*Playboy* Interview: Joseph Heller." June 1975: pp. 59 +.

Nagel, James. "The *Catch-22* Note Cards." *Studies in the Novel*. 8 (1976): pp. 394–405.

——. "Two Brief Manuscript Sketches" *Modern Fiction Studies*. 20 (1974): pp. 221–224.

O'Neill, Patrick. *The Comedy of Entropy: Humour/Narrative/Reading*. Toronto: University of Toronto Press, 1990.

Phelan, James. *Reading People, Reading Plots*. Chicago: University of Chicago Press, 1989.

Rabinowitz, Peter. "Truth in Fiction: A Reexamination of Audiences." *Critical Inquiry*, 4 (1977): pp. 121–141.

Rougement, Denis de. *Love in the Western World*, trans. Montgomery Belgion. New York: Pantheon, 1956.

Ruas, Charles. "Joseph Heller." *Conversation with American Writers*. New York: Knopf, 1984.

Said, Edward. *Beginnings: Intention and Method*. New York. Basic Books, 1975.

Seed, David. *The Fiction of Joseph Heller*. New York: St. Martins, 1989.

Tolstoy, Leo. *The Death of Ivan Ilych and Other Stories*. New York: Signet, 1960.

Weatherby, W. J. "The Joy Catcher," *Guardian*. 20 November 1962: p. 7.

Wilson, Edmund. *The Wound and the Bow*. New York: Oxford University Press, 1947.

DANIEL GREEN

A World Worth Laughing At:
Catch-22 *and the Humor of Black Humor*

One can't help but note that in the commentary about the fiction conventionally identified with the mode of "black humor" there is much discussion of what makes such fiction black, but little of its humor. The most famous expression of this tendency occurs in probably the most frequently cited book on black humor, Max Schulz's *Black Humor Fiction of the Sixties*. "I have shied away from the humor in Black Humor," writes Schulz. Choosing instead to focus on what he calls the "cosmic labyrinth," Schulz claims that "to give equal value to humor in any consideration of this literature is possibly to let oneself be trapped by a term that came into being somewhat capriciously and may not accurately describe that literature."[1] While it may be true that several of the novels labeled as black humor at one time or another are not "humorous" in a narrow sense, or that the term itself was adapted somewhat arbitrarily, Schulz's reluctance to deal at length with books such as *Catch-22* or Stanley Elkin's *A Bad Man*, clearly *funny* books by any measure, evidences a common scholarly preference for the "cosmic" at the expense of the comic.

It might reasonably be assumed that criticism of individual novels would confront more directly the vital role of comedy in their aesthetic and rhetorical operations. Such attention would seem to be in order especially for *Catch-22*, which relies so systematically on what Frederick Karl has cata-

Studies in the Novel, Vol. 27, number 2; (Summer 1995): pp. 186–196. © 1995 University of North Texas.

logued as "puns, high jinks, slapstick, [and] witty dialogue. However, by far most writing about *Catch-22* has focused like Schulz on more portentous issues of politics, philosophy, economics, and even theology. In fact, to the extent that aesthetic or expressly literary issues are raised seriously at all, they tend to be restricted to relatively traditional studies of sources and precursors, or broadly thematic discussions of Heller's sense of what critics have chosen to term "the absurd." While the novel clearly has affinities with absurdism, these affinities have generally been used to *distance Catch-22* from the kind of comedy associated with the devices Heller exploits for absurdist effect.[2] While not everyone who has written about the novel has dismissed its plain comedic qualities, it is not unfair to cite the following statement by Leon F. Seltzer as typical of the general thrust of opinion about the role of comedy in *Catch-22:* "the novel's absurdities—comic and otherwise—operate almost always to expose the alarming inhumanities which pollute our political, social, and economic systems."[4]

My intention is not to deny that *Catch-22* does expose such inhumanities (clearly it does just that for many readers), nor even for that matter to criticize the substance of previous commentary on the novel, but to point out the implicit dichotomy between the "comic" and the "serious" created by this commentary. Precisely because *Catch-22* seems to most readers a fundamentally serious work, I would argue, a reflexive critical assumption comes into play whereby comedy and humor are seen as necessarily in service of something ostensibly more worthwhile, more identifiably meaningful. In short, the logical inference to draw from the kinds of statements I have quoted is that the comic cannot itself be serious.

An exception to the approach taken by the bulk of those in the first wave of *Catch-22* criticism is Morton Gurewitch in his book *Comedy: The Irrational Vision.* Gurewitch sees *Catch-22* as above all a "mad farce" so unrelenting as to effectively overwhelm any narrower didactic or satiric impulses. "The satire," writes Gurewitch, "is devoured . . . by omnivorous nonsense."[5] In some ways this view could seem reminiscent of early responses to the novel which deemed it unworthy of sustained attention. However, Gurewitch intends his assertion to be taken as a laudatory judgement, and as such it is welcome recognition that the "merely funny" pervades *Catch-22,* to the extent that analysis focusing on world view or ideology are at the very least problematic. At the same time, Gurewitch's use of the word "nonsense" risks propping up the same opposition between the comic and the serious I have described. It implies a comedy defined by the absence of any positive content (although it must be said that Gurewitch celebrates comedy for what he calls its "irrational freedom").[6] Opposing "sense" with "nonsense" does not finally overcome what seems to be an inherent devaluation—embedded in critical discourse itself—of the comedic impulse.

Despite the foregrounding of more solemn issues by critics such as Schulz and Seltzer, *Catch-22* provides ample opportunity to explore this impulse. In fact, in my analysis *Catch-22* is first and foremost a comic novel whose primary structural principle is the *joke* and whose design and execution are most appropriately construed as the vehicles of mirth. This description is also intended to underscore the book's accomplishment, but without divorcing its comedy from its overall seriousness of purpose. In my attempt to establish the inherent respectability of comedy as a mode creating its own kind of meaning, I will draw on Jerry Palmer's analysis in his *The Logic of the Absurd*,[7] which develops a convincing account of both the internal mechanism of the joke and the effect successful jokes have on our reception of the texts which employ them. Although Palmer's book focuses on film and television comedy, the burden of much of the discussion that follows is precisely that *Catch-22* shares essential characteristics with these forms. (As does, moreover, an entire strain of contemporary American fiction, encompassing loosely American "postmodern" writers and including Joseph Heller, which not only uses comedy extensively but relies on strategies and conventions derived as much from popular sources such as film and vaudeville as from purely literary traditions.)

Few novels in fact offer comedy as pure as that in *Catch-22*. No situation, not even the bloodiest or most fearful, is insulated from the further indignity of the joke, or exempt from the comedic *reductio ad absurdum;* no character, not even the apparent protagonist, escapes the ravages of mockery and ridicule. While such thoroughgoing comedy is familiar to us in film—particularly the American comic film descended from Mack Sennett—it is undoubtedly disconcerting to find it in a purportedly "serious" work of literature depicting a subject as forbidding as war and its consequences. Nevertheless, this brand of comedy distinguishes *Catch-22* from the primary line of twentieth-century comic fiction which uses comedy as a strategy to clearly satirical or otherwise discursive ends, and it is here that Palmer's view of the comic process is most illuminating.

Palmer argues for the necessity of a theory of comedy which values it for its own sake: "by reducing comedy to the play of serious values (attacking A, promoting B) the nature of the process, the pleasure which is specific to comedy and humour [sic], is lost."[8] Palmer contends that comedy has a pull of its own which inevitably muddies the thematic waters a text might otherwise seem to be navigating. His book's thesis, he writes, is that "ambiguities are built into the reception of comedy and humour, and this for reasons that are fundamental to their nature" (p. 18). He goes on to analyze in impressive and compelling detail the operations inherent in comedy's fundamental nature, constructing a model which provides a basis for understanding the way jokes and gags unfold, and which also explains their success or failure. On one level,

Palmer's account seems remarkably simple, as he divides the comic event into two distinct moments, one during which occurs a disruption of narrative or contextual expectations, and a second which leads to a laugh-producing contradiction: that the cause of the disruption—either a verbal remark or visual image—is implausible yet at the same time contains a kind of plausibility after all (p. 43). The clarity provided by this formulation, however, as well as its potential relevance in a wide range of contexts and across generic boundaries, make it an effective tool for gauging the reach and depth of the comic impulse. It is particularly provocative when applied to a text like *Catch-22*, where this impulse has struck so many as being at best in conflict with other, more overarching forces.

That *Catch-22* engages in broad comedy is readily apparent from its first chapter, indeed its very first sentence. But the reader attentive to comic structure and pattern, not simply as adjunct to thematics but as source of intrinsic narrative and aesthetic pleasure, will not fail to appreciate a passage such as the following:

> The colonel dwelt in a vortex of specialists who were still specializing in trying to determine what was troubling him. They hurled lights in his eyes to see if he could see, rammed needles into nerves to hear if he could feel. There was a urologist for his urine, a lymphologist for his lymph, an endocrinologist for his endocrines, a psychologist for his psyche, a dermatologist for his derma; there was a pathologist for his pathos, a cystologist for his cysts, and a bald and pedantic cetologist from the zoology department at Harvard who had been shanghaied ruthlessly into the Medical Corps by an faulty anode in an I.B.M. machine and spent his sessions with the dying colonel trying to discuss *Moby Dick* with him.[9]

One almost waits for the rimshots at the end of such a performance (it has the feel in particular of a more verbally playful Woody Allen joke). Although the ultimate effect of humor such as this may be to contribute to the novel's overall sense of absurdity, it should be emphasized that the immediate effect is laughter, and that the novel's knitting together of such moments is its primary narrative strategy.

While "jokes" in the most conventional sense do not necessarily dominate the pages of *Catch-22*—they are nevertheless plentiful—the spirit and substance of comedy like the above does inform much of the novel's exposition, as well as many of its character exchanges. Chapter II, "Clevinger," for example, opens to a brief dialogue between the title character and Yossarian, echoed in subsequent dialogue, which embodies and ultimately comments on this spirit:

Clevinger had stared at him with apoplectic rage and indignation and, clawing the table with both hands, had shouted, "You're crazy!"

"Clevinger, what do you want from people?" Dunbar had replied wearily above the noises of the officers' club.

"I'm not joking," Clevinger persisted.

"They're trying to kill me," Yossarian told him calmly.

"No one's trying to kill you," Clevinger cried.

"Then why are they shooting at me?" Yossarian asked.

"They're shooting at *everyone*," Clevinger answered. "They're trying to kill everyone."

"And what difference does that make?" (pp. 11–12)

The tone of this interchange is suggestive of nothing so much as the patter of a vaudeville team, and the humor evoked by such a passage clearly relies on the basic strategies of comedy, surprise and incongruity. In replying "what difference does that make?" to Clevinger's declaration, Yossarian is clearly disrupting the logical case Clevinger is trying to make for Yossarian's "craziness." At first we find Yossarian's defense quite implausible (and therefore are perhaps inclined to agree with Clevinger) but on second thought it makes its own kind of sense. What difference *does* it make to Yossarian if he is in fact killed that everyone else is a target? The ambiguity ensuing from these disparate responses provokes our laughter. It is this instinctive, largely subconscious reaction which is prompted by what Palmer terms the "logic of the absurd" (p. 44).

Moreover, Clevinger's disclaimer—"I'm not joking!"—ultimately works to highlight his position as the butt of the joke being set up at his expense, both by Yossarian and by the shape of the scene's own comic trajectory. Ironically, by the end of Chapter II Yossarian finds the tables turned as he himself becomes the butt of the joke whose absurd but ruthless logic provides the novel its title and controlling metaphor: Catch-22. Doc Daneeka informs him that the required number of missions has been raised (from 44 to 50 at this point), and throughout the rest of the book Yossarian struggles against the inescapable force of Catch-22, sometimes resisting actively and at others more passively cutting his losses in his effort to somehow get the last laugh on the system it represents. Doc Daneeka's explanation of the principle of Catch-22 suggests further the relevance of Palmer's schema; indeed, what is most disturbing about the whole idea of Catch-22 is explicable through its terms. We—and the airmen on Pianosa—are surprised by the obvious manipulation and injustice embodied in this unofficial law. Its main tenet—that anyone who would continue to fly missions after what Yossarian, Orr, and the others have been through would be crazy, but that "anyone who wants to get out of combat duty isn't really crazy" (p. 41)—seems a perversely implausible distortion of logic, but at the same time has a certain monstrous plausibility as well. Even Yossarian is moved to admire such a catch, and Doc Daneeka pronounces it "the best there is" (p. 41). If the world of *Catch-22* is indeed "crazy," it is largely because it is so thoroughly informed by the rigorous logic of comedy.

Not only is Yossarian repeatedly taken aback by the ubiquity of this logic, but readers of *Catch-22* must also be surprised by the unremitting manifestations of its all-encompassing joke in an incongruous setting of bloody air war and inhuman exploitation where fear and misery are translated into comic pratfalls. A large part of the book's artistic interest, I would argue, lies precisely in the way in which Heller sustains his comic routines over the course of nearly 500 pages, as well as the way in which he joins these routines into a compelling, albeit highly fragmented, narrative. Heller succeeds both in creating consistently startling comic moments and in tying these moments together in a way which reflects and reinforces the fundamental nature of the joke itself. Palmer describes two kinds of narrative which incorporate gags and jokes. The first gathers such gags into an essentially self-sufficient sequence, while the second subordinates the gags to an otherwise non-comic story. In the former case, comedy is presumed to be capable of producing its own kind of satisfaction; in the latter, the comedy is employed as a supplement to the story's non-comic core (pp. 141–142). While Palmer is perhaps correct to contend that narratives of the first kind are rarely found in practice (especially in literature), *Catch-22* comes as close to this kind of narrative as any text in modem fiction. Further, while such a strategy might seem a threat to narrative unity, in *Catch-22* it can actually be seen to provide a kind of unity that has previously been overlooked. What has appeared to be an excessively fragmented narrative (or at least a too randomly fragmented one) can be read as a mammoth orchestration of individual comic bits and routines into a kaleidoscopic comedy revue, the cumulative effect of which is to situate Yossarian ever more irretrievably in the world defined by Catch-22. The chronological fluidity of the story is partly induced by the logic of an absurdity as overwhelming as this, and is partly an opportunity for the reader to reflect on the logic of the absurd itself as played out under this text's conditions: that a world so irrational, where distinctions between past, present, and future collapse, could actually exist seems implausible in the extreme, yet when judged by the terms of its governing framework, the confusions of such a world seem plausible indeed.

Thus does one of the most basic of comedic devices—the joke—serve both as the foundation of individual scenes and episodes and as a central organizing principle of the novel as a whole, with consequent ramifications not only vis-á-vis its aesthetic framework but also for any philosophical or political positions it may be presumed to be advancing. Even more examples of scenes and situations in *Catch-22* explicable in terms of jokes and related kinds of "low" humor could be adduced here—the "atheist" scene between the chaplain and Colonel Cathcart, for example, in which the Colonel "plays dumb" (although he isn't really playing) in his astonishment that atheism is legal, that the enlisted men pray to the same God as the officers, etc. But while many readers might reluctantly acknowledge the book's reliance on such humor, it is the marginal status of this kind of comedy that provokes even admirers to attribute supplemental value to its use in order to "raise" the text to a more respectable and more suitably meaningful level of discourse.

Again, examining the mechanism of the joke can help to explain why this happens. The balance between the plausible and the implausible in a given joke is often delicate, and can itself determine the impact of that joke. Palmer argues, for example, that contemporary audiences may see only the implausible in silent film comedies, and therefore judge them to be merely silly. Some audiences at the time, however, attended mostly to the plausible—that is, currently relevant—features and thus, notably, "found them excessively 'black,' too abrasive to be funny" (p. 57). Substituting "serious" or "disturbing" for "abrasive" in this statement, we can perhaps begin to see how contemporary literary critics avoid or overlook the humor of black humor.

Implicit in Palmer's account of the operation of comedy is a kind of self-consciousness which if not expressed directly *through* the text is potentially induced on the reader's side *by* the text. Thus while comic fiction is not necessarily self-reflexive in the mode of more strictly defined metafictions (e.g., John Barth's *Lost in the Funhouse* or Robert Coover's *Universal Baseball Association*), that which, like *Catch-22,* unleashes the logic of the absurd does encourage an awareness of textuality in those moments when the very mechanism of this logic compels the reader to note the disruption of textual continuity. When the joke opens an especially wide gap—that is, when the imbalance between the plausible and the implausible seems, initially at least, very pronounced—the degree of such awareness can only increase. Here is perhaps the source of both the primary effect of humor—laughter—*and* the temptation to devalue mere laughter among "serious" readers, an apparent paradox that can be illustrated by looking at a scene skeptical readers could well point to as fundamentally non-comic.

The scene inside Yossarian's airplane after it has been hit and his fellow airman Snowden wounded is probably one of the most memorable episodes in *Catch-22*. Although portions of this scene are replayed throughout the novel, its full impact is registered near the end in a final flashback. Yossarian's memory does indeed for the most part unfold with appropriate sobriety:

> Yossarian bent forward to peer and saw a strange colored stain
> seeping through the coveralls just above the armhole of Snowden's
> flak suit. Yossarian felt his heart stop, then pound so violently he
> found it difficult to breathe. Snowden was wounded inside his flak
> suit. (p. 457)

But even here the solemnity and outright horror of the situation can easily
be interrupted by a joke:

> A chunk of flak more than three inches big had shot into his other
> side just underneath the arm and blasted all the way through,
> drawing whole mottled quarts of Snowden along with it through
> the gigantic hole in his ribs it made as it blasted out ... Here was
> God's plenty, all right [Yossarian] thought bitterly as he stared—
> liver, lungs, kidneys, ribs, stomach, and bits of the stewed tomatoes
> Snowden had eaten that day for lunch. Yossarian hated stewed
> tomatoes and turned away dizzily and began to vomit, clutching
> his burning throat. (p. 457)

No doubt such a moment can, and has, been interpreted differently. Some
might find it merely tasteless; most probably assume it has some compre-
hensible relationship to the scene's—and the book's—aesthetic or thematic
design, and look to subordinate it to that design—thus the joke serves to
heighten the horror, reinforce the anti-war message, etc. While I would
not deny that it does either or both of these things, what gets overlooked
in such an interpretation is the sheer disruptiveness of the joke, the way it
actually takes our attention away from the grossness of "God's plenty" to
contemplate the implausibility of the joke itself entering the narrative space
otherwise occupied by Snowden's internal organs. As Palmer has it, "any gag
works by contradicting discursively defined expectations" (p. 155), and the
starkness of the contradiction involved here makes for a particularly strong
sense of implausibility—so much so that Heller might seem to risk alienat-
ing readers for whom such a situation "deserve[s] only serious treatment or
behavior" (p. 206). Yet reflection does indeed suggest it is plausible after all
that Yossarian, continuously immersed as he is in death and mayhem, would
be sickened only at the sight of the less familiar stewed tomatoes.

In a scene like this, the comedic element is so unsettling that one's
awareness of the discordant note introduced can produce either the sense
that Yossarian's squeamishness is mordantly funny or that its origin in the
repulsiveness of war makes its comic quality secondary. Readers whose response is the latter are likely to find that perceptual gap created by the logic
of the absurd to be an abyss into which received notions of literary signifi-

cance could disappear. But those whose immediate response is laughter are acknowledging the integrity and the vitality of comedy, although it would not be accurate to say such readers thus ignore the potentially provocative insinuations of context—in fact, a definition of "black humor" would have to emphasize the obvious way in which this particular brand of levity *depends* on a corresponding contextual gravity.

Certainly not all scenes in *Catch-22* are comic in the way I have described. Yossarian's descent into the underworld on the streets of Rome, for example, seems clearly meant to convey a sobering picture of the human predicament (although even here his obvious helplessness finally only reinforces an overall view of him as a comic figure). Furthermore, comedy as absolute as *Catch-22* at its most extreme does almost unavoidably provoke consideration of its implications, formal and thematic. It is finally only testimony to the impact of comedy, its capacity to be meaningful in a variety of contexts, that the novel has drawn the weighty interpretations I adduced previously. Misunderstanding and distortion result when the hermeneutic operations involved in forming such interpretations are insufficiently distinguished from the operations of comedy proper, or these latter operations are disregarded entirely. In effect, humor is erased as a significant element of the text, becoming merely an incidental effect. Certainly joking in a context perceived as especially serious or disturbing could elicit laughter resonant with questions (not only "Why am I laughing?" but undoubtedly following from that immediate response), but the joke itself remains separate from such questions, its structure independent of context. The force of a given joke may indeed be related to its context, of course; the blackness of black humor, while often overemphasized, cannot be ignored and is obviously meaningless except through reference to context. The term "black humor," then, is perhaps most appropriately defined as an unapologetic, unalloyed use of comedy in extreme situations which implicitly raise very large, even profound, questions. Black humor of the sort found in *Catch-22* neither trivializes such questions nor foregrounds them, but rather broadens the range of experience to which comedy is relevant.

The conclusion to *Catch-22* has struck many readers as a particularly extreme situation, or at least one with important implications for the novel's ostensible thematic emphasis. Many who see *Catch-22* as a satire or a philosophical treatise find the ending a cop-out. Why does Yossarian choose to run away, they implicitly ask, rather than stay and work to change the system? (Although such criticism overlooks the fact that the chaplain proposes to do just that.) Should one conclude that the book is insufficiently serious from the outset, the ending could conceivably seem a transparent attempt to graft on an explicitly antiwar message. A more accurate assessment would conclude that the ending does leave a message, but also point out that it is a message entirely consistent with the novel's preponderant use of comedy. If the world depicted on Pianosa could be changed, surely by the end of this long novel a sign of such a change would reveal itself. Yet Yossarian's lived-world remains essentially the same at the end as it was when we first experienced it in the hospital ward. Nor are we as readers likely to feel that the conditions of that lived-world have been neutralized, much less altered, by the extended comic treatment of them. Instead, the comedy of *Catch-22* is ultimately nonregenerative: its relentless, frequently black humor does not finally call attention to situations, issues, or problems that could be improved, resolved, or eliminated through increased human effort. The blackness of the humor, in fact, may be a function of this final despair. In the face of a world so wholly irredeemable, Yossarian's only alternative is to abandon it in a gesture of personal survival. He may have managed to get the last laugh, but it is a feeble one, and his apparent optimism about the possibilities of "Sweden" make this reader feel the joke is still on him.

Palmer ultimately addresses what he calls the "effectivity" of comedy. He concludes that humor "is neither essentially liberatory nor conservative, for its nature is such that it always refuses to make any commitment to any 'opinion' about anything (except of course the opinion that levity is appropriate under these circumstances)" (p. 213). Possibly what has driven scholars to neglect the role of comedy in *Catch-22* is the sense that under the circumstances portrayed by this novel—war, death, systemic oppression—"levity" does *not* seem appropriate. Perhaps there are situations, attitudes, and beliefs that are off limits to comic treatment, but surely comic art can be served *only* by those who reject taboos of decorum and give free rein to the logic of comedy; the unrestrained play of this logic once unleashed achieves the *only* truly serious purpose of comedy, which is finally to expose the potentially ridiculous even if what is exposed proves disturbing or offensive. Joseph Heller does so unleash the inherent force and energy of the comic impulse, and this more than its concern with the "alarming inhumanities" of the system makes *Catch-22* a sobering work of literature. Thus, while "black humor fiction" may do little to enhance our knowledge of the "cosmic labyrinth," it does greatly enhance our understanding of the legitimate reach of comedy: even the most grave or the most exalted of subjects can be subjected to the logic of the absurd. *Catch-22* will not tell you how to live or what to think or even what's worth thinking about. It will tell you what's worth laughing at.

NOTES

1. Max Schulz, *Black Humor Fiction of the Sixties* (Athens: Ohio University Press, 1973): p. x.

2. Frederick R. Karl. "Joseph Heller's *Catch-22:* Only Fools Walk in Darkness," *A "Catch-22" Casebook*, eds. Frederick Kiley and Walter McDonald (New York: Crowell, 1973): pp. 159–165.

3. Robert Brustein's early assertion that *Catch-22* "penetrates the surface of the merely funny" ("The Logic of Survival in a Lunatic World," Kiley and McDonald, pp. 6–11) has been echoed by many subsequent critics and scholars: "*Catch-22* goes beyond just capturing the form of absurdity, it moves toward a metaphysical statement about reality and truth in the contemporary world" (Howard Stark, "The Anatomy of *Catch-22*," Kiley and McDonald, pp. 145–158); "The *Catch-22* joke is not even very funny the first time, and in fact . . . it is no joke" (Vance Ramsey, "From Here to Absurdity: Heller's *Catch-22*," Kiley and McDonald, pp. 221–236); "[T]he comic anarchy which provokes it is only the surface of *Catch-22*, not its sustaining structure" (Clinton S. Burhans Jr., "Spindrift and the Sea: Structural Patterns and Unifying Elements in *Catch-22*," Nagel, pp. 40–51).

4. Leon F. Seltzer, "Milo's 'Culpable Innocence': Absurdity as Moral Insanity in *Catch-22*," *Critical Essays on Joseph Heller*, ed. James Nagel (Boston: G. K. Hall, 1984): pp. 74–92.

5. Morton Gurewitch, *Comedy: The Irrational Vision* (Ithaca: Cornell University Press, 1975): p. 126.

6. Gurewitch, p. 223.

7. Jerry Palmer, *The Logic of the Absurd* (London: BFI Publishing, 1987).

8. *Ibid.*, p. 14. Much of Palmer's analysis is directed toward identifying and preserving humor's specificity. Although Palmer insists that his book is not a critique of Freud's view of jokes in *Jokes and their Relation to the Unconscious* and that he is pursuing "latent implications of Freud's theory" (p. 219), he nevertheless argues that Freud failed to discriminate sufficiently between the impact of jokes and other verbal phenomena on psychic processes. Palmer strongly believes that jokes, and humor generally, have a discernible structure and signifying capacity independent of any role in the signifying system of the unconscious as a whole.

9. Joseph Heller, *Catch-22* (New York: Simon & Schuster, 1961): pp. 9–10.

JAMES NAGEL

The Early Composition History of Catch-22

In 1978, the *Wilson Quarterly* conducted a survey of professors of American literature to determine the most important novels published after World War II. To be sure, the result was a most impressive list, but Joseph Heller's *Catch-22* was ranked first.[1] Its position in this survey indicates the esteem and seriousness with which literary scholars have come to regard Heller's first novel since it appeared in October 1961. Only two months later, on December 7, 1961, Heller took obvious pleasure in writing to the dean of the College of Arts and Letters at the University of Notre Dame that "*Catch-22* is already being discussed in literature courses at Harvard, Brown, and two universities here in New York City."[2] Since Heller had taught for two years in the Department of English at Pennsylvania State University, he was fully conversant with the academy, with both its genuine intellectual stimulation and its professional excesses. Indeed, in the early stages of planning *Catch-22*, Heller had planned a satiric scene in which Major Major "meets an old drunk at an MLA convention who was ruined by a man who said he liked Henry James."[3] In another section Major Major "was from the winter wheat fields of Vermont and a former teacher of English. Made the mistake of stating publicly that he did not like Henry James," and there is a suggestion that Major Major "never realized that Proust and Henry James were the same man." Although these comments did not survive to the final version

---

Biographies of Books: The Compositional History of Notable American Writings, Barbour and Quirk (eds), University of Missouri Press (1996): pp. 262–290. © 1996 University of Missouri Press.

of the novel, no one would have enjoyed the satire more than Heller's former colleagues in the academy.

Beyond its high regard in universities throughout the world, *Catch-22* has become an enormous commercial success as well, selling well over ten million copies in just the first two decades after it was published. Such enormous popularity seems to have come as something of a surprise to both author and publisher, since Simon and Schuster is reported to have ordered a first printing of only 4,000 copies. The financial arrangements, too, suggest modest expectations for all concerned; Heller's advance for the novel was only $1,500, $750 upon signing the contract and another $750 when the manuscript was delivered.[4] Nor did the novel enjoy immediate success: it did not make the best-seller list in hardbound and did not become an international sensation until the paperback edition was released. Some of the attention paid to the novel was surely due to its satiric treatment of war and to the escalating antiwar feeling throughout the 1960s, what Pearl K. Bell labeled "that passionately antiwar decade and its nay-saying, antinomian, black-comic Zeitgeist."[5]

It was a fortuitous coincidence, for nowhere in the *Catch-22* materials is there any reference to the Vietnam War or anything like it, although the novel and the manuscripts resonate with antiwar sentiments, including a notation Heller recorded in 1955 that Douglas MacArthur, in his seventy-fifth-birthday speech, urged "people to let their leaders know that they will refuse to fight wars."[6] But even without the Vietnam War, *Catch-22* would have been notable on purely artistic grounds, for writers and literary scholars quickly responded to its robust wit, devastating satire, and complex satiric method that hearkened to the eighteenth century as well as to the twentieth. John Steinbeck, for example, wrote to Heller in July of 1963 to say that he felt peace had become as ridiculous as war and that he found the novel "great" for both its attitude and its writing. Among others, James Jones, himself the author of a highly regarded war novel, wrote to Simon and Schuster to express his sense of awe at the conflict of tragedy and comedy in the book, finding it "delightful" and "disturbing. Perhaps illustrative of the broad appeal of the novel, actor Tony Curtis wrote to Heller as early as 1962 expressing an interest in doing the movie and calling himself Yossarian.[7]

Despite the enormous popularity of Heller's first novel, and the volume of critical attention it has received in the three decades since it was published, relatively little attention has been paid to the composition history of *Catch-22*, even though the record of the growth of the manuscripts reveals a great deal about the development of the central themes and devices as the concept grew over the years.[8] Of particular importance are the early notes and drafts of the manuscript, for they are enormously detailed and complex, often direct in stating Heller's objectives and reservations about what he was doing with his material. Heller's memories of the beginning of his first novel have been recorded many times in interviews, always with the same basic story:

> I was lying in bed in my four room apartment on the West Side when suddenly this line came to me: "It was love at first sight. The first time he saw the chaplain 'Someone' fell madly in love with him." I didn't have the name Yossarian. The chaplain wasn't necessarily an army chaplain—he could have been a *prison* chaplain. But as soon as the opening sentence was available, the book began to evolve clearly in my mind, even most of the particulars—the tone, the form, many of the characters, including some I eventually couldn't use. All of this took place within an hour and a half. It got me so excited that I did what the cliché says you're supposed to do: I jumped out of bed and paced the floor. That morning I went to my job at the advertising agency and wrote out the first chapter in long hand. Before the end of the week, I had typed it out and sent it to Candida Donadio, my agent. One year later, after much planning, I began chapter two.[9]

The idea was to offer it as the first chapter of a book, and, as a result, it appeared as "Catch-18" in *New World Writing* later that year.[10]

Precisely when the original composition of the novel began has been a matter of some confusion, since Heller has indicated both 1953 and 1955 as the starting dates for the novel, probably referring to different stages in the development of the concept. There are indications in the manuscript, however, that Heller started working on the idea in 1953, trying out many different approaches to the novel before he arrived at the strategy used in the first chapter that was published two years later. By this time Heller had drafted hundreds of note cards outlining virtually every character and incident in the novel along with pages of sketches, conversations, time schemes, and the development of various themes.[11] It is clear that by 1955 he had a first chapter to publish but did not have a major section of the novel completed until 1957, when he submitted it to Robert Gottlieb at Simon and Schuster. Gottlieb was only twenty-six at the time, and a junior editor, but he expressed his interest in the project, made some suggestions, and Heller signed a contract the following year. It took him three more years to complete work on the novel. After publication in late 1961, Heller became an international sensation, and Robert Gottlieb became editor-in-chief of Alfred A. Knopf.

The initial composition of *Catch-22* is important in several senses. On the simplest, perhaps the most important, level, it records the process of invention of one of the most remarkable novels of the twentieth century. It is no inconsequential body of papers that will reveal the process of significant creation at work, and the manuscripts clearly show Heller suggesting ideas to himself, discarding them, outlining possible structures for the shape of his narrative, trying out absurd conversations that underscore important themes. There is much to be learned about both characters and themes in material that was never published, for the manuscripts often are clear about motivations for various actions that are unclear in the novel, why Yossarian went into the hospital with a false liver ailment, for example. In many instances scenes and speeches in the manuscripts elucidate an episode in the published novel. A world of biographical reference in the manuscripts is largely lost in the published novel (in which the setting and the names of characters were changed): references to the places and people Heller knew during his service in the Army Air Corps in World War II, depictions of some of the men in his unit, some of the notable events that preoccupied them during the summer of 1944. These various documents, written in Heller's hand, provide an invaluable guide to understanding the composition and meaning of a monumental contemporary novel.

One point that should be made at the inception of any discussion of the stages of composition of Heller's first novel is that from beginning to end the title of the book was "Catch-18," a title with somewhat richer thematic overtones than "Catch-22." The early drafts of the novel, particularly the sketches and note cards, have a somewhat more "Jewish" emphasis than does the published novel. In Judaism, "eighteen" is a significant number in that the eighteenth letter of the Hebrew alphabet, "chai," means "living" or "life." Eighteen thus has a meaning for Jews that it does not have for other people: the *Mishnah* promotes eighteen as the ideal age for men to marry, and Jews often give personal gifts or charitable contributions in units of eighteen. Thematically, the title "Catch-18" would thus contain a subtle reference to the injunction in the *Torah* to choose life, a principle endorsed by Yossarian at the end of the novel when he deserts.[12]

It is also clear that the title was changed not because Heller had second thoughts but because a few weeks before the scheduled printing of the novel, Heller's publisher learned that Leon Uris, who had earlier written *Exodus*, was coming out with a novel entitled *Mila-18*. A change had to be made, and there was discussion of using "Catch-11" in that the duplication of the digit "1" would parallel the structural use of the repetition of scenes. But "11" was rejected because of the movie *Ocean's Eleven* and the now familiar concern for using a number already current in the public imagination.[13] Then Heller found a new title he liked, "Catch-14," and on January 29, 1961, he wrote to his publisher in defense of it: "The name of the book is now CATCH-14. (Forty-eight hours after you resign yourself to the change, you'll find yourself almost preferring this new number. It has the same bland and nondescript significance of the original. It is far enough away from Uris for the book to establish an identity of its own, I believe, yet close enough to the original title to still benefit from the word of mouth publicity we have been giving it.)" For whatever reason, and legend has it that Robert Gottlieb did not find "14" to be a funny number, the title was finally changed once again, this time to "Catch-22," recapturing the concept of repetition. Since the central device of the novel is *déjà vu*, with nearly every crucial scene, until the conclusion, coming back a second time, the title was once again coordinate with the organizational schema of the narrative. As Heller remarked, "the soldier in white comes back a second time, the dying soldier sees everything twice, the chaplain thinks that everything that happens has happened once before. For that reason the two 2's struck me as being very appropriate to the novel.[14] On this logic, and a decidedly accidental series of events, the phrase "catch-22," rather than "catch-18," became the term for bureaucratic impasse the world over.

It did so, however, only because readers found in the novel something they felt was important, a level of humor that was painfully resonant of their own experience, a grim reality that, in the 1960s, seemed all too close to current events. But even these aspects of the novel would not have had much impact were it not for the craft of the book, an artistry won through years of Heller's meticulous attention to the details of his novel. Indeed, one of the remarkable aspects of the writing of *Catch-22* is that Heller seems not to have discarded anything from the very beginning of composition, as though he somehow knew even from the start what a sensation his first attempt at extended fiction would be. As a result, the *Catch-22* manuscripts contain literally thousands of pages of materials, note cards, early sketches, drafts of scenes, outlines of chapters, detailed lists of the appearance of each character in each chapter, outlines of thematic progressions, chronologies in which the events of the novel are measured against actual events in 1944, and hundreds of other pages dealing with proposed scenes and characters. They constitute a truly remarkable creative record, one unmatched in the papers of any other important American novel.

One of the most fascinating stages in the growth of the manuscript is a collection of note cards on which Heller, writing at his desk at work, planned the structure of the novel before composition and then analyzed its contents after the first complete draft.[15] The most important of these is a group of thirty-seven cards, written in Heller's hand, headed "CHAPTER CARDS (outlines for chapters before they were written.)" Based on what Heller has said in a letter, these cards would have been assembled in 1953, at the earliest stage of composition, two years before the "sudden inspiration" that resulted in "Catch-18."[16]

Perhaps the most striking feature of these cards, especially in light of the frequent charges that the novel is "unstructured," "disorganized," or even "chaotic," is the detail of the initial plan. Not only are the main events in each chapter suggested, but characters are named and described, and such matters as structure, chronology, and various themes (including sex and "catch-18") are set into a complex pattern. Other cards indicate the relationships among events, with key sentences written in. A typical card, about twelfth from the beginning,[17] treats the characters and events for what was projected to be a single chapter:

1.   Cathcart's background & ambition. Puzzled by ——— de Coverley.

2.   Hasn't a chance of becoming a general. Ex-corporal Winter green, who evaluates his work, also wants to be a general.

3.   For another, there already was a general, Dreedle.

4.   [Arrow up] Tries to have Chaplain say prayer at briefing.[Arrow up]

5.   Description of General Dreedle. His Nurse.

6.   Dreedle's quarrel with Moodis [sic].

7.   Snowden's secret revealed in argument with Davis.

8.   Dreedle brings girl to briefing.

9.   Groaning. Dreedle orders Korf shot.

10.   That was the mission in which Yossarian lost his balls.

The section of the published novel that relates to these items now comprises much of chapters 19 ("Colonel Cathcart") and 21 ("General Dreedle"), with chapter 20 ("Corporal Whitcomb"), unrelated to these matters, interspersed between them. Thus the ten items on the card resulted in roughly twenty-one pages of the novel.[18]

The business of Colonel Cathcart's background and ambition now begins in chapter 19 with a description of him as a "slick, successful, slipshod, unhappy man of thirty-six who lumbered when he walked and wanted to be a general" (*Catch*, 185). These matters cover a bit over two pages and then give way to item 4 on the card, "Tries to have Chaplain say prayer at briefing." To demonstrate how closely Heller worked with the note cards, this item had directional arrows pointing up on both sides of it, and, indeed, in execution the matter listed was moved forward in the chapter. This move underscores the logical relationship between the two concerns: "Colonel Cathcart wanted to be a general so desperately he was willing to try anything, even religion . . ." (*Catch*, 187). The idea develops systematically: Cathcart is impressed by a photograph in *The Saturday Evening Post* of a colonel who has his chaplain conduct prayers before each mission and he reasons, "maybe if we say prayers, they'll put my picture in *The Saturday Evening Post*"(*Catch*, 188). The humor of the situation progresses as Cathcart's thinking begins to take shape in his conversation with the chaplain:

> "Now, I want you to give a lot of thought to the kind of prayers we're going to say . . . I don't want any of this kingdom of God or Valley of Death stuff. That's all too negative. What are you making such a sour face for?"
>
> "I'm sorry, sir," the chaplain stammered. "I happened to be thinking of the Twenty-third Psalm just as you said that."
>
> "How does that one go?"
>
> "That's the one you were just referring to, sir. 'The Lord is my shepherd I——.'"
>
> "That's the one I was just referring to. It's out. What else have you got?" (*Catch*, 189)

Cathcart's logic leads him to an admission that "I'd like to keep away from the subject of religion altogether if we can" and to the true object of his desires: "Why can't we all pray for something good, like a tighter bomb pattern?" (*Catch*, 190). But the plan for prayers is abandoned altogether when the chaplain reveals that the enlisted men do not have a separate God, as Cathcart had assumed, and that excluding them from prayer meetings might antagonize God and result in even looser bomb patterns. Cathcart concludes "the hell with it, then" (*Catch*, 193). Thus the first item on Heller's note card and the elevated matter regarding prayer grew to make up all of chapter 19. The secondary notions of each of these items were moved: Cathcart's puzzlement at ——— de Coverley was delayed to chapter 21, and the revelation that Milo is now the mess officer was placed earlier, in chapter 13, when Major ——— de Coverley promotes him out of a desire for fresh eggs.

The remaining items on the card became chapter 21, "General Dreedle." This chapter presents two main issues: the first is the string of obstructions to Cathcart's promotion to general, one of which is General Dreedle; the second is General Dreedle himself. In the novel, the chapter develops the topics equally. The balance is enriching: the ambitious colonel trying to get promoted contrasts the entrenched general trying to preserve what he has. Cathcart's problems in the novel reflect precisely what Heller listed as items 2 and 3 on his note card:

> Actually, Colonel Cathcart did not have a chance in hell of becoming a general. For one thing, there was ex-P.F.C. Wintergreen, who also wanted to be a general and who always distorted,

destroyed, rejected or misdirected any correspondence by, for, or about Colonel Cathcart that might do him credit. For another, there already was a general, General Dreedle, who knew that General Peckem was after his job but did not know how to stop him. (*Catch*, 212)

Heller demoted Wintergreen from "ex-corporal" in the notes to "ex-P.F.C." in the novel. General Peckem, called P. P. Peckenhammer throughout the note cards and the manuscript, has been added as a further complication.

The business of General Dreedle, note card items 5 through 9, now occupies the last half of the chapter (*Catch*, 212–220) with only minor alterations from the notes. "Moodis" is changed to "Moodus"; in the incident of the "groaning" at the staff meeting, Dreedle orders Major Danby, not "Korf," shot for "moaning" (*Catch*, 218). Two items are not treated: the business of Snowden's secret was saved for the conclusion of the novel (*Catch*, 430), where it becomes climactic of the *déjà vu* technique and the most powerful scene in the novel. Placed where it is now, the further revelation of Snowden's secret, that man is matter, emphasizes the theme of mortality just when Yossarian is most concerned with death and survival.

The second idea not treated, relating to Yossarian's castration, Heller later rejected in manuscript revision. The incident of Yossarian's wound was ultimately moved to chapter 26: Aarfy, called "Aarky" throughout the note cards, gets lost on the mission to Ferrara and, before McWatt can seize control of the plane, flies back into the flak and the plane is hit. Yossarian's wound in the novel is in his thigh, but his first assessment follows the suggestion of the note card:

> He was unable to move. Then he realized he was sopping wet. He looked down at his crotch with a sinking, sick sensation. A wild crimson blot was crawling rapidly along his shirt front like an enormous sea monster rising to devour him. He was hit! . . . A second solid jolt struck the plane. Yossarian shuddered with revulsion at the queer sight of his wound and screamed at Aarfy for help.
> "I lost my balls! I lost my balls! . . . I said I lost my balls! Can't you hear me? I'm wounded in the groin!" (*Catch*, 283–284)

Heller changed a terrible reality to an understandable confusion that represents a normal fear in war. In its revised state the idea unites the sexual theme with the dangers of war and the destructive insensitivity of Aarfy. Yossarian's wound also serves the plot in getting him back into the hospital, where the themes of absurdity, bureaucracy, and insanity are explored:

Nurse Cramer insists to Yossarian that his leg is "certainly . . . not your leg!
. . . That leg belongs to the U.S. government" (*Catch*, 286). It would have
been difficult to make this conversation humorous if Yossarian had been
castrated. Nonetheless, the relationship of the published novel to the suggestions on the note card reveals that although Heller continued the creative
process throughout the composition and revision of his book, the final product is remarkably consistent with his initial conception. The central tone,
the key events, the characters (although often with changed names), and the
underlying themes are essentially what Heller recorded on a note card eight
years prior to the publication of the novel.

Another note card of particular interest is one entitled "Night of Horrors" in the notes and the manuscript chapter derived from it but "The
Eternal City" in the published novel. The card contains seven entries, the
first four of which concern matters not eventually made part of the chapter.
These have to do with the discovery of penicillin (which Yossarian apparently needs for syphilis), Yossarian's attempts to get the drug through Nurse
Duckett, and the acquisition of it by "Aarky." The discovery by Yossarian
that the old man in the whorehouse is dead, and that the girls have been
driven out of the apartment by the vagaries of "catch-18," thus would have
been the result of his search for a cure. He has come to the apartment in
Rome to see Aarky. The villain in this episode turns out to be Milo, as item
7 explains: "Milo is exposed as the source of penicillen [*sic*], tricking both
Aarky & Yossarian, and as the man who infected the girl to create a demand
for his new wonder drug. Yossarian breaks with him." This concept, finally
rejected, would have been an interesting but perhaps unnecessary further
development of Milo's corruption. It would also have been an overt expression of Yossarian's underlying values, one not in the novel because Milo
simply leaves Yossarian in Rome out of a desire to make money from the
traffic in illegal tobacco.

This idea and all but one of the other suggestions on the card were
finally abandoned or subordinated to what appears as item 5: "Yossarian finally walks through the streets of Rome witnessing various horrors, among
them the maid, who has been thrown from the window by Aarky." It is this
concept that ultimately became the heart of "The Eternal City" (*Catch*, 396–
410). Yossarian, in Rome to look for Nately's whore's kid sister, in an attempt
to keep her from a life of prostitution, discovers a nightmare world. In the
novel Milo shares these generous motives until he learns of the smuggling
of illegal tobacco (*Catch*, 402). What emerges in the chapter is Yossarian's
"night of horrors," his surrealistic walk through Rome at night, in which
greed, violence, corruption, insanity, and death, prime themes throughout
the novel, converge on his consciousness from all sides, and he is arrested
for being AWOL.

There are numerous other note cards as intriguing and significant as these two and several individual ideas that were developed or abandoned after their first conception in the notes. That Snowden will be killed on the mission to Avignon, that in response Yossarian will parade in the nude and sit naked in a tree during the funeral, are all established on a card entitled "Ferrara." An example of the kind of minor detail that Heller frequently changed is the suggestion on this card that when Yossarian is awarded his medal, still standing naked in formation, "Dreedle orders a zoot suit for him." Another such revision concerns what is finally chapter 30, "Dunbar" (*Catch*, 324–333), but is called "McAdam" in the notes. (The name "Mc-Adam," of course, was later changed to "McWatt.") The two most dramatic events of the chapter are here suggested: McAdam dives low over the beach, slicing Kid Sampson in half, and then commits suicide. The note card indicates an indefinite "man" as the victim and also suggests that "McAdam kills himself & Daneeker," which was revised, but the main focus of the published chapter is all there. This card also contains a fascinating suggestion: "Nurse Cramer's family tree traced back to include all known villains in History. She completes the line by being a registered Republican who doesn't drink, smoke, fornicate, or lust consciously & [is] guiltless of similar crimes."

An entry for chapter 40, entitled "Catch-18" in the notes, reads "in the morning, Cathcart sends for Yossarian and offers him his deal. Big Brother has been watching Yossarian." The concluding phrase makes explicit an underlying thematic allusion to George Orwell's *1984*, one now more subtly beneath the action of the novel. The same card contains the suggestion that Nately's whore will stab Yossarian as he leaves Cathcart's office, which occurs in the novel, and that she will shout "olé" as she plunges the knife in, which does not.

The note for the final chapter, "Yossarian," contains not only plot suggestions but some interpretive remarks as well. There is a good deal of interest in Yossarian's mortality: "Yossarian is dying, true, but he has about 35 years to live." Another provocative entry, one rejected, suggests that "Among other things, he really does have chronic liver trouble. Condition is malignant & would have killed him if it had not been discovered." It is fortuitous that this idea was changed, for Yossarian's trips to the hospital are now linked to his protest against the absurdity of the war and his personal quest for survival; to add to those ideas the serendipitous saving of his life through the discovery of his cancer in a military hospital he has falsely entered would have been to compound too many levels of irony. Perhaps the most important comments on this note card are those relating to the thematic significance of Yossarian's refusal of Cathcart's deal. In the note card, Yossarian discusses the ethics of the deal and his alternatives with an English deserter: "Easiest would be to go home or fly more missions. Hardest would be for him to fight for identity without sacrificing moral responsibility." The following entry reads "He chooses the last, after all dangers are pointed out to him."

In the novel, the English deserter has been replaced by Major Danby, who, since he does not appear in the preliminary notes, would seem to be a late invention. The conception of the "fight for identity" has been altered: Yossarian says, "I've been fighting all along to save my country. Now I'm going to fight a little to save myself. The country's not in danger any more, but I am" (*Catch*, 435). The "identity" motif has been submerged into the "survival" theme, one centered on Yossarian's physical and moral survival. Thus Yossarian can now claim, "I'm not running away from my responsibilities. I'm running to them" (*Catch*, 440). In thematic terms, this change is among the most important ideas in the preliminary note cards. What is remarkable about them as a group, however, is how closely they correspond to what Heller eventually published some eight years later. It is a dramatic testimony to the clarity of his initial conception, for, although there were many early changes and deletions, along with alterations in the final version of the manuscript, the finished product is well described by the note cards Heller developed in his advertising office, shaping and defining and trying out his idea in miniature before he actually wrote the first draft.

In addition to the note cards, Heller also worked on a number of other documents prior to writing the first full draft of his novel. One group of these that is particularly important is composed of "plans," outlines, sketches, brief exchanges of dialogue, summaries of the role of a character, ideas for plot developments, checklists on which Heller indicated that a certain idea had or had not been included in the first draft. These pages, somewhat more than a hundred, allowed Heller more room than did the note cards to expand on concepts and outlines, although to some extent they serve the same function. For example, on the sheet for "Catch-18" Heller recorded his ideas for the permutations of that concept:

A. Censoring letters
B. Increases Wintergreen's punishment
C. Colonel must request transfer
D. Sanity in soldier
E. Drives girls out
F. Will send Nately Back
G. Deal With Yossarian.[19]

Heller had thus decided before he began writing that the matter of "catch-18" would occur at least seven times in the novel. Further, as the outline indicates, the general direction of the recurrence progresses from humor to tragedy, from the business of having Wintergreen dig holes to contain the dirt created from previous holes to the final matter of Yossarian's being trapped in a moral dilemma in which his self-respect and his very life are seriously threatened.

Some of Heller's notations to himself reveal a considerable interpretive intelligence. On a page about Corporal Snark, Milo's first chef in the novel and the character who poisons the squadron with soap in the mashed potatoes to prove that the men have no taste (*Catch*, 63), Heller records his comments about this relatively minor character. It is clear that Snark is to be thematically opposed to Milo in that Snark cooks for the "art" of his craft and Milo is interested only in the commercial aspects of food. Heller wrote that Snark "would like to forge within the smithy of his soul the uncreated soufflés of the world." Another entry is particularly ironic: "Spots the significance of Milo's enterprises. An egg, in case the critics have missed it, is a symbol of creation. A hard-boiled egg is the symbol of the creative process frozen. A scrambled egg is the symbol of creation scrambled. A powdered egg is the symbol of the creative process pulverized—destroyed." No one reading through Heller's plans would doubt that he gave extraordinary attention to every detail of his novel, including the role and thematic impact of every character in every scene. This pertains even in instances in which Heller did not follow his suggestions, as with some of his ideas for Snowden: "Snowden's innards are loathsome things brought up through a crack in the earth. . . . Snowden's luggage in the bedroom at the enlisted men's apartment . . . Snowden's secret is that they are out to kill Yossarian." These ideas, particularly the last, are not implemented in the novel, nor are such related plans as the notion that General Eisenhower and Harry Truman want Yossarian dead.

One of the documents deals with the war novel that Yossarian and Dunbar struggle to write, a matter suggested on a note card and developed in Heller's plans but not incorporated into the final novel. The note cards contained two suggestions that relate to this document: one entry, item 7, suggests that "Yossarian & Dunbar write novel, although Jew won't conform & they still lack a radical" and the second, item 10, indicates a "parody of Hemingway in introduction of attempt to assemble cast for war novel." In the brief sketches derived from the note-card entries, Heller wrote a half-page developing each idea, the first of which, entitled "Perfect Plot," begins

> now they had just about everything to make a perfect plot for a
> bestselling war novel. They had a fairy, they had a slav named
> Florik from the slums, an Irishman, a thinker with a Phd, a cynic
> who believed in nothing, a husband who's [*sic*] wife had sent him
> a Dear John letter, a clean-cut young lad who was doomed to die.
> They had everything there but the sensitive Jew, and that was

enough to turn them against the whole race. They had a Jew but there was just nothing they could do with him. He was healthy, handsome, rugged, and strong, and if anybody else in the ward wanted to make something out of anything he could have taken them in turn, anybody but Yossarian, who didn't want to make anything out of anything. All he cared about was women and there was just nothing in the world you could do with a Jew like that.[20]

Several matters are of interest in the paragraph, including the suggestion that Yossarian is Jewish, an idea buttressed by Heller's comments in a letter in 1974.[21] That Yossarian and Dunbar would be writing a novel about war would be thematically awkward in the context of the progressive immediacy of danger and death. The writing of fiction implies remoteness, the vantage of the observer, more than direct involvement. Heller's idea that an outfit with an ethnic distribution would somehow parody Hemingway seems confused, since Hemingway never wrote any novels along those lines. The parody would seem better directed at some of the popular war movies that circulated in the 1950s. Another important dimension to this scene is that Yossarian and Dunbar are in the hospital, implying either that they are ill or wounded or, more likely, that they are feigning illness to escape hazardous duty, a ruse that runs throughout the novel.

Another Heller document, however, explores alternative reasons why Yossarian wants to go into the hospital. On a page entitled "Conspiracy to Murder Him, " Heller outlined some thoughts about Yossarian's growing preoccupation with death:

Grows aware of it with Snowden's death. They were all shooting at him, and when they hit someone else it was a case of mistaken identity. They wanted him dead, there was no doubt about it and there was no doubt that it was all part of a gigantic conspiracy. . . . Colonel Cathcart wanted him dead. General Dreedle wanted him dead. . . . Eisenhower and Harry S Truman wanted him dead. It was the one thing upon which even the enemies were agreed. Hitler wanted him dead because he was Assyrian, Stalin wanted him dead because he wasn't. Mussolini wanted him dead because he was Mussolini, and Tojo wanted him dead because he was short and far away and couldn't make himself understood. . . . The only safe place for him in the whole world was in the hospital, because in the hospital nobody seemed to care whether he lived or died.

This material has genuine comic potential, even in Heller's brief outline of it, although it makes Yossarian's fear of death somewhat more paranoiac than in the novel, where his continuous proximity to death is a matter of circumstance rather than malevolence. Heller's decision not to develop this idea was part of a general pattern of excision of references to real persons. Without the resonance of the names, the humor of the passage is greatly diminished.

Several of the other sketches Heller worked on are also intriguing documents, including a page on which Yossarian, Orr, and Hungry Joe all move the bomb line before the mission to Bologna. This page, entitled "Rebukes Yossarian for moving bomb line," contains dialogue in which Clevinger argues with his obtuse good sense that Yossarian was unfair to the others in moving the line on the map. In the following paragraph the plot thickened in a way it does not in the novel:

> It was another clear night filled with bright yellow stars he knew he might never see again. Moving the bomb line was not fair to the other men in the squadron, men like Orr, who tiptoed out into the darkness and moved the bomb line up an inch, and like Hungry Joe, who moved it up another inch, and the steady stream of all the others, each one moving it one inch so that it was up over Sweden when daylight glowed.

Yossarian alone is culpable in the novel, but this passage establishes the universality of his apprehension in a manner that may have enriched this motif. On the other hand, Heller's ultimate rejection of a scene in which Yossarian explains to the chaplain how much he enjoyed touching Snowden's torn flesh and organs, and how he rubbed blood over himself to impress everyone back at the base, was wisely deleted. In this sketch Heller seems to have been exploring the possibilities of his material, developing ideas before discarding them. The obvious thematic incongruence of Yossarian being pleased by the very death that transforms him would have considerably weakened the Snowden scenes.

There are other related documents that seem to have been written at this stage, after the note cards but before the first draft of the novel. Heller was obviously very concerned about the chronology of the action, not only that it progress in accord with certain key scenes but that these events be consistent with the history of the actual war. At one point he constructed a detailed outline of events in the European theater from 1943 to 1945. He begins in 1943 with the landings in Sicily on June 11 and follows with the Anzio landings in January of 1944, the Normandy invasion on June 6, and the stabilization of German forces in Italy (which necessitated the bombing of transportation lines). He did a separate page on events in Italy between May and August of 1944 (the period of his own bombing missions), outlining the objective of the Italian campaign ("tie down Germans; gain air bases near S. Germany") and the stalemate in southern Italy that delayed the Allied advance. He particularly notes the taking of Rome on June 4, 1944, D-Day two days later, and the victories in Pisa and Florence. His broad outline continues through 1945 and the Battle of the Bulge, the advance of the Russians on the eastern front, the execution of Mussolini, the crossing of the Po, and the fall of Berlin on May 3.

With the historical facts clear, he worked on the chronological outline of his own narrative, using the closest paper large enough to contain his detailed notations, the blotter on his desk. On this document Heller recorded not only the general events of the novel but, within a grid crossing time values with characters, the action for each character at the time of the central events. Heller's chart would then tell him, as he worked on a given scene, what all of the characters were doing. For example, the entries indicate that when Yossarian is wounded he comes into contact with Nurse Duckett and gets psychoanalyzed by Major Sanderson, Dunbar cracks his head in the hospital, Nately refuses to enter the hospital, Aarky gets lost on the mission, Orr has a flat tire, the Soldier in White reappears, and the old man of the Roman brothel continues to be a mystery. Reading the chart down, Heller could follow the activities of any character he chose; reading it across, he could coordinate their activities and keep a complex chronology straight. In this he did not entirely succeed, but, given the intricate time structure of the novel, he needed a method of organizing the complex events.[22]

At some point Heller constructed other documents that also clarify the actions of the characters and the key themes of the novel. Taking their interaction in the plot apart, he meticulously recorded the progression of events involving each character. These documents cover nearly a hundred pages and reveal the painstaking care and detailed attention that Heller gave to the structure of his fiction. Many of these entries contain humorous ideas not in, or submerged in, the novel, one being that Major Major "was from the winter wheat fields of Vermont and a former teacher of English. Made the mistake of stating publicly that he did not like Henry James." Another entry explores the idea that "Rome was a sort of school for sexual experience." Other entries explore the "Night of Horrors," later changed to "The Eternal City," and others the concept of free enterprise. One outline reveals Heller's plan for the ending, which begins "Yossarian is wounded, recovers, and continues flying combat missions until he completes seventy." The emphasis is on Nately's whore, how she tries to stab him when he tells her of Nately's death. That sketch takes him through to the end:

> Yossarian can lend himself obediently to all Colonel Cathcart's designs and lose his life; he can accept Colonel Cathcart's proposi-

tion and lose his character. Or, he can desert, and risk losing both when he is eventually apprehended, as he knows he will probably be. There is no way he can remain a citizen in good standing without falling victim to one dishonorable scheme or another of his legal superior.

In the end, he runs off, closely pursued by Nately's mistress, the embodiment of danger and of a violent conscience that will never leave him in peace.

As these comments indicate, Heller often gave his ideas critical substance even before he wrote the scenes, acting as creative writer and interpreter simultaneously in a manner rarely equaled for detail and insight in American fiction.

The most important manuscript of *Catch-22* is a handwritten draft a good deal longer than, but essentially the same as, the published novel. It is complete save for the first chapter, which was published separately as "Catch-18" in *New World Writing* in 1955, and for chapter 9, which is simply missing from this draft although present in the typescript. This manuscript displays the additions, deletions, insertions, typeovers, misspellings, and informal punctuation of the type normally found in first drafts.[23] It is essentially handwritten, although there are paragraphs and occasionally pages that are typed, indicating, perhaps, some revision simultaneous to the initial composition. Two chapters of the manuscript do not appear in the novel (as a result the numbers of the chapters are different in each case) and hundreds of brief passages were deleted. Indeed, Heller's revisions consisted more of deletion and addition than of alterations in scenes. The pages are numbered sequentially by chapter, although as other pages were inserted, varying numbering and lettering schemes were used to keep order so that pages frequently have several numbers or letters on them. As was true on the note cards, many of the names of characters differ in the manuscript from the novel: Aarfy appears consistently as Aarky; Peckem is known throughout the manuscript as P. P. Peckenhammer. Nately is a more important character in the manuscript than in the novel, and an entire chapter about his family was deleted. One important character in the manuscript, Rosoff, does not appear at all in the novel. But the central point is that Heller's first draft remains remarkably close to what he outlined in his note cards and to the published novel.

There are other matters in the early composition stages that are significant. One of them is that the location of Yossarian's base throughout the note cards and manuscript is Corsica, where Heller himself had been stationed. Pianosa was not introduced until the manuscript and even the typescript had been completed. The manuscript is more detailed than the novel in describing features of the setting, since Heller had been to Corsica himself and knew the topography intimately; there is no evidence that he ever visited Pianosa. Yossarian's unit in the manuscript is also Heller's old outfit, the Twelfth Air Force, whereas in the novel it is the Twenty-seventh, a nonexistent unit. In the manuscript there is a much more "literary" frame of reference than in the final novel, and Yossarian is compared to Ahasuerus, Gulliver, and Samson Agonistes, reflecting Heller's graduate training in literature. The manuscript is also somewhat more sexually explicit than the published version, as in the scene in which Daneeka shows the newlyweds how to make love. In the manuscript Daneeka says, I showed them how penetration was accomplished and explained its importance to impregnation." This reference was dropped in the final draft. In a similar vein, the manuscript has more scatological dialogue, so that when Milo maneuvers a package of dates away from his friend, "Yossarian always did things properly, too, and he gave Milo the package of pitted dates and told him to shove his personal note up his ass." This passage, and this tone, did not survive to publication (*Catch*, 64).

Another area of frequent revision is the final paragraphs of the chapters, which show a great deal of revision, more than any other section of the manuscript. For example, in the first draft the last paragraph of chapter 7, which concludes a section on Milo's complex investment schemes, reads

> the only one complaining was Milo. And the only ones who were happy, as it turned out, were Milo and the grinning thief, for by the time McWatt returned to his tent another bedsheet was gone, along with the sweet tooth and a brand new pair of red polka dot pajamas sent him with love by a wealthy sister-in-law who despised him for what he had been told was his birthday.

Heller crossed all of that out in his manuscript and substituted "but Yossarian still didn't understand." By the time the novel appeared the passage had become

> but Yossarian still didn't understand either how Milo could buy eggs in Malta for seven cents apiece and sell them at a profit in Pianosa for five cents (*Catch*, 66),

which better conveys the absurd humor.

One way in which the manuscript differs from the novel is that there are more passages of interpretive comment in the first draft, such as a comment in chapter 2 about the Texan. In the manuscript the narrator says

> that's what was wrong with the Texan, not that he never ended kneeding [his jowls], but that he overflowed with goodwill and

brought the whole ward down trying to cheer it up. He was depressing. He was worse than a missionary or an uncle. <The Texan> {He} wanted everybody in the <ward> {hospital} to be happy. He was really very sick.

In the novel this passage has been reduced in a manner typical of Heller's changes:

The Texan wanted everybody in the ward to be happy but Yossarian and Dunbar. He was really very sick. (*Catch*, 16)

In shortening this passage, Heller also changed its impact, making the Texan's illness ambiguous. The manuscript implies that his unrestrained ebullience and goodwill are so out of keeping with reality as to be pathological; the novel seems to suggest that because he does not want Yossarian and Dunbar to be happy there must be something wrong with him.

Another expository assertion of theme originally opened chapter 3:

Colonel Cathcart wanted fifty missions, and he was dead serious about them. Yossarian had one mission, and he was dead serious about that. His mission was to keep alive. His mission was to keep alive as long as he could, for he had decided to live forever or die in the attempt. Yossarian was a towering one hundred and ninety-two pounds of firm bone and tender flesh, and he worshipped the whole bloody mess so much that he would have lain down his life to preserve it. Yossarian was no stranger to heroism. He had courage. He had as much courage as anyone he'd ever met. He had courage enough to be a coward, and that's exactly what he was, a hero.

This assessment of Yossarian's character is the kind of comment reserved for the other characters in the published novel, with Yossarian's role revealed dramatically. Heller deleted this passage and presented the idea with the remark that Yossarian "had decided to live forever or die in the attempt, and his only mission each time he went up was to come down alive" (*Catch*, 29), a more concise formulation. Heller made scores of alterations in the manuscript along these lines, nearly always with the result of reducing expository comment, compressing a scene without losing the effect, or clarifying the motivation of one of the characters.

Occasionally Heller's original ideas were abstract and the revisions concrete and specific, lending realistic detail where there had been only generality. For example, in chapter 3 Heller had written a passage about

> General Peckenhammer's directive requiring all tents in the
> Mediterranean Theatre of Operations to be pitched with entrances
> facing back proudly toward the future along imaginary parallel
> lines projected perpendicular to the chain of events that had made
> the present inevitable.

In terms of the setting of the novel, always very specific, this passage makes
little sense and is not humorous. Whatever philosophical value there might
be in these abstractions, they do not comment in any important way on
Yossarian's situation, nor does the deterministic suggestion carry much thematic weight since if circumstances are inevitable there is little point in pro-
testing against them. Heller's revision works better: it is clear that General
Dreedle is angry about

> General Peckem's recent directive requiring all tents in the
> Mediterranean theater of operations to be pitched along parallel
> lines with entrances facing back proudly toward the Washington
> Monument. (*Catch*, 26)

This version is more deeply comic, with its absurd patriotism motivated
by Peckem's unbridled ambition. Dreedle's anger has more to do with his
struggle for power with Peckem than with whether the directive makes any
sense, although "to General Dreedle, who ran a fighting outfit, it seemed a
lot of crap." On another level it also parodies the regimentation of all aspects
of military life.

Some passages had an element of humor but were deleted anyway in the
revision of the first draft. In the published novel, "Yossarian shot skeet, but
never hit any. Appleby shot skeet and never missed" (*Catch*, 35). Heller does
not do much with this business, although the passage reinforces the general
idea that Appleby is capable and very competitive, whereas Yossarian is me-
diocre and not at all competitive. In the manuscript, however, Heller made
more extensive comment:

> Yossarian couldn't shoot a skeet to save his ass. The only time
> Yossarian ever shot a skeet was the time he discharged his
> shotgun accidentally and shot a whole box full of skeet right out
> of Appleby's hands ten minutes before the firing was scheduled
> to begin. Appleby, one of those who never missed, was impressed
> profoundly.

This incident makes Yossarian's innocence somewhat more dangerous
than in the novel, and it also gives Appleby a more generous spirit.[24] The

joke in the manuscript surpasses that in the novel, but it comes at the cost of making Yossarian a dangerous threat. In the final version he is essentially a life-affirming character fighting for survival in a hostile and threatening world.

Another important revision relates to the conclusion of chapter 8, which contains the scene known as "Clevinger's Trial," an intense and shocking section in which Clevinger appears before the Action Board for such crimes as "mopery'" "breaking ranks while in formation," and "listening to classical music" (*Catch*, 74). The board consists of Lieutenant Scheisskopf, Major Metcalf, and a "bloated colonel with the big fat mustache." What disturbs Clevinger is not only that he is presumed guilty, in fact *must* be guilty or he would never have been charged, but that he senses the intense hatred of his superior officers. In the novel, that point is emphasized in the conclusion, in which Clevinger realizes that nowhere in the world, not even in Nazi Germany, "were there men who hated him more" (*Catch*, 80). This conclusion is sharp and effective, perhaps the best final line in any of the chapters. It is also a major improvement over what Heller had originally written, which was that

> these were men who were on his side, who pledged allegiance to the same flag. It was a ruinous, shattering encounter, for that was the one thing Clevinger had not learned at Harvard, how to hate, and the one thing Yossarian could not teach him. They were not the enemy soldiers he had enlisted to fight, yet he was the enemy they had enlisted to fight, and it gave them the decisive advantage in whatever incomprehensible struggle they had plunged themselves into against him.

Although there may be elements of tragic wisdom in this insight, its verbosity diffuses the impact of the shorter and more pointed conclusion. Here, as in many instances, Heller demonstrated his considerable skill at revision, making the concluding paragraph in the novel much better than that in the first draft.

Many of Heller's deletions from the manuscript are essentially compressions retaining the same basic themes and the same attributes of character. The reductions thus have the effect of leaving some matters unstated but nonetheless consistent with the passages that appear in the published version. For example, chapter 8 of the novel begins "not even Clevinger understood how Milo could do that, and Clevinger knew everything," referring to Milo's ability to sell eggs for less than he pays for them and still make a profit. The manuscript went on to detail various categories of what Clevinger knew:

Clevinger knew who was fighting the war and why, who had started the war and when, who would pay for the war and how, and why the war had to be one [won] and by whom, even though winning the war would mean giving everything back to the same sinful people of poise, power, and pretension all over the world who had helped get it started in the first place, just so they could fuck things up all over again with a brand new one that would make it necessary for Yossarian to dump his wet, warm blood out still one more time in <senseless> {meaningless} payment for their headstrong and supercilious blunders. It would all go back to them by default, for they were the only ones willing enough to work full time at getting, keeping, and misusing authority.

In addition to unnecessarily elaborating on an idea inherent in the events, this passage introduces an element of futility in both the war itself and Yossarian's protest. Since everything will revert to its original condition even if the Allies win the war, every level of the action is absurd. In the conclusion of the published novel, Yossarian takes a rather different stance, stating, "I've been fighting all along to save my country." He clearly feels that it does make a difference who wins; that conflict having been resolved, however, he now must devote himself to saving both his life and his integrity, which explains his desertion. The final portion of the deleted passage, a protest against oligarchy and a call for political activism, remains only by implication.

Some of Heller's deletions constitute a pattern that, in effect, diminishes the role of characters or themes. For example, the triumvirate of Scheisskopf, his wife, and the accommodating Dori Duz is more important in the manuscript than in the novel. Many passages involving Yossarian and Dori Duz were deleted in chapter 8, for example, most dealing with Yossarian's lust and her capacity to tantalize him. In another section Dori replaces Mrs. Scheisskopf in bed so that the wife can go out on the town with *Buddenbrooks* looking for someone interesting "to shack up with." Despite the humor in these passages, Dori has less moment than Mrs. Scheisskopf, and Heller diminished her role appropriately in the novel.

Mrs. Scheisskopf gets more attention in the manuscripts than in the published version. Much of what was cut about her, however, contained generalized comments about women that would have introduced tangential issues, and Heller wisely deleted them. For example, he originally wrote in chapter 8 that

like all married women who have been denied the essential childhood advantages of a broken home and a tenement environment, she yearned to be a slut with lovers by the thousand. Unlike all married women, she had the vision, courage, and intelligence to make a gallant try.

Although this passage would have provided a plausible explanation for her promiscuity, it would have done so in a school of red herrings. So, too, a related section Heller deleted. He originally wrote that

she was pleasant and confused, with a misplaced sex urge located somewhere in her frontal lobe in the unyielding nut of some trite and treasured neurosis in which only she had any curiosity. She was the sort who in olden times would undoubtedly have run off with her colored chauffeur. What stopped her from doing it now was her colored chauffeur. He couldn't stand her. He found her too bourgeois.

Beyond the humor in the etiology of her insatiable desire, there are again unfortunate racial and socioeconomic implications in the chauffeur business that had to be deleted. It seems probable that Heller, unfailingly liberal and humane in his personal views, was initially inspired by some stereotypic comic strategies that, upon reflection, were inconsistent with the themes he was developing.

The role of Scheisskopf in this chapter was also reduced somewhat, although not fundamentally altered. There was originally more of his obsession with marching and winning parades, with the men being forced to drill in the dead of night with their feet wrapped in burlap bags to muffle the sound. Heller's style in some of this material took on an anomalous tone:

Not a human voice was distinguishable throughout the whole clandestine operation; in place of the usual drill commands, Lieutenant Scheisskopf substituted the sigh of a marsh hen, the plash of a bullfrog, and the whir of quails' wings on a slumbrous Friday afternoon.

The rhapsodic mood of the passage is inconsistent with the inhumane, even unhuman, ambition of Scheisskopf, who cares nothing for the men in his unit and would gladly nail them in formation if it would help win the weekly prize in the Sunday parades.

Heller also deleted a good deal of material from chapter 10, which deals with an array of matters starting with Clevinger's death in a cloud, the Grand Conspiracy of Lowery Field, and ex-P.F.C. Wintergreen's devotion to digging holes in Colorado, and proceeding through to the ominously escalating number of missions required in Pianosa. There was originally a good deal more elaboration on Wintergreen's prodigious digging, with several pages detailing how he would dig until he could find the match, thrown by a Lieutenant Tatlock (who did not survive to the published novel), at the bottom of a hole. All of this proceeds from the fact that "it was ex-P.F.C. Wintergreen's military specialty to keep digging and filling up [pits] in punishment for going AWOL every time he had the chance." There was much elaboration in the manuscript on all of this, even to the point that "Staff Sergeants Bell and Nerdlinger set up a bookmaking stand several yards away and gave odds to all comers on how long it would take him to find each match."

Two other deleted passages in chapter 10 of the manuscript are of particular interest, including one that explains why Milo chose his own squadron to bomb and strafe after he convinced the Germans to conduct the war on a businesslike basis:

> Actually, Milo bombed all five squadrons in the Group that night, and the air field, bomb dump, and repair hangars as well. But his own squadron was the only one built close enough to the abandoned railroad ditch for the men to {take shelter there} seek safety there and be machine gunned repeatedly by the planes floating in over the leafy trees blooming in luxuriant silhouette against the hard, cold, <spectral> {ivory} moon.

The diffusion of Milo's attack in this passage to the entire Group generates rather different values than the more focused raid on the squadron in the novel, in which the danger and threat to life are immediate and devastating.

But a more important passage was cut from this chapter, one that deals with Yossarian's mental condition as it relates to the Snowden scene. A three-page section in the manuscript was deleted that develops some of the causes of Yossarian's "insanity" as seen by others, in this case Sergeant Towser:

> Yossarian had gone crazy twice, in Sergeant Towser's estimation. The symptoms began subtly with a morbid hallucination about a dead man in his tent right after the mission to Orvieto, where the dead man in his tent was really killed, and erupted disgracefully into outright insanity on at least two occasions with which Sergeant Towser was personally familiar, first on the mission to Avignon, when Snowden was killed in the rear of his plane, and again shortly afterward when Yossarian's close friend Clevinger {was} <had been> lost in that mysterious cloud.

What is explicitly clear here is that Yossarian is "insane" only because Towser is insensitive to Yossarian's grieving for a lost friend, to his remorse for the death of a man he did not know, to his feelings about the horrible death of Snowden, and to his general sense of the immediacy of death in their lives. There are further explanations in the deleted sections clarifying the point that Yossarian initially discarded his clothes because they were covered with Snowden's blood and that Yossarian's subsequent retreat into the hospital was occasioned by Clevinger's death. In the published novel this event supports other interpretations: for example, that Yossarian took off his uniform to indicate his rejection of his military role.

This section continues from Towser's point of view, and, since Towser works in Major Major's office, it deals with Yossarian's vigorous attempts to confront his commanding officer. A related passage, also deleted, explores Towser's memories of Mudd, the dead man who lives in Yossarian's tent: "He looked exactly like $E=MC^2$ to Sergeant Towser because he had traveled faster than the speed of light, moving swiftly enough to go away even before he had come and say so long even before he had time to say hello." There is more of this on Mudd, including a scene in which Yossarian returns from a mission to discover that the man in his tent has been killed, and all of these passages were deleted. The effect is that the novel now says little about the details of the Mudd incident or the background of how Yossarian came to walk around naked. A perceptive reader has a sense of the motivational line, but it is not as definite as in Heller's first draft.

One incident that Heller revised rather substantially is the Glorious Loyalty Oath Crusade in chapter 11, an obvious parody of the American loyalty statements of the 1950s and not of military practice in World War II. In the manuscript this crusade targets Communists in the squadron and is not, as in the novel, simply an attempt by Captain Black to discredit Major Major. In the manuscript Black several times asserts that his duty as intelligence officer requires him to identify Communists and to prevent them from examining the bombsights in the planes. Heller repeatedly deleted references to Communism in this section. He also somewhat softened the inconvenience caused to the men by the crusade. He cut out a passage in which the men had to get up at midnight for morning missions and at dawn for afternoon flights because of the necessity to sign so many oaths.

Heller made literally thousands of revisions of this kind as he worked and reworked his material, drawing nearer to publication. In some cases entire chapters were deleted, one involving a calisthenics instructor named Rosoff, who in many ways duplicated Scheisskopf in his excessive zeal for regimentation, and another in which Nately writes home to his father, which shifted some attention away from the theater of war and toward the United States. Many references to actual persons were dropped, including prominent military figures, and the names of men in Heller's unit were changed to avoid any chance of libel suits. But the fact remains that, over the nine years of composition of the novel, the central characters, themes, and incidents that Heller had initially planned in the early stages of the novel remained essentially intact, and in these documents resides one of the most complete, and fascinating, records of the growth of an American classic.

NOTES

1. See Richard Ohmann, "The Shaping of a Canon: U.S. Fiction, 1960–1975," *Critical Inquiry* 10:1 (1983): p. 206.

2. See Joseph Heller's letter to Dean Sheedy (December 7, 1961), in the Heller Manuscripts at Goldfarb Library, Brandeis University. Unless otherwise indicated, all manuscript references are to this collection. I am grateful to Joseph Heller for permission to quote from these documents.

3. Joseph Heller, planning document. Prior to actually beginning the composition of the novel, Heller wrote hundreds of note cards and manuscript pages on which he proposed scenes, defined characters, organized the chronology, and outlined the structure of the novel. Unfortunately, such documents are not sequentially numbered and are not organized into a discrete unit, making precise reference to them problematic. I will, therefore, minimize documentation to them in routine cases. Similarly, in composing his manuscripts, Heller frequently deleted sections, started over (using a new numbering scheme), moved material, or otherwise revised in such a way that reference to specific manuscript page numbers is all but useless. Indeed, Heller interspersed numbered pages with lettered pages, sometimes going through the alphabet twice in a given chapter before returning to numbered pages once again.

4. On early sales, see William Hogan, "*Catch-22:* A Sleeper That's Catching On," *San Francisco Chronicle*, May 3, 1962: p. 39; on financial arrangements, Chet Flippo, "Checking in with Joseph Heller," *Rolling Stone*, April 16, 1981: pp. 51–52.

5. Pearl K. Bell, "Heller's Trial by Tedium," *The New Leader*, October 28, 1974: p. 17.

6. This document is on file in the Heller Manuscripts.

7. John Steinbeck, letter to Joseph Heller, July 1, 1963, Heller Manuscripts. The letter from James Jones is also in this file. Tony Curtis to Joseph Heller, October 16, 1962, Heller Manuscripts.

8. Indeed, three recent books on Heller's fiction ignore the composition history of his work. See Robert Merrill, *Joseph Heller* (Boston: Twayne, 1987); Stephen W. Potts, *Catch-22: Antiheroic Antinovel* (Boston: Twayne, 1989); David Seed, *The Fiction of Joseph Heller: Against the Grain* (New York: St. Martin's Press, 1989).

9. Joseph Heller, quoted in George Plimpton, "How It Happened," *New York Times Book Review*, October 6, 1974: p. 3.

10. See Heller's comments in Richard B. Sale, "An Interview in New York with Joseph Heller," *Studies in the Novel*, 4 (1972): pp. 63–74. Joseph Heller, "Catch-18," *New World Writing*, 7 (April 1955): pp. 204–214.

11. About the beginning date of the book's composition, see Sale, p. 67, where Heller suggests that he started the novel in 1955, and Josh Greenfeld, "22 Was Funnier than 14," *New York Times Book Review*, March 3, 1968: p. 1, where 1953 is given

as the beginning date. Some of my comments about the note-card stage of development were previously published, in somewhat different form, in "The *Catch-22* Note Cards," *Critical Essays on Joseph Heller,* ed. James Nagel (Boston: G. K. Hall, 1984): pp. 51–61 (reprinted from *Studies in the Novel,* 8 [1976]: pp. 394–405).

12. On the significance of the number *18,* see Melvin J. Friedman, "Something Jewish Happened: Some Thoughts about Joseph Heller's *Good as Gold,*" in *Critical Essays on Joseph Heller,* p. 196.

13. For the discussion of the change of title from "Catch-18" to "Catch-11" to "Catch-22," see Ken Barnard, "Joseph Heller Tells How *Catch-18* Became *Catch-22* and Why He Was Afraid of Airplanes," *Detroit News Sunday Magazine,* September 13, 1970: pp. 18–19, 24, 27–28, 30, 65.

14. Heller's letters to Alfred A. Knopf are on deposit in the Heller Manuscripts. See Barnard, "Joseph Heller Tells," 24. Although the manuscript of the novel was entitled "Catch-18" for nearly the entire period of composition, I will refer to the manuscript materials as the "Catch-22" manuscripts unless I specifically wish to indicate the chapter entitled "Catch-18" or the story published under that title.

15. On Heller's writing at his desk at work, see Alden Whitman, "Something Always Happens on the Way to the Office: An Interview with Joseph Heller," *Pages,* 1 (1976): p. 77. My comments here closely follow those in "The *Catch-22* Note Cards," pp. 51–61. The note cards are lined, 5" x 8" Kardex cards of a type used by the Remington Rand office Heller worked in during the composition of the novel. Heller's comments on the cards are variously in blue, red, and black ink, with occasional pencil notations. The variations in ink would suggest that the planning progressed slowly, during which the implements on Heller's desk changed. The cards might also suggest that some of the planning work was done in the office, whereas Heller has indicated that the writing of the novel was done at home, in the evenings, whenever he felt like it. He did not rush, and the development of the novel was stretched over eight years.

16. Joseph Heller, letter to author, March 13, 1974: p. 2, Heller Manuscripts.

17. Given the disorganized state of the Heller manuscripts, it is difficult now to determine the precise order of the cards and even, in some cases, whether a given card was written before or after the initial draft. All references to the numbers and groups of cards are therefore based on my own judgment of the most likely function of the cards when they were written. Heller's comments to me in conversation about the manuscripts has guided my judgment, but even he was unable to remember precise details after a lapse of many years.

18. Joseph Heller, *Catch-22* (New York: Simon & Schuster, 1961): pp. 185–192, 206–220. Hereafter cited parenthetically in the text as *Catch*.

19. These sheets are not organized or numbered in any coherent fashion, suggesting that they were written at various times and not as a discrete stage of composition. Some pages are not numbered, while others begin the numbering or lettering scheme all over again. The "Catch-18" sheet is numbered 17, which is crossed out, and renumbered 15. The letters on the outline are enclosed in circles, which I do not indicate in my text.

20. This entry is on a sheet entitled "Hospital." For a more detailed transcription of Heller's paragraphs, see James Nagel, "Two Brief Manuscript Sketches: Heller's *Catch-22,*" *Modern Fiction Studies,* 20 (1974): pp. 221–224.

21. Joseph Heller, letter to Daniel Walden. I have read this letter but do not have a copy. In it Heller says that he always thought of Yossarian as Jewish. How-

ever, in other places Heller has said directly that he wanted Yossarian to be without ethnic identity.

22. For copies of Heller's blotter, I am indebted to Colonel Frederick Kiley of the United States Air Force, who was generous with both his time and materials when I spoke with him in Washington, D.C. Kiley used the blotter for the cover of his book *A 'Catch–22' Casebook,* ed. Frederick Kiley and Walter McDonald (New York: Crowell, 1973).

23. I will use the term *manuscript* to designate the handwritten draft of the novel, distinct from the *typescript.* Some of the pages of the manuscript have been typed and inserted; some paragraphs were typed with handwriting following, suggesting a revision during the process of composition. In my quotations I will attempt to represent the manuscript accurately, adding only periods to end sentences (sometimes on the manuscript it is not clear if there is a period or not). Throughout my transcriptions, [ ] will be used for editorial interpolations, < > to indicate additions made to the text, and { } to denote deletions by Heller.

24. There is a suggestion in the deleted dialogue that Havermeyer and Appleby discuss the incident and agree that Yossarian shot the gun on purpose, which would change the attitude of Appleby.

NORMAN PODHORETZ

Looking Back at Catch-22

This past December, upon hearing that Joseph Heller had just died at the age of seventy-six, James Webb took to the op-ed page of the *Wall Street Journal*, where he delivered himself of a fervent tribute to *Catch-22*, Heller's first, best (by far), and still most famous novel. There was nothing peculiar or remarkable in itself about Webb's gesture; tributes to Heller were appearing everywhere at the same time. And like Webb's, almost all of them dwelled entirely on *Catch-22*, which came out in 1961 and which subjected World War II to a satirical treatment whose hilarity was matched only by its savagery. Scarcely a mention was made by anyone of the five lesser novels Heller published in the following thirty-eight years of his life—his seventh is scheduled for posthumous publication in the fall—or of the two plays and the two works of nonfiction he also wrote. (The only exception I came across was a little obituary by David Remnick in the *New Yorker* that entered a plea for Heller's second novel, *Something Happened*.)

No doubt many other pieces about *Catch-22* will have been produced by the time this one gets into print. No doubt, too, most of them will be as effusive as Webb's. Indeed, the day before he pronounced it a "masterpiece" and a "great novel," an appreciation in the *Washington Post,* run as a sidebar to Heller's obituary, ended with the similarly confident assertion that *Catch-22* would "live forever."

Commentary Magazine, February 2000, pp. 32-37. © 2000 *Commentary Magazine.*

For all that, however, Webb's piece was special—and what made it special was that it came from a graduate of the Naval Academy who went on to fight with great bravery as a marine in Vietnam, where he was wounded and much decorated, and who later was appointed Secretary of the Navy by Ronald Reagan. One might have thought that such a person with such a background would have a reservation or two about a book that ridicules war and the military with a relentlessness that must surely have inspired the envy of many a pacifist.

Not a bit of it. So far as Webb is concerned, *Catch-22* is without sin of any kind, and its "lasting greatness is beyond dispute." It is a greatness that lies in the truths Heller reveals about war:

> His message . . . was that all wars dehumanize. That few soldiers march happily to their fate. And that once the bullets start to fly, all battlefields become apolitical. For while there may be few atheists in a foxhole, there are even fewer politicians.

This, as we shall soon see, is actually a rather toothless paraphrase of Heller's far more brutal "message." Slightly more biting, but still misleading, is Webb's praise of *Catch-22* for having "stripped away cant and hypocrisy from the telling of how difficult it is to serve" in war. In Webb's judgment, Heller thereby performed a salutary exorcism on the "national mindset that was nothing short of adamant in its insistence on the fatalistic bravado with which our soldiers had faced death" in World War II.

Webb, like Heller, is convinced that this mindset was delusory. But was it? I would concede that it may well have been romantically one-sided, but was it any more unbalanced than Heller's own mindset, or Webb's?

To get some notion of what is omitted from *Catch-22,* let alone from Webb's sanitized rendering of Heller's "message," one need only glance at the work of literature that Heller himself said had exerted (in the words of one obituary notice) "perhaps the longest-lasting impression on him." This was a prose translation of Homer's *Iliad* that he read as a boy, and that inspired in him the ambition to be a writer.

Now it is certainly the case that the side of war upon which *Catch-22* dwells exclusively and obsessively—its grisly horrors, and the human pettiness it can elicit—are vividly recorded in the *Iliad.* (Remember Achilles sulking in his tent and refusing to join in battle because one of his concubines has been taken from him by the commanding general Agamemnon?) But in Homer's epic, all this is intermingled with the great virtues that war also elicits, and of which the poem sings even more melodiously. These virtues—courage, honor, sacrifice, nobility—also make an occasional appearance in *Catch-22*, but mainly in order to be given as ferocious a beating by Heller as the one he administers to war itself.

So ferocious, indeed, that no one deeply influenced by this novel would ever be able to understand why a self-professed American pacifist like the philosopher William James could come to believe in the great need for a "moral equivalent of war" in addressing the problems of a society at peace. Furthermore, James insisted,

> One cannot meet [the arguments of the militarists] effectively by mere counter-insistency on war's . . . horror. The horror makes the thrill; and . . . the question is of getting the extremest and supremest out of human nature. . . . The military party denies neither the bestiality nor the horror . . . ; it only says that these things tell but half the story.

Even more puzzling to a reader entirely under the sway of *Catch-22* would be the remark made by another pacifist philosopher, Bertrand Russell. Sitting in a British jail for having agitated against conscription in World War I, Russell later wrote, "I was tormented by patriotism. The successes of the Germans . . . were horrible to me. I desired the defeat of Germany as ardently as any retired colonel."

And yet, bewildering as such sentiments might seem to anyone caught up in the worldview of *Catch-22*, they nevertheless mainly account for the less than enthusiastic reception of the novel when it was first published in 1961. Having become embroiled in the debate over it then, I can testify that one of the reasons for this lack of enthusiasm was precisely the uneasiness caused by its portrayal of World War II.

This was to be expected. In 1961, there were very few people around who took a negative view of the war against Hitler and Nazism; or to state it more strongly, practically everyone thought it had been a just and necessary war and that we as a nation had every reason to be proud of our part in it. To be sure, admitting that they were denigrating *Catch-22* because they were offended by its "message" would have violated the literary canons of the day, according to which a work of art was supposed to be judged strictly on aesthetic grounds. Consequently, many of the early reviewers pounced instead on *Catch-22*'s literary weaknesses of structure and narrative. The *New York Times Book Review*, for example, gave it only a short notice on page 50 complaining of its "want of craft and sensibility."

What kept the novel from getting lost as a result of this largely dismissive reception was that a few critics sprang to its defense. I was one of them. But the line of argument we tended to follow did not focus on war in general or World War II in particular. Forgetting the critical rule that *Moby-Dick*, whatever symbolic meaning it may have, is first of all about the hunt for a whale, I even claimed that *Catch-22* was only "ostensibly" about an air-force squadron in World War II. Its real subject, I maintained, was the nature of American society in the mid-20th century.

Nor was I the only defender of *Catch-22* who advanced this interpretation. As participants in a nascent new radicalism, some of us took our cue from an essay by Heller's younger contemporary and fellow novelist Philip Roth, which lamented that this country sometimes seemed like a gigantic insane asylum that was virtually impossible for the writer of fiction to describe "and then make credible."[1] Heller's achievement, we argued, was that he had found a way to do just that. And that he should have done it through a portrayal of what was then almost universally regarded as America at its best—here was where World War II came in—rather than firing easy shots at the obvious shortcomings and faults of the country, seemed to us veritably heroic. This was why my own main criticism of Heller was not that he had defamed World War II but that, instead of carrying this breathtakingly brazen enterprise to its logical conclusion, he had suffered a loss of nerve at the end that did serious damage to the integrity of his novel as a satire.[2]

As all the world knows by now, the hero of *Catch-22* is a bombardier named Yossarian who is convinced that everyone is trying to kill him. This makes various people angry, especially his friend Clevinger, who is serving in the same squadron. Clevinger is a man who believes passionately in many principles and who is also a great patriot:

> "No one is trying to kill you," Clevinger said.
> "Then why are they shooting at me?" Yossarian asked.
> "They're shooting at everyone," Clevinger answered. "They're trying to kill everyone."
> "And what difference does that make?"

Clevinger and Yossarian are each certain that the other is crazy. In fact, so far as Yossarian is concerned, everyone is crazy who thinks that any sense can be made out of getting killed. When Yossarian is told that people are dying for their country, he retorts that as far as he can see, the only reason he has to fly more combat missions is that his commanding officer, Colonel Cathcart, wants to become a general. Colonel Cathcart is therefore his enemy just as surely as the German gunner shooting at him when he drops his bombs.

Everywhere, Yossarian reflects in contemplating the war,

men went mad and were rewarded with flying medals. Boys on every side of the bomb line were laying down their lives for what they had been told was their country, and no one seemed to mind, least of all the boys who were laying down their young lives.

But Yossarian minds so powerfully that he himself is carried to what might seem the point of madness. Not, however, in Heller's eyes. There is not the slightest doubt that he means us to regard Yossarian's paranoia (even though it extends to a nurse in the field hospital who dislikes him and to bus drivers everywhere, all of whom are trying to do him in) not as a disease but as a sensible response to real dangers. For example, we are shown that his diagnosis of Colonel Cathcart—and all the other senior officers whom he also dismisses as insane—is accurate. The madness lies not in him but in them and the system over which they preside.

This system is governed by "Catch-22," which contains many clauses. The most impressive we learn about when the flight surgeon Doc Daneeka explains to Yossarian why he cannot ground a crazy man, despite the fact that the rules require him to ground anyone who is crazy. The reason is that the crazy man must ask to be grounded, but as soon as he asks he can no longer be considered crazy—because, according to *Catch-22*, "a concern for one's own safety in the face of dangers that are real and immediate is the process of a rational mind."

Doc Daneeka's terror of death is almost as great as Yossarian's, and his attitude toward the world is correspondingly similar: "Oh I'm not complaining. I know there's a war on. I know a lot of people are going to suffer for us to win. But why must I be one of them?"

What is the war in *Catch-22* all about? For approximately the first three-quarters of this 442-page novel, the only answer anyone ever seems able to offer is that, in an armed conflict between nations, it is a noble thing to give your life for your own. This proposition Heller takes considerable pleasure in ridiculing.

"There are now 50 or 60 countries fighting in this war," an ancient Italian who has learned the arts of survival tells the idealistic and patriotic nineteen-year-old Lieutenant Nately. "Surely so many countries can't *all* be worth dying for." Nately is shocked by such cynicism and tries to argue, but the old man shakes his head wearily. "They're going to kill you if you don't watch out, and I can see now that you are not going to watch out." (As though to nail down his acceptance of the ancient Italian's perspective, Heller makes sure that this prophecy later comes true.) And in response to Nately's declaration that "it's better to die on one's feet than to live on one's knees," the old man tells him that the saying makes more sense if it is turned around to read, "It is better to *live* on one's feet than die on one's knees."

The interesting thing, as I noted at the time in my own review, is that until the novel begins winding down to its conclusion, there is scarcely a mention of Nazism and fascism as evils that might be worth fighting against, or of anything about America that might be worth fighting—never mind dying—for. If Heller had raised any of these considerations earlier, his point of view would have been put under more pressure and a greater degree of resistance than he actually allows it to encounter throughout most of the book.

That he was aware of this evasion becomes obvious from a dialogue between Yossarian and Major Danby ("a gentle, moral, middle-aged idealist") that takes place in the closing pages. Danby reminds Yossarian that the Cathcarts are not the whole story. "This is not World War I. You must never forget that we're at war with aggressors who would not let either one of us live if they won." To which Yossarian replies:

> I know that. . . . Christ, Danby, . . . I've flown 70 goddam combat missions. Don't talk to me about fighting to save my country. I've been fighting all along to save my country. Now I'm going to fight a little to save myself. . . . From now on I'm thinking only of me.

This statement comes as a great shock, since Heller had given the reader every reason to believe that Yossarian had been thinking only of himself *throughout* the novel. In fact, if we take seriously what this new Yossarian is saying, then the whole novel is trivialized. Its remorselessly uncompromising picture of the world, written under the aegis of the idea that survival is the overriding value and that all else is pretense, lying, cant, and hypocrisy, now becomes little more than the story of a mismanaged outfit and an attack on the people who (as Yossarian so incongruously puts it with a rhetoric not his own) always cash in "on every decent impulse and every human tragedy."

Catch-22, then, was not as heroic as it seemed at first sight. On closer examination, it became clear that Heller simply did not have the full courage of his own convictions—a courage that would have enabled him to go all the way with the premise that lay at the basis of his novel. When it came right down to it, he felt a great need to seek conventional moral cover, and could not bring himself to represent World War II itself as a fraud, having nothing whatever to do with ideals or principles.

Yet, for the aesthetic purposes of this novel, it would have been better if he *had* so represented it. For in shrinking from the ultimate implication of the vision adumbrated by *Catch-22*—the conviction that nothing on earth is worth dying for, especially not a country—he weakened the impact of his book. And when, suddenly and out of nowhere, he went on to endow Yossarian with a sense of honor in refusing to cooperate to his own advantage with the Cathcarts of this world, Heller also weakened the credibility of his protagonist.

None of this, however, seemed to bother any of *Catch-22*'s new crop of admirers, whose numbers swelled as the involvement of the United States in Vietnam escalated. It is easy to see why. Heller's novel played perfectly into the conviction of the radical movement of the 60's that this country, and its armed forces above all, were ruled by an "establishment" made up of madmen and criminals. Moreover, in identifying sanity with an unwillingness to serve the purposes of this insane society, Heller was also perfectly in tune with a doctrine that was being preached by most of the major gurus of the era, including writers like Allen Ginsberg and Ken Kesey, and psychiatrists like R. D. Laing. As Heller himself, speaking directly in his own voice, once put it in summarizing what he had been getting at in *Catch-22:* "Frankly, I think the whole society is nuts—and the question is: what does a sane man do in an insane society?"

But perhaps most important of all, *Catch-22* also justified draft evasion and even desertion as morally superior to military service. After all, if the hero of *Catch-22,* fighting in the best of all possible wars, was right to desert and run off to Sweden (as Yossarian does in the end), how much more justified were his Vietnam-era disciples in following the trail he had so prophetically blazed?

Unlike most of them, James Webb was actually in Vietnam when he read *Catch-22* in 1969. "From that lonely place of blood and misery and disease," he now recalls, "I found a soul mate who helped me face the next day and all the days and months that followed." Well, as one who served in the army but never saw combat, I have no desire—or any right—to begrudge a war hero like Webb the solace he derived from Heller. I can also imagine why and how, discovering *Catch-22* while fighting in so mismanaged a war as Vietnam, Webb could feel that deep was calling unto deep.

Even so, I fear that both this feeling and the solace *Catch-22* brought him were based on a sanitized misreading of the book's "message," which, as I hope has become obvious by now, has nothing whatsoever to do with the difference between soldiers and "politicians," or with the "apolitical" nature of battlefields. I also have to say that when a professional military man adopts so worshipful an attitude toward a book that is as nihilistic in its conception of war as *Catch-22,* a certain lack of self-respect is surely being exposed: should he not be defending his own when it comes under attack?

True, Webb happens to be a published author, with five novels under his belt, so this might be a case of one part of his own trumping the other, with the writer in him, not content with a fair share of respect, hogging the half that should rightly go to the soldier. Anyhow, where the failure of self-respect is concerned, Webb's encomium to *Catch-22* is as nothing compared to what happened at the Air Force Academy in Colorado Springs in 1986, on the occasion of the 25th anniversary of the novel's publication.

When I first heard back then that the Academy was planning a conference to celebrate this event, I thought it must surely be playing some kind of joke, to get even with Heller's cruel satire of its own branch of the service. But as it turned out, the only joke the Academy was playing was on itself, and on the profession it presumably exists to serve.

For *Catch-22* is perhaps even rougher on the air force (then a part of the army rather than the independent branch it later became) than it is on war. To stress it yet again, the air force as portrayed in this novel is an organization headed by idiots and lunatics like Colonel Cathcart who send countless young boys to their deaths for no reason—none whatsoever—other than the furthering of their own personal ambitions. Even more bizarre (and lest we forget about the evils of American capitalism), Heller gives us Milo Minderbinder, who, from his position as mess officer, runs a huge business in which the enemy has a share; from this enemy, Minderbinder actually accepts a contract to bomb his own outfit. And so it goes, up and down the chain of command.

It was to ponder and applaud the book in which this portrait is painted of their branch of the service that 900 future air-force officers were brought together for an entire weekend in 1986. In the course of that weekend, the cadets were also subjected to learned disquisitions from a troupe of literary scholars who repeatedly assured them—as did Heller himself, making a triumphal appearance, and relying on the prudential retreat he had executed from his true convictions at the end of the novel—that *Catch-22* was neither anti-military nor opposed to World War II.

Admittedly, the novel was not totally absolved of fault by the Air Force Academy. One member of its faculty criticized Heller's attitudes toward women as lacking in proper sympathy and respect.

Asked by a not unreasonably puzzled reporter why the Air Force Academy should have singled out *Catch-22*, of all books, for such reverential attention, the head of its English department explained that you "don't want dumb officers out there protecting your country." A dumb officer, it seems, was one who failed to understand that "the historical distinctions between good guy and bad guy" had been hopelessly blurred, and who had not yet learned that "the enemy is everywhere and nowhere."

By then I stood in a very different place from the one I had occupied in 1961; and from that place it struck me as an even greater lunacy than any Heller himself attributed to the air corps that a man with a head full of notions like this should have been entrusted with the education of young people who were being trained to lead their fellow good guys into battle against their country's enemies. But even more absurd and more disheartening were the cheers that greeted Heller's appearance at the celebration.

If the cadets were cheering him because they were fooled by his disingenuous interpretation of the novel as a "story of military bureaucracy run amok," then they were showing themselves incapable of recognizing a savage attack on everything they were supposed to stand for, even when it hit them smack in the face. If, on the other hand, the cadets were cheering because they understood what Heller was really saying, then they were endorsing a set of notions that made a mockery of their future profession: that love of country is a naive delusion, that the military is both evil and demented, and that for a soldier to desert is morally superior—more *honorable*—than to go on serving in the face of mortal danger.

Since 1986, the anti-military ethos of which *Catch-22* is the *locus classicus* for our time has grown weaker and less pervasive, and the original "mindset" about World War II, so sharply criticized by Webb, has returned with great force. Tom Brokaw of NBC has made a small fortune with a book hailing the men who fought that war as "the greatest generation" we have ever produced in this country (the very accolade formerly bestowed on the draft dodgers of the Vietnam era). Steven Spielberg's film, *Saving Private Ryan,* while stressing (as though in deference to what we might call the Heller version) the gruesomeness of the war, gives equal—well, almost equal—weight to the determination of the soldiers to do their duty and the heroism they sometimes exhibited in the course of it. And out of the Vietnam era itself has come Senator John McCain, whose wonderfully honorable behavior as a prisoner of war has made him a viable challenger to George W. Bush for the Republican presidential nomination and has attracted the admiration even of people who disagree with many of his policies.

Nevertheless, the influence of the Heller version lingers on in a gutted American military and in a culture that puts the avoidance of casualties above all other considerations. (How often have we been told that the only military engagements the American people will tolerate are those that do not result in the shipping-home of any "body bags"?) Of course, Heller cannot be given all the "credit" for this situation. But there is no denying that through the brilliance of his comic gifts, and the gusto and exuberance with which he deployed them, he made a mighty contribution to it. More specifically, he did as much as anyone to resurrect the pacifist ideas that had become prevalent after World War I and had then been discredited by World War II: that war is simply a means by which cynical people commit legalized murder in pursuit of power and profits; that patriotism is a fraud; and that nothing is worth dying for (this last sentiment, according to Nietzsche, being a mark of the slave).

I do not often agree with the novelist E. L. Doctorow, but I think he was entirely right in his comment upon learning of the death of his friend Joseph Heller:

> When *Catch-22* came out, people were saying, "Well, World War II wasn't like this." But when we got tangled up in Vietnam, it became a sort of text for the consciousness of that time. They say fiction can't change anything, but it can certainly organize a generation's consciousness.

The success of *Catch-22* in accomplishing this feat was undoubtedly a measure of its power as a work of art, about which I have never changed my mind (though not even when I joined in its defense in 1961–62 did I think its "greatness was beyond dispute" or that it "would live forever"). What I have come to question, however, is whether the literary achievement was worth the harm—the moral, spiritual, and intellectual harm—*Catch-22* has also undoubtedly managed to do, and to the "consciousness" of, by now, more generations than one.

Notes

1. "Writing American Fiction," *Commentary*, March 1961.

2. I wrote a long review of *Catch-22* soon after it was published, and another, much briefer piece on Heller in 1986. In what follows, I draw in part on both of them.

SANFORD PINSKER

Once More Into the Breach: Joseph Heller Gives Catch-22 a Second Act

F. Scott Fitzgerald famously observed that there are no "second acts" in American lives, and much the same thing can be said of most literary sequels. They are usually a risky business because such books call even more attention to the original work and thus are destined to suffer by comparison. Granted, there are exceptions—one thinks of John Updike's Rabbit tetralogy or Philip Roth's ongoing novels about Nathan Zuckerman—but most of the time an author ends up as Joseph Heller did when he tried to breathe a second life into *Catch-22* (1961) by reuniting the merry band of absurdist pranksters who had made his first novel such a commercial and critical success.

Closing Time (1994) not only reunites us with Yossarian, Milo Minderbinder, and Chaplain Tappman, but also adds figures drawn from Heller's Coney Island childhood: Sammy Singer, Lew and Claire Rabinowitz and a character named "Joey Heller." As their flesh is increasingly held hostage to the vagaries of old age, recurrent words such as "cancer" point simultaneously to the sorrow of individual conditions and to the larger forces of imperialism that suggest malignancy on a much wider scale. In theory, the realistic elements and their surrealistic counterparts ought to have fused, but in fact they do not make a good fit. Why so? Because Heller's darkly playful account of an elaborate wedding in the bowels of the Port Authority Bus Terminal (PABT) is both arbitrary and insisted upon. We don't believe it in the same

Topic: A Journal of the Liberal Arts, Volume 50 (2000): pp. 28–39. © 2000 *Topic.*

233

way that we "believe" in Lew and Sammy, Claire and "Joey." Taken together, memory proves more powerful, more likely to release Heller's writing at its best, than do his forays into the supernaturally zany. It is, after all, one thing to invoke George C. Tilyou as the emblematic Coney Island entrepreneur (he was the force behind Coney Island's legendary Steeplechase ride), and quite another to resurrect him from the grave so that he might interact with characters living (Lew) and long dead (J. P. Morgan, Henry Ford). Put a slightly different way: *Then* consumes Heller's imagination whether defined as growing up in the ethnic conclave of Coney Island or his days as a World War II bombardier. *Now*, by contrast, is consumed with a protracted waiting for the end as Heller's aging protagonists, to paraphrase Shakespeare, sit on the ground and tell the sad stories of their former lives. They are war veterans of a very specific sort, and as such, painfully aware that their reference points are not remembered, much less widely shared. As Sammy puts it in *Closing Time*'s opening paragraphs:

> When people our age speak of the war it is not of Vietnam but of the one that broke out more than half a century ago and swept in almost all the world. . . . Thank God for the atomic bomb, I rejoiced with the rest of the civilized Western world . . . when I read the banner newspaper headlines and learned it had exploded. By then I was already back and out, unharmed and, as an ex-GI much better off than before. I could go to college. I did go and even taught college for two years in Pennsylvania; then returned to New York and in a while found work as an advertising copywriter in the promotion department of *Time* magazine (11).

The biographical connections between Sammy and Heller are confirmed in *Now and Then*, Heller's memoir about the educational doors that the GI Bill opened, his stint as an English composition teacher at Penn State University, and the career change that had him pounding out ad copy for *Time*. At the same time, however, the tissue of correspondences is not enough to regard Sammy as indistinguishable from Heller. Sammy is, as it were, his own man, however much his essential attitudes often mirror those of Heller. What matters much more is that Heller's boyhood chums, real and imagined, represent a spectrum of adjustment to the dying of their individual lights. Sammy lives fourteen years suffering the ravages of Hodgkin's disease, just as Heller himself continues to battle against the residual weakness occasioned by his publicly chronicled bout with Guillain-Barré Syndrome. Disease, in short, is the tie that binds Heller's *alte kochers* (old farts) together. Unlike "the whole sick crew" who yo-yo their way through Thomas Pynchon's *V*, Heller's characters arc physically sick, quite apart from any metaphorical value their collective "sickness" might have. By contrast, it is the contemporary world, in its shameless greed and thorough-going corruption, that is sick in the ways that social satirists like Heller use the term.

Closing Time is largely rendered from the clear-eyed perspective of World War II veterans who, in other respects, have increasing difficulty reading the fine print of contracts or *TV Guide* codings. Sammy Rabinowitz speaks for them all when be muses, with painful specificity, about the toll that time takes. In twenty more years,

> we will all look pretty bad in the newspaper pictures and television clips, kind of strange, like people in a different world, ancient and doddering, balding, seeming perhaps a little bit idiotic, shrunken, with toothless smiles in collapsed, wrinkled cheeks. People I knew are already dying and others I've known are already dead. We don't look that beautiful now. We wear glasses and are growing hard of hearing, we sometimes talk too much, repeat ourselves, things grow on us, even the most minor bruises take longer to heal and leave telltale traces.
>
> And soon after that there will be no more of us left. (13)

Heller's title points directly to this obsession with the cumulative effects of what poet Andrew Marvell called "Time's winged chariot drawing near"— but without allowing Sammy to make such analogies himself. That role is largely assigned to John Yossarian, the cock-eyed optimist who waged his comic war against the powers that be, and kill, in *Catch-22*, and who now has made a separate peace (of sorts) with Milo Minderbinder. At the same time, Yossarian's first appearance in *Closing Time* is a conspicuous echo of the hospital scene that first endeared him to Heller's readers:

> In the middle of his second week in the hospital, Yossarian dreamed of his mother, and he knew again that he was going to die. The doctors were upset when he gave them the news.
>
> "We can't find anything wrong," they told him.
>
> "Keep looking," he instructed.
>
> "You're in perfect health."
>
> "Just wait." (19)

The banter has Heller's thumbprint all over it, just as its ominous foreshadowings suggest that Yossarian is headed for yet another a peck of problems. Hospitals remain what they have always been in Heller's fiction—temporary respites from the world and places where floating anxiety can operate at full throttle; but in this case, the nervous energy speaks directly to the Heller

who is a world-class hypochondriac and who, following his divorce, set up
bachelor digs on West End Avenue:

> Yossarian was back in the hospital for observation, having retreated
> there once more beneath another neurotic barrage of confusing
> physical symptoms to which he had become increasingly susceptible
> since finding himself dwelling alone again for just the second time
> in his life, and which seemed, one by one, to dissipate like vapor
> as soon as he described or was tested for each. Just a few months
> before, he had cured himself of an incurable case of sciatica merely
> by telephoning one of his physicians to complain of his incurable
> case of sciatica. He could not learn to live alone. He could not make
> a bed. He would rather starve than cook. (19)

At one point in *Now and Then*, Heller's memoir of those times, those places,
he confesses that "All my life it's been . . . much easier to let other people
attend to all such duties [e.g., packing a suitcase] for me" (105)—and that
he and Yossarian are, in certain respects, mirror images of one another: "I
say of a character, Yossarian, that he couldn't learn to make a bed and would
sooner starve than cook. *That* is autobiography" (105).

If one thinks of these reflections of Heller as fun house mirrors, able to
encompass aspects of Sammy Singer as well as those of little Joey Heller, the
result is a more akin to self-composite than to autobiography. What, then,
should readers do (if anything) to keep the various incarnations of Heller
straight? Just as the novel's overall structure splits himself into a realistic half
and a more fantasy driven counterpart (thus suggesting. among other things,
the composition of the human brain), so too does Heller divide aspects of
his personality among several characters. Like the name "Michael," Heller's
all-purpose, nearly omnipresent moniker for children of a younger generation, what may matter is that it does *not* matter. Call him Sammy, call him
Yossarian, call him Ishmael—the important thing is that Heller is out to
play his end game on two nearly simultaneous fronts: the first is memory,
warmly evocative and filled with gritty realism; and the second is wilder,
more given to the odd contours of dream. When these dimensions collide,
or nearly collide—as in the scene when Chaplain Tappman and George C.
Tilyou brush very close to one another—the result is a fusion that suggests
a model of the human mind

Closing Time is experimental enough to provoke a wide range of critical speculation about its narrative structure and literary devices. About
some matters, however, there is firmer ground for agreement. For example,
Heller insists that he knows where a novel is going when he gets a precise
opening sentence locked in his head. That has been the case, he tells us,

with each of his novels, and *Closing Time* is no exception. It had to begin with Sammy's voice (rather than, say, with Yossarian's); just as the novel's symmetry demands that we circle back to him at the end. Also, because Yossarian is the narrative cement that binds disparate aspects of the novel together, he is the character who usually introduces the literary allusions that will haunt the novel's final apocalyptic pages. For the last twenty-five years Yossarian has been working for Milo Minderbinder (talk about how far the formerly idealistic have fallen!), well aware that "surplus stale commodities like old chocolate and vintage Egyptian cotton" (19) no longer make Milo's heart beat faster. Now, he has a fabulous killing machine of an airplane to peddle to the highest bidder—regardless of creed or national origin. The man who turned World War II into a giant Ponzi scheme is back in the free enterprise saddle once again, and with considerably larger fish to fry. Yossarian is no longer the outraged innocent he once was not only because he has come to the realization that people are *always* out to kill other people (including him), but also because he has learned how to go along to get along. Still, he worries about death-and-dying in ways that are simultaneously addressed to the larger world and privately pitched to the local habitation of himself.

> The vision of the morbid vision he had experienced was of a seizure or a stroke and had set him reminiscing again about durable old Gustav Ashenbach alone on his mythical strand of Mediterranean beach and his immortal death in Venice, worn out at fifty in a city with a plague nobody wished to talk about. In Naples far back, when assembled in line for the troopship sailing him home after he'd flown seventy missions and survived, he'd found himself behind and older soldier named Schweik and a man born Krautheimer who had changed his name to Joseph Kaye to blend more securely into his culture, and his name, like Schweik's, had meant not much to him then. (20)

Unlike the playful allusions to Jaroslav Hasek's *The Good Soldier Svejk and his Fortunes in the World War,* a novel often compared with *Catch-22,* and the insider jokes about Franz Kafka's angst-ridden Joseph K, Thomas Mann's *Death in Venice* will become an integral part of *Closing Time*'s death-haunted vision. Again, individual dying is amplified by the death of culture, and ultimately, by the teasing possibility of the death of *everything.*

Meanwhile, Yossarian dutifully swallows "baby aspirin," a detail meant to suggest his deeply regressive tendencies, and muses about the bad pickle the world is going through. His screed might have been lifted wholesale from similar outbursts in *Picture This*:

Another oil tanker had broken up. There was radiation. Garbage. Pesticides, toxic waste, and free enterprise. There were enemies of abortion who wished to inflict the death penalty on everyone who was not pro-life. There was mediocrity in government, and self-interest, too. There was trouble in Israel. These were not mere delusions. He was not making them up. Soon they would be cloning human embryos for sale, fun, and replacement parts. Men earned millions producing nothing more substantial than changes in ownership. The cold war was over and there was still no peace. Nothing made sense and neither did everything else. People did things without knowing why and then tried to find out. (20)

This is Heller talking, or to be more precise, Heller *railing*.

He is hardly alone in his sour assessments. Among contemporary novelists of a certain age and temperament, unpacking one's cultural griefs has an appeal too delicious to resist. What John Updike, Philip Roth, the late Stanley Elkin, Mordecai Richler, and Joseph Heller have in common—other, that is, than their breathtaking talent and deservedly wide reputations—is a bad case of cultural crankiness. At bottom they believe that History will end when they do—and the process of decline-and-fall is apparent to anyone with eyes to see. The condition afflicts many, writers and non-writers alike, in what is charitably called "late middle age." The difference is that gifted writers do more than whine about an age which has passed them by. Instead, they *rant*, and perhaps more important, chart in vivid detail what has happened since their respective paradises were lost. Everything that was once spontaneous and natured, uncomplicated and simple, has turned pinch-faced, mean-spirited, and politically correct.

Put a slightly different way, the vagaries of contemporary culture are fat softballs served up to world-class hitters. Small wonder that Roth's Mickey Sabbath or Updike's aging Rabbit Angstom, become characters we love to hate. They just don't give a fig about niceties, nor will they swallow their collective tongues when solemn folks tsk-tsk them for swilling single-malt scotch, puffing away on overpriced cigars, wife-cheating, or cracking off-color, socially offensive jokes. They have sweaters older than their critics.

With a snip here, a tuck there, I have just described the general tendencies you will find in a good deal of fiction by what I call "the old farts' club," but I have also captured a good many of the specifics that, taken together, add up to the outrageous John Yossarian of *Closing Time*. Poked and prodded by medical specialists, Yossarian is declared to be a "perfect human being":

There was champion cardiologist who found no fault with him, a pathologist for his pathos, who found no cause for concern either, an enterprising gastroenterologist who ran back to the room for a second opinion from Yossarian on some creative investment strategies he was considering in Arizona real estate, and a psychologist for his psyche, in whom Yossarian was left in the last resort to confide. (23)

After all, Yossarian insists, he is no longer interested in current events (I wish the daily newspapers were smaller and came out weekly" [23]), and he no longer laughs at the jokes comedians crack: "what about these periodic periods of anomie and fatigue and disinterest and depression?" he wonders. His perspective is simultaneously shared and widened by cronies like Lew Rabinowitz and Sammy Singer. For example, Lew adds the experience of the Dresden firebombing to Yossarian's close encounter with death when he ripped open Snowden's flight jacket and learned that "man was garbage." The difference is that Lew goes down laughing while Yossatian largely remains the same study in neurotic comic contradiction that he was in *Catch-22*. Interchanges such as the following between Yossarian and Milo Minderbinder's son, M2, suggest that conversation remains the same slippery slope it was when Heller first concocted his brand of absurdist dialogue:

> [M2] "Will Michael [Yossarian's son] come with me?"
> [Yossarian] "If you pay him for the day. Are things all right?"
> [M2] "Wouldn't I want to tell you if they were?"
> [Yossatian] "But would you tell me?"
> [M2] "That would depend."
> [Yossarian] "On what?"
> [M2] "If I could tell you the truth."
> [Yossarian] "Would you tell me the truth?"
> [M2] "Do I know what it is?"
> [Yossarian] "Could you tell me a lie?"
> [M2] "Only if I knew the truth."
> [Yossarian] "You're being honest with me."
> [M2] "My father wants that." (57)

If *Catch-22* demonstrates anything, it is that language is power, and that those who control the ebb and flow of words have dominion over life and death. In *Catch-22*, the power brokers were officers; in *Closing Time* they are either politicians (Heller's sophomoric insistence that the President be dubbed The Big Prick is only one example of his contempt for life inside the Washington, D.C. Beltway) or the top bananas of conglomerates.

Consider, for example, the following "catches" that wrap themselves around the ironically named Freedom of Information Act: "The Freedom of

Information Act, the chaplain [Tappman] explained, was a federal regulation, obliging government agencies to release all information they had to anyone who made application for it, except information they had that they did not want to release" (61). The echoes to "catch-22," with its labyrinthine justifications to keep aviators flying ever move missions, are obvious; but should some readers miss the point, Heller adds a paragraph that recalls Yossarian's days as a playful, subversive censor of enlisted men's mail:

> Hundreds of thousands of pages each week went out regularly to applicants with everything blacked out on them but punctuation marks, prepositions, and conjunctions. It was a good catch, Yossarian judged expertly, because the government did not have to release any information about the information they those not to release, and it was impossible to know if anyone was complying with the liberalizing federal law called the Freedom of Information Act. (61)

If *Closing Time* included more passages of this sort, the term "sequel" might have made sense and the resulting novel might have enjoyed greater sales. But to his credit, Heller had larger ambitions. The result is that snippets of *Catch-22*'s linguistic anarchy are sprinkled through the book as nostalgic reminders, while the novel itself moves in quite other directions.

Unfortunately, what Heller gains by widening his canvas he loses in terms of coherence. The nether world hidden in the bowels of the Port Authority bus terminal works not only against the novel's structural grain, but also against its meaning. As one character puts it, "You sound so bitter these days. You used to be funnier." She might well have been speaking about Heller himself, as he revisits the book that established his credentials as a literary comedian and then strains to transcend them. David M. Craig's *Tilting at Morality* is a valuable study of the various ways that Heller gives narrative shaping to the defeats lurking around the edges of every victory or the ways that language emerges as its own laughingstock. How one decides to tell a tale is, for Craig, at least as important as the saga itself. With *Closing Time*, Heller employs an omniscient narrator who knows his world as intimately as did the narrators of novels by Charles Dickens. Thus, Heller's narrator

> guides the readers through the secret corridors of MASSPOB (Military Affairs Special Secrets Project Office Building) power and into the labyrinthine Port Authority sub-basement rather than through dilapidated London streets like Tom-all-Alone's or into Lady Dedlock's boudoir at Chesney Wold. But, like a Dickens narrator, the narrator of *Closing Time* insists that everything is connected: the Time-Life Building and the Port Authority sub-

basements; the Pentagon (Heller's MASSPOB) and Kenosha, Wisconsin; the Coney Island on which Lew, Sammy, and Heller grew up and its infernoesque re-creation; the Port Authority Bus Terminal (PABT) homeless and Yossarian. The entire society is as interconnected as M&M Enterprises was in the famous coals-to-Newcastle section of *Catch-22*, in which Milo's syndicate spreads out to cover the globe. (Craig 231)

Insofar as every detail, symbolic or otherwise, in *Closing Time* seems to point toward the novel's apocalyptic conclusion, Craig has a point; but his extended bow toward Dickens does not convince, nor does his insistence that the novel's overly complicated plotting finally holds together. What we get, instead, are moments worth savoring for their satiric value and absurdist charm, and characters who derive their particular strengths from being rendered as one-dimensional. Take, for example, the scenes that revolve around Milo and his latest scam, "A Sub-Supersonic Invisible and Noiseless Defensive Second-Strike Offensive Attack Bomber" (or *Shhhhh*, for short):

> "We can give you a plane," promised Wintergreen [now one of Milo's underlings] "that *will* do it [i.e., bomb a target] yesterday."
> "Shhhhh!" Milo said.
> "The Shhhhh?" said the expert on military nomenclature. "That's a perfect name for a noiseless bomber"
> "Then the Shhhhh! is the name of our plane. It goes faster than sound."
> "It goes faster than light."
> "You can bomb someone before you even decide to do it. Decide it today, it's done yesterday." (249)

Reading such passages one is much more likely to think of Lewis Carroll's "Wonderland" than of the Dickensian novel. Thus, when a Pentagon king-pin wonders if this newfangled plane could "destroy the world," Milo is forced to admit that, alas, it cannot: "We can make it uninhabitable, but we can't destroy it." Good enough—or as one high officer puts it, "I can live with that!"

Ethical matters aside (and Heller remains convinced that morality is not and never was, much of a consideration in hatching up Big Deals), there's money to be made in promoting a bomber that can't be seen or heard, and that flies so fast that it can (presumably) bomb targets yesterday—even if Milo knows that none of the surrealistic claims are true. But in a context where Dr. Strangelove, meant to echo the madman in Stanley Kubrick's film of the same name, is pushing the virtues of his B-Ware bomber, *Shhhhh* makes as much sense as anything else. What matters, of course, is how the funding it generates will be split: the Air Force procurement people will want to get their usual cut; no doubt certain politicians will insist that their palms be greased; and Milo's empire will, once again, increase-and-multiply.

In *Catch-22*, "military intelligence" turns out to be a contradiction in terms, and Heller has lost none of his animus—or for that matter, his self-righteousness—when such themes are reprised in *Closing Time*. Things have worsened considerably. Here, the sadly funny story of Chaplain Tappman and the "heavy water" he now urinates raises the ante that formerly got him into hot water. He is a human resource for tritium, an essential ingredient in nuclear weaponry: it took two people to lift an eyedropper of Tappman's urine, and he produced it at the rate of several quarts a day. Small wonder that he is spirited away to Wisconsin so that for-your-eyes-only people can watch over him. Rather like the arguments between Yossarian and Sammy about whether the proper term is "nauseous," or "nauseated," what such moments come to are running gags—repetitions that keep circling around themselves. In this regard, Yossarian gives as good as he gets. More important, however, is his observation that what he can never quite trust about "high comedy . . . is that people say funny things, and the others don't laugh. They don't even know they are part of the comedy." The description surely fits those in *Catch-22* who wear clichés as if they were body armor, or earnest fools such as Clevinger who die before they understand that the joke is on them. That beat, widened considerably, goes on in *Closing Time*.

The result is a novel made up of several "novels," each presumably resting in the narrative framework of the others. However, rather than a set of neatly inter-fitting Chinese boxes or Russian dolls, *Closing Time* cannot quite pull its varied threads into a coherent whole. What moves us are Heller's vivid memories of Coney Island and the boyhood friends now dying off one by one. Here, the sorrow is palpable enough for us to touch it, and this is especially true in the case of Lew and Claire Rabinowitz. Cancer always lurks around the edges, not only in the form of Hodgkin's disease, but also as an indicator of our malignant times. Heller, to his credit, does not make the connection explicit because doing so would confuse the stridency of propaganda with the subtlety of art.

The same, alas, can not be said of *Closing Time*'s surrealistic excesses. For example, the elaborate (and elaborately described) wedding planned for the PABT recalls the parties that Jay Gatsby hosted at his Long Island mansion, but now with the homeless and those who revel in "homeless chic" rubbing elbows. At that point, anything can go, and does: Wagnerian opera, computer games (e.g., Triage) that presumably have started World War III; references to Leverkuhn's *Apocalypse*. Heller has given us dips in Dantesque waters before (one thinks of his dark descriptions of Rome, the "eternal city," in the final pages of *Catch-22*), but these sections of *Closing Time* pile too much fantasy into too wide a space. Let me hasten to add that this is *not* a matter of narrative credibility, as if we are asked to "believe" that dead people walk around in a world forty miles beneath the surface; rather it is a question of proportion, of artfully balancing the novel's human portraiture with its inclination to make final statements as the world itself goes down. One indicator of advancing age, I am told, is a tendency to think that history itself will end when you do. With *Closing Time,* Heller greatly expands both the world and the formula he used to successfully indict the darkly comic faces of *Catch-22*. *Closing Time* means to be even darker in its sequel-continuation, but this is a case in which the single oft-repeated note of *Catch-22*, which forces its characters—and us—to "see everything twice" gradually unfastens from its moorings and becomes something approaching *pure* fantasy. Unfortunately, purity of the sort that my adjective implies works against the grain of the nuancing that art requires. In addition, one begins to wonder if such a wide, ambitious canvas allows Heller to be more self-indulgent than he might have been.

True enough, excess has always been Heller's asset, and also his liability. *Closing Time* received respectful (though greatly qualified) reviews, but it did not fill the large shoes of its predecessor. Part of the reason is that Heller's vision of an absurdist world had been incorporated into the population at large; another part is that he found himself straining to find ways of taking the old absurdities to ever-new heights. Milo Minderbinder's entanglements with weapons procurement ought to have done it for him but with the exceptions of isolated scenes, it didn't. On a much lower level, even keeping the novel's various "Michaels" straight (every son, it seems, bears that moniker) became a reader-unfriendly chore, and the difficulties only deepened as Heller pulls out all the narrative stops. Add a character such as Angela Morecock and one quickly concluded that *Closing Time* was the sort of novel that an unrepentant sophomore might write.

Still, what works to perfection in *Closing Time* are the memories of growing up in Coney Island. Heller would return to them in *Now and Then,* a memoir as vivid in many ways as it is disappointing in others. Meanwhile, the long shadow that *Caich-22* cast over his subsequent work became a problem Heller could only write about but not lick.

Works Cited

Craig, David M., *Tilting at Morality: Narrative Strategies in Joseph Heller's Fiction.* Detroit: Wayne State University Press, 1997.

Heller, Joseph. *Closing Time.* New York: Simon and Schuster, 1994.

———. *Now and Then: From Coney Island to Here.* New York: Knopf, 1998.

MICHAEL C. SCOGGINS

Joseph Heller's Combat Experiences in Catch-22

In the forty-one years since the initial publication of *Catch-22*, Joseph Heller's best-selling 1961 novel about World War II, the book has been a favorite subject for analysis and commentary, and an enormous body of literary criticism on the work has been published. There have been numerous essays on the novel's structure, its debt to other works of literature, its humor and logic, its moral and ethical values, and its religious themes and mythical overtones (Nagel 4). However, Heller's treatment of the war itself has received scant attention by most critics. A few writers have compared *Catch-22* to other war novels, especially the novels of Ernest Hemingway (Nolan 77–81; Aubrey 1–5), and David M. Craig has written two essays for *War, Literature and the Arts* demonstrating how *Catch-22* incorporated some of Heller's own combat experiences (Craig "Revisited," 33–41; Craig "Avignon," 27–54). But the majority of Heller's critics have taken the stance that *Catch-22* has very little to do with World War II and is in fact not a war novel at all (Kiley and McDonald v; Merrill *Joseph Heller*, 11). Heller himself consistently minimized the war's influence on the novel in many of his statements and interviews. For instance, in a 1970 speech in New York City, he told his audience that " *Catch-22* is not really about World War II" (Heller "Translating," 357), and in a 1975 interview he reiterated those sentiments: "As I've said, *Catch-22* wasn't really *about* World War Two. It was really

War, Literature & the Arts, 15:1-2 (2003): pp. 213–227. © 2003 *War, Literature & the Arts.*

about American society during the Cold War, during the Korean War, and about the possibility of a Vietnam" (Merrill "Interview," 68).

Thus it is not surprising to find that very few critics have actually studied the characters and plot elements in *Catch-22* that Heller borrowed from his own experiences as an Army Air Force bombardier. In this essay I will demonstrate that Heller's military career played a much greater role in the concept and structure of *Catch-22* than most critics have ever suspected. Many of the characters and incidents in *Catch-22* were in fact drawn directly from Heller's tour of duty, and were simply modified or exaggerated for dramatic effect. Heller's interviews and reminiscences about the novel, as well as secondary sources like the unit histories of Heller's squadron and bomb group, provide a wealth of such examples. In the same speech quoted above, Heller gave a rare confirmation of this influence: "I would say all the physical details, and almost all of what might be called the realistic details do come out of my own experiences as a bombardier in World War II. The organization of a mission, the targets—most of the missions that are in the book were missions that I did fly on" ("Translating" 356). Heller's untimely death in 1999 has now silenced his voice, and like so many of our World War II veterans, he is no longer around tell his stories. However, we still have his novels, essays and interviews, and with these tools I hope to bring some of those stories back to life.

In the introduction to *Catch-22* Heller states, "The island of Pianosa lies in the Mediterranean Sea eight miles south of Elba. It is very small and obviously could not accommodate all of the actions described. Like the setting of this novel, the characters, too, are fictitious" (6). As we shall see, both the setting and the characters of *Catch-22* are less fictitious than Heller led us to believe in 1961. Pianosa is a real island, situated between the larger islands of Corsica and Elba in the Ligurian Sea off the northwest coast of Italy. In the novel, Pianosa is the base for the fictional 256th Bombardment Squadron of the fictional 27th Air Force. The year is 1944, and the 256th Squadron is flying North American B-25 "Mitchell" twin-engined bombers on tactical missions in support of Allied operations in northern Italy and southern France. One of the men attached to this squadron is the novel's hero, Lieutenant (later Captain) John Yossarian, an "Assyrian-American" bombardier who has been flying combat missions since late 1943; by the time the novel ends in December 1944, he has logged a total of seventy-one missions (Craig 44–45; Burhans 45–47). Heller admitted in later years that the name "Yossarian" was derived from the name of one of his Air Force buddies, Francis Yohannon, but that the character of Yossarian himself was "the incarnation of a wish" (*Now and Then* 175–176). Although there are some minor inconsistencies, the internal chronology of *Catch-22* is detailed and coherent enough that Clinton Burhans Jr. was able to create a timeline of Yossarian's entire military career, from his enlistment in 1941 until his desertion from his squadron in December 1944 (Burhans 45–47). This timeline bears a remarkable similarity to Heller's own Air Force career as revealed in various published and unpublished sources.

Joseph Heller was a nineteen-year-old Jewish-American from Brooklyn, New York when he enlisted in the US Army Air Corps in 1942; his three years of military service included a tour of duty as a wing bombardier in the Mediterranean theater of operations. From early May 1944 until December 1944, he was stationed on the island of Corsica where he flew sixty combat missions in B-25 "Mitchell" bombers with the 488th Bombardment Squadron, 340th Bombardment Group, 57th Bombardment Wing, 12th Air Force (*Now and Then* 165–185; Ruderman 16–17; *History of the 57th Bomb Wing*). Like Yossarian's fictional 27th Air Force, the real 12th Air Force was engaged in flying tactical support missions over northern Italy and southern France. After Heller completed his required quota of missions, the Air Force rotated him back to the States under the point system in December 1944. "After short service as a public relations officer in San Angelo, Texas, Heller was discharged from the air force as a first lieutenant, with an Air Medal and a Presidential Unit Citation" (Ruderman 16).

While most *Catch-22* readers will remember Captain John Yossarian as a man who is deathly afraid of being killed and who wants out of combat at all costs, it is clear that at the beginning of the war he was as patriotic as anyone else. This patriotism is apparent in a conversation Yossarian has with Major Danby, the group operations officer, near the end of the novel:

> "I mean it, Yossarian. This is not World War One. You must never forget that we're at war with aggressors who would not let either of us live if they won."
>
> "I know that," Yossarian replied tersely, with a sudden surge of scowling annoyance. "Christ, Danby, I earned that medal I got, no matter what their reasons were for giving it to me. I've flown seventy goddamn combat missions. Don't talk to me about fighting to save my country. I've been fighting all along to save my country. Now I'm going to fight a little to save myself. The country's not in danger any more, but I am." (455)

In his 1975 interview, Heller revealed his own feelings at the beginning of the war. "I actually *hoped* I would get into combat," he related. "I was just 19 and there were a great many movies being made about the war; it all seemed so dramatic and heroic. . . . I saw it as a war of necessity. Everybody did. . . . Pearl Harbor united this country in a strong and wholesome and healthy way" (Merrill "Interview," 60). Later in the same interview, he reaffirmed his belief that World War II was a necessary war. "It offended some people, during the Vietnam war, that I had not written a truly pacifist book," he told Merrill. "But I am not a true pacifist. World War Two was necessary at least to the extent that we were fighting for the survival of millions of people" (64). Heller also made it clear that Yossarian's views about the war were not his own: "Yossarian's emotions, Yossarian's reaction to the war in the squadron were not those I experienced when I was overseas" (Heller "Translating," 357).

During the course of the novel, two important catalysts are responsible for changing Yossarian's attitude towards flying combat. The first is the continually increasing number of missions that the men are required to fly. When Yossarian first arrives in Europe, the airmen are required to complete only twenty-five missions before being rotated home. In order to impress his superiors, the fanatical group commander, Colonel Cathcart, raises the number of missions from twenty-five to thirty, and he continues to increase the number in increments of five, until by the end of the novel the men are required to fly eighty missions before they can go home (Burhans 45–47; *Catch-22* 383–384). Yossarian becomes increasingly frustrated and despondent because, each time he gets close to his maximum, Cathcart raises the number again, so his chances of survival become smaller and smaller. When Yossarian reaches fifty-one missions, Cathcart raises the number to fifty-five, and Yossarian decides to take a stand and absolutely refuse to fly any more. He visits the group medical officer, Doc Daneeka, hoping to be grounded for medical reasons. "Why don't you at least finish the fifty-five before you take a stand?" Doc Daneeka advises. "With all your bitching, you've never finished a tour of duty even once." "How the hell can I?" Yossarian asks. "The colonel keeps raising them every time I get close" (180).

The number of missions required of the aircrews in *Catch-22* is an accurate reflection of the reality of the war in southern Europe. In northern Europe, the crews of the 8th Air Force's B-17 and B-24 heavy strategic bombers flew deep into Germany and were often in the air for eight to ten hours at a time. Until long-range escort fighters like the P-51 "Mustang" became available late in the war, they suffered terrible losses from German fighters and antiaircraft fire. As a consequence, for most of the war the B-17 and B-24 crews were required to fly only twenty-five missions before being rotated home (Freeman 29–32). In comparison, the shorter range B-25s in southern Europe flew missions lasting for only a few hours, and they often flew several missions per day *(Now and Then* 185–186). As Heller noted in his autobiography, his quota was raised several times during his own tour. When he arrived in Corsica in early 1944, the number of missions for his group was up to fifty, and during his tour it went from fifty to fifty-five, and then to sixty.

By the time he was taken off combat status, the number of required missions had reached seventy (185).

By late 1944 the German Air Force, or Luftwaffe, was no longer a threat over southern Europe, and German fighters no longer blasted American bombers out of the skies by the dozens as they had done earlier in the war. However, antiaircraft fire, or "flak" as it was popularly called, was still a danger; and one target where flak was a particular problem was Avignon in southern France. It is over Avignon that Yossarian experiences the other catalytic moment in his tour of duty, an episode that absolutely terrifies him and that makes him realize he might not survive the war after all (Craig 28–29). This mission over Avignon is referred to in ever increasing detail throughout the novel, as Heller gradually reveals more and more about the experience until, near the end of the novel, we finally come to understand just what it is that drives Yossarian to feel the way he does.

Yossarian's pilot on the Avignon mission is Lieutenant Huple. Although Huple is a good pilot, he is also a fifteen-year-old kid who has enlisted illegally—a fact that does not exactly inspire confidence among his fellow airmen. The copilot is Yossarian's friend Dobbs, and in the rear of the plane is a young radio operator/turret gunner named Snowden. Early in the novel Heller tells us that "Snowden had been killed over Avignon when Dobbs went crazy in mid-air and seized the controls away from Huple" (36). Later, we learn more about this mission "when Dobbs went crazy in mid-air and began weeping pathetically for help":

> "Help him, help him," Dobbs sobbed. "Help him, help him."
>
> "Help who? Help who?" called back Yossarian, once he had plugged his headset back into the intercom system, after it had been jerked out when Dobbs wrested the controls away from Huple and hurled them all down suddenly into the deafening, paralyzing, horrifying dive which had plastered Yossarian helplessly to the ceiling of the plane by the top of his head and from which Huple had rescued them just in time by seizing the controls back from Dobbs and leveling the ship out almost as suddenly right back in the middle of the buffeting layer of cacophonous flak from which they had escaped successfully only a moment before. *Oh, God! Oh, God, Oh God,* Yossarian had been pleading wordlessly as he dangled from the ceiling on the nose of the ship by the top of his head, unable to move.
>
> "The bombardier, the bombardier," Dobbs answered in a cry when Yossarian spoke. "He doesn't answer, he doesn't answer. Help the bombardier, help the bombardier."
>
> "I'm the bombardier," Yossarian cried back at him. "I'm the

bombardier. I'm all right. I'm all right."

"Then help him, help him," Dobbs begged. "Help him, help him." (51–52)

About midway through the novel, Heller gives us some more details, telling us that the Avignon mission "was the mission on which Yossarian lost his nerve" (230). After several subsequent references to "Snowden's secret," which serve to build up the reader's suspense and anticipation, Heller finally gives us the rest of the story, and we find out the true nature of this "secret." After Huple regains control of the aircraft, Yossarian crawls to the back of the plane to check on the wounded gunner. Snowden is lying in the back of the aircraft with a large gash in one of his thighs, caused by a piece of flak that tore through the side of the plane and cut into his leg. Behind him, the tail gunner is on the floor in a "dead faint," having passed out from the shock of seeing Snowden's wound. Yossarian treats the wound as best he can with a first-aid kit and tries to reassure the wounded gunner, who keeps complaining, "I'm cold, I'm cold." When Yossarian opens up Snowden's flak suit to look for another wound, Snowden's "secret" becomes apparent: a second piece of flak has torn into Snowden's body from the other side, and as Yossarian unzips his suit, Snowden's intestines spill out onto the floor of the aircraft in a "soggy pile" (449–450).

As Heller was to reveal in later interviews and his autobiography, this incident was a synthesis of several of his own combat experiences. Heller actually flew two missions to Avignon to bomb railroad bridges over the Rhône River in support of the Allied invasion of southern France, and both missions made a lasting impression on him. His initial mission to Avignon occurred on 8 August 1944, and it was on this mission that he first saw one of his comrades shot down by flak (Heller "Chronology," 1; Heller "*Catch-22* Revisited," 56; Craig 29). "I was in the leading flight," Heller recalled, "and when I looked back to see how the others were doing, I saw one plane pulling up above and away from the others, a wing on fire beneath a tremendous, soaring plume of orange flame. I saw a parachute billow open, then another, then one more before the plane began spiraling downward, and that was all." Two men, the pilot and copilot, did not escape from the aircraft, and both were friends of Heller's (*Now and Then* 181–182).

But it was Heller's second mission over Avignon, on 15 August 1944, that provided most of the details for the Snowden incident in *Catch-22*. For both Yossarian and Heller, it was their thirty-seventh mission (Craig 29). As the B-25s approached the target, the German antiaircraft fire was once again accurate and deadly. As his squadron began its bomb run, a B-25 in another squadron was hit by flak and one of its wings broke off. The plane nosed over and plunged to earth, and none of the crew escaped. Two other planes also went down during the mission, again with no survivors. Heller's squadron dropped their bombs and then quickly banked up and away from the target (*Now and Then* 179; "Revisited" 330). He describes what happened next in *Now and Then:*

> And then the bottom of the plane just seemed to drop out: we were falling, and I found myself pinned helplessly to the top of the bombardier's compartment, with my flak helmet squeezed against the ceiling. What I did not know (it was reconstructed for me later) was that one of the two men at the controls, the copilot, gripped by the sudden fear that our plane was about to stall, seized the controls to push them forward and plunged us into a sharp descent, a dive, that brought us back down into the level of the flak.
>
> I had no power to move, not even a finger. And I believed with all my heart and quaking soul that my life was ending and that we were going down, like the plane on fire I had witnessed plummeting only a few minutes before. I had no time for anything but terror. And then just as suddenly—I think I would have screamed had I been able to—we leveled out and began to climb away again from the flak bursts, and now I was flattened against the floor, trying frantically to grasp something to hold on to when there was nothing. And in another few seconds we were clear and edging back into formation with the rest of the planes. But as I regained my balance and my ability to move, I heard in the ears of my headphones the most unnatural and sinister of sounds: silence, dead silence. And I was petrified again. Then I recognized, dangling loosely before me, the jack to my headset. It had been torn free from the outlet. When I plugged myself back in, a shrill bedlam of voices was clamoring in my ears, with a wail over all the rest repeating on the intercom that the bombardier wasn't answering. "The bombardier doesn't answer!" "I'm the bombardier," I broke in immediately. "And I'm all right." "Then go back and help him, help the gunner. He's hurt." (179–180)

Heller made his way to the rear of the airplane and found the radio gunner lying on the floor with a large oval wound in his thigh; a piece of flak had punched through the side of the plane and torn open the gunner's leg, just as recounted in *Catch-22*. Fighting down his own nausea at the sight of the wound, Heller poured sulfa powder into the cut, bandaged it and gave the gunner a shot of morphine. When the young man began to complain of feeling cold, Heller reassured him that they would be home soon and that he would be all right. Once the plane landed, the wounded gunner was taken to the base hospital and eventually made a full recovery. It was apparently this action that netted Heller his Air Medal (177–178, 180–181). Heller took the rest of the Snowden story, the part about the horrible intestinal wound, from an incident that occurred on an earlier mission over Ferrara, Italy, on 16 July 1944. A radio gunner in Heller's squadron, Sergeant Vandermeulen, had his midsection sliced open by a burst of flak and died in the back of his aircraft, moaning that he was cold ("Chronology" 1; *Now and Then* 177). "For my episodes of Snowden in the novel," Heller stated, "I fused the knowledge of that tragedy with the panicked copilot and the thigh wound to the top turret gunner in my own plane on our second mission to Avignon" (*Now and Then* 177). After this mission, Heller came away with a new appreciation of the dangers of combat:

> I might have seemed a hero and been treated as something of a small hero for a short while, but I didn't feel like one. They were trying to kill me, and I wanted to go home. That they were trying to kill all of us each time we went up was no consolation. They were trying to kill *me*.
>
> I was frightened on every mission after that one, even the certified milk runs. It could have been about then that I began crossing my fingers each time we took off and saying in silence a little prayer. It was my sneaky ritual. (181)

This dread of combat was to later show up as a trademark characteristic of Heller's *Catch-22* alter ego, Yossarian. Once he completed his required sixty missions, Heller had no interest in volunteering for any more (*Now and Then* 175). He chose to return home by ship, not airplane, and for many years afterwards he refused to ride in any airplanes at all—he had grown terrified of flying (171–172). Heller's attitude was not unique among air combat veterans. About ten years ago, I had a conversation with a former World War II Air Force pilot at an air show in Charlotte, NC. I asked the old veteran if he had maintained his pilot status after the war, and he said "No." When I asked him why, he replied, "I felt like I had used up all my luck during the war, and I didn't want to push it any further."

Many of Heller's other combat experiences found their way into *Catch-22*, including a mission to bomb an Italian ship that is recounted almost identically in both his novel and his autobiography. As Heller tells the story in *Catch-22*:

> Intelligence had reported that a disabled Italian cruiser in drydock at La Spezia would be towed by the Germans that same morning to a channel at the entrance of the harbor and scuttled

there to deprive the Allied armies of deepwater port facilities when they captured the city. For once, a military intelligence report proved accurate. The long vessel was halfway across the harbor when they [Yossarian's bomb group] flew in from the west, and they broke it apart with direct hits from every flight that filled them all with waves of enormously satisfying group pride until they found themselves engulfed in great barrages of flak that rose from guns in every bend of the huge horseshoe of mountainous land below. (*Catch-22* 384–385)

In the novel, Yossarian's friends Dobbs and Nately are both killed on the mission to La Spezia. Heller's description of this mission in his autobiography is virtually identical to the account in *Catch-22*, with one important exception: although there was heavy flak, none of his friends were killed. He tells us that this mission, one of the last he flew, filled him with both "military and civilian pride, the civilian pride bred of my sole assertion of leadership and authority as an officer" (183). The La Spezia mission was flown on 23 September 1944 to destroy the Italian cruiser *Taranto,* and the 340th Bomb Group won its second Presidential Distinguished Unit Citation for this mission, a citation in which Heller shared ("Chronology" 2; *History of the 340th Bomb Group*). As he relates in *Now and Then:*

The assignment that morning was a hurried one. The destination was the large Italian seaport of La Spezia. The target was an Italian cruiser reportedly being towed out into a deep channel of the harbor by the Germans, to be scuttled there as an obstacle to approaching Allied ground forces pressing steadily north. . . . When I looked behind us after we had flown through the flak at La Spezia and turned off, I was greatly satisfied with myself and all that I saw, and with all the others as well. We were unharmed; the turbulent oceans of dozens and dozens of smutty black clouds from the countless flak bursts were diffused all over the sky at different heights. The other flights were coming through without apparent damage. And down below I could watch the bombs from one cascade after another exploding directly on the ship that was our target. (183–185)

One of the most memorable episodes in *Catch-22* is the incident where Milo Minderbinder, a pilot in Yossarian's squadron, bombs his own airbase at night. After being appointed the base mess officer, Milo forms an international business syndicate that includes as members not only the Allied nations but the German government as well. He signs a contract with the German military to bomb and strafe his own men in order to save his syndicate from bankruptcy (264–266). It is no coincidence that Alesan Airfield on Corsica, the base for Heller's own 340th Bomb Group, was bombed and strafed by the Luftwaffe in the early morning hours of 13 May 1944. Although Heller's base was not bombed by friendly aircraft as in the novel, it is interesting to note that the first enemy plane over the field was actually a Bristol "Beaufighter," a twin-engined British night fighter operated by both Great Britain and the United States in the Mediterranean Theater. The 340th Bomb Group staff officers speculated that the Beaufighter had been captured by the Germans and put to use as a "pathfinder" aircraft, whose job it was to drop lighted flares over the target before the main force came in for the attack. The Germans apparently left the British markings on the Beaufighter intact in order to fool the Americans into mistaking it for a friendly plane. The German aircraft used in the raid were identified as twin-engined Junkers JU-88 medium bombers, similar in function to the American B-25s, and Focke-Wulf FW-190 fighter planes. In addition, there were unconfirmed reports of Dornier DO-217 and Heinkel HE-111 medium bombers and Messerschmitt ME-109 fighters *(History of the 340th)*. Twenty-two men in Heller's group were killed, and two hundred and nineteen were wounded; only seven aircraft were airworthy the next day ("Chronology" 1). The description of the attack on the 340th Group's online history bears a close similarity to Heller's description of Milo's raid in *Catch-22*. Although I am not aware of any instances where Heller alluded to this similarity in print, the conclusion seems inescapable that Heller has once again has taken an episode from his own combat background and, with some important changes for dramatic effect, incorporated it into his novel.

Heller was also quite capable of making use of his Air Force memories to describe the day-to-day operations of a B-25 bomber group. Take, for instance, this colorful description of the bombers warming up and taking off on a mission, a description obviously written by a man who has "been there and done that" many times:

> Engines rolled over disgruntledly on lollipop-shaped hardstands, resisting first, then idling smoothly awhile, and then the planes lumbered around and nosed forward lamely over the pebbled ground like sightless, stupid crippled things until they taxied into the line at the foot of the landing strip and took off swiftly, one behind the other, in a zooming, rising roar, banking slowly into formation over mottled treetops, and circling the field at even speed until all the flights of six had been formed and then setting course over cerulean water on the first leg of the journey to the target in northern Italy or France. The planes gained altitude

steadily and were above nine thousand feet by the time they crossed into enemy territory. One of the surprising things always was the sense of calm and utter silence, broken only by the test rounds fired from the machine guns, by an occasional toneless, terse remark over the intercom, and, at last, by the sobering pronouncement of the bombardier in each plane that they were at the I.P. [initial point] and about to turn toward the target. There was always sunshine, always a tiny sticking in the throat from the rarified air. (*Catch-22* 49)

One memorable episode that was *not* incorporated into *Catch-22* occurred on 22 March 1944, when Mt. Vesuvius erupted and destroyed most of the 340th Bomb Group's seventy-nine aircraft. The group's base was located on the Italian mainland at the time, and the eruption of Vesuvius forced the group to move, first to Paestum for three weeks and then to Corsica on 16 April ("Chronology" 1). It seems odd that Heller did not use this incident in his novel—such an occurrence could only have served to convince the paranoid Yossarian that not only were the Germans and his superiors out to kill him, but God and Nature as well.

A study of Heller's writings and interviews reveals that Yossarian was not the only *Catch-22* character based on Heller's wartime acquaintances, in spite of some of his statements to the contrary. For example, in his 1975 *Playboy* interview Heller told Sam Merrill that the only character he took from real life was a pilot named "Hungry Joe" (Merrill 61). In *Catch-22* Hungry Joe has terrible nightmares whenever he is due to be shipped home and tries to pass himself off as a *Life* photographer so he can take revealing pictures of USO girls (52–56). Heller revealed that Hungry Joe was based on a good friend of his named Joe Chrenko, who actually did try to pass himself off once as a *Life* photographer so he could photograph girls. Joe Chrenko also lived in the same tent as Francis Yohannon, Heller's eponymous inspiration for Yossarian. Yohannon owned a pet cocker spaniel he bought in Rome, which became Huple's cat in the novel "to protect its identity" (*Now and Then* 176; Merrill 61).

As for the other characters, Heller told Merrill, "They're not based on anyone I knew in the war. They're products of an imagination that drew on American life in the postwar period" (Merrill 61). But later in the same interview Heller contradicted this statement when he described the Italian prostitute Luciana, whom Yossarian patronizes in the novel. As Heller related to Merrill:

> His encounter with Luciana, the Roman whore, corresponds exactly with an experience I had. He sleeps with her, she refuses money and suggests that he keep her address on a slip of paper.

When he agrees, she sneers, "Why? So you can tear it up?" He says of course he won't and tears it up the minute she's gone—then regrets it bitterly. That's just what happened to me in Rome. (64)

In *Now and Then*, Heller gives additional examples of *Catch-22* characters who were based on his fellow airmen. One of these is the squadron executive officer, Major ——— de Coverly. The men of Yossarian's squadron are able to enjoy themselves immensely while on furlough in Italy thanks to Major ——— de Coverly, whose most important duty apparently involves renting apartments for his men to use while on leave:

> Each time the fall of a city like Naples, Rome or Florence seemed imminent, Major ——— de Coverly would pack his musette bag, commandeer an airplane and a pilot, and have himself flown away, accomplishing all this without uttering a word . . . . A day or two after the city fell, he would be back with leases on two large and luxurious apartments there, one for the officers and one for the enlisted men, both already staffed with competent, jolly cooks and maids. (*Catch-22* 135)

As it turns out, Major ——— de Coverly was closely patterned after Heller's own squadron exec, Major Cover, who performed an identical role for his men:

> The first American soldiers were in Rome on the morning of June 4 [1944], and close on their heels, perhaps even beating them into the city, sped our congenial executive officer, Major Cover, to rent two apartments there for use by the officers and enlisted men in our squadron . . . with cooks and maids, and with female friends of the cooks and maids who liked to hang out there. . . . (*Now and Then* 176)

One of the realities of the air war over Europe was the attrition of high ranking officers, which even included group commanders and wing commanders. In *Catch-22*, Yossarian's original group commander, Colonel Nevers, is killed on a mission over Arezzo and is replaced by Colonel Cathcart, who becomes notorious for steadily increasing the number of missions his men are required to fly (*Catch-22* 54). Not surprisingly, the commander of Joseph Heller's own 340th Bomb Group, Colonel Charles D. Jones, was shot down by the Germans on 10 March 1944 while on a bombing mission over the Littorio marshalling yards in Rome. Jones had only been the group's commander for three months. One of the group's earlier commanders, Colonel William C. Mills, was shot down and killed on a mission over Algeria in May 1943. On 16 March, Jones was replaced by Colonel Willis F. Chapman, who was Heller's group commander throughout his tour ("Chronology" 1; *History of the 340th*). Like Cathcart, Chapman also increased the number of missions his men were required to fly, but in accordance with Air Force policy, not his own whims.

One of the most memorable characters in *Catch-22 is* Yossarian's tent mate Lieutenant Orr, a bashful and optimistic young pilot who has a penchant for crash-landing his airplanes and a mechanical aptitude that drives Yossarian crazy. During the course of the novel, Orr assembles a homemade gasoline stove for the tent they share, and he builds an ornate fireplace complete with a mantelpiece. "He had constructed andirons for the fireplace out of excess bomb parts and had filled them with stout silver logs, and he had framed with stained wood the photographs of girls with big breasts he had torn out of cheesecake magazines and hung over the mantelpiece" (*Catch-22* 322). As Heller admitted in his autobiography, the character of Orr was based on a pilot named Edward Ritter who shared Heller's tent. Just like Orr, Ritter was a "tireless handyman," building the fireplace in their tent, assembling their gasoline stove, and creating a washstand out of a bomb rack and a flak helmet. Just like Orr, Ritter also had a penchant for ditching in the water and crash-landing safely on land without losing a single crewman:

> Remarkably, through all his unlucky series of mishaps the pilot Ritter remained imperviously phlegmatic, demonstrating no symptoms of fear or growing nervousness, even blushing with a chuckle and a smile whenever I gagged around him as a jinx, and it was on these qualities of his, his patient genius for building and fixing things and these recurring close calls in aerial combat, only on these, that I fashioned the character of Orr in *Catch-22*. (*Now and Then* 175)

The analogy is complete even down to the pictures of the girls on the mantelpiece, who are documented graphically in a photograph of Heller's tent interior reproduced on the dust jacket and inside covers of *Now and Then*. In this photo, which was used for the squadron's annual Christmas card in 1944, three pinup photographs of female models are clearly seen behind a uniformed Heller, and the pictures are hanging over the mantel-piece that Ritter constructed from an old railroad tie.

Throughout *Catch-22*, Yossarian is plagued by the presence of a "dead man in his tent." This dead man is a pilot named Mudd, who reports for duty in Yossarian's squadron, places his gear in Yossarian's tent, and is then sent on a mission without officially checking in with squadron headquarters.

When Mudd's plane is blown up by flak on this same mission, his presence in the squadron cannot be officially confirmed; thus his gear remains in Yossarian's tent as a haunting reminder throughout most of the novel (*Catch-22* 111–112). Like Yossarian, Heller also had a vacant cot in his own tent until Ritter showed up to fill it. The cot had previously belonged to a bombardier from Oklahoma named Pinkard, who was shot down and killed on a mission over Ferrara (*Now and Then* 177).

Toward the end of the novel, Yossarian's squadron receives some replacement airmen, several of whom are billeted in Yossarian's now almost vacant tent. "The moment he saw them, Yossarian knew they were impossible. They were frisky, eager and exuberant, and they had all been friends in the States. They were plainly unthinkable. They were noisy, overconfident, emptyheaded kids of twenty-one. . . . They reminded him of Donald Duck's nephews" (*Catch-22* 356–357). Similarly, at the end of his tour, as he was awaiting orders to return home, Heller received as roommates two "chaste beginners," young replacement pilots "not long past twenty" (*Now and Then* 169, 172–173). As Heller noted, there was a "huge divide" between him and the new replacements. He was through with his missions and was going home, and the replacements were just getting started. Heller had completed sixty missions, and the number of required missions for combat airmen in his bomb group had just been raised to seventy (185). But one of Heller's new roommates had brought with him a bonus that the dour Yossarian would not have appreciated: a typewriter (169). While his roommates were away flying combat missions, Heller was able to spend time alone with the typewriter, reviving a penchant for writing that he had pursued before the war and was anxious to renew (185). This desire to write would ultimately result in a best-selling novel about World War II called *Catch-22* and a long and distinguished career as a writer of fiction, a career that sadly ended only a year after the publication of his autobiography *Now and Then*.

In an even stranger quirk of fate, Heller's decision to incorporate his war experiences into a novel would ultimately guarantee that a large number of authentic World War II bombers would be saved from the scrap heap and restored to flying status, an occurrence that Heller certainly could not have anticipated when he first wrote *Catch-22*. In 1968, Paramount Pictures and director Mike Nichols began filming a movie version of *Catch-22* that was released to theaters in 1970. To lend authenticity to the movie, Nichols and Tallamantz Aviation of California assembled a fleet of eighteen vintage B-25 bombers for the aerial combat sequences. Over 1500 hours of flying time went into the production of the film, of which less than ten minutes actually appeared in the movie (Thompson 19–22). During the production of this movie, Nichols's B-25 group constituted the twelfth-largest air force in the world (Merrill 60). By producing *Catch-22* for the silver screen, Paramount rescued these veteran aircraft from oblivion and guaranteed their survival into the twenty-first century. Most of these B-25s have been meticulously restored to their original military condition and are regular attractions on the air show circuit today. Their continued existence helps to keep alive the memory of Joseph Heller and the thousands of his comrades who fought and died in the aerial battles of World War II.

WORKS CITED

A History of the 340th Bombardment Group. Online Air Force unit history. 16 November 2001. <http://members.tripod.com/jkoppie/340.htm>.

A History of the 57th Bombardment Wing. Online Air Force unit history. 29 June 2002; <http://members.tripod.com/jkoppie/57th.htm>.

Aubrey, James R., "Heller's 'Parody On Hemingway' in *Catch-22*." *Studies in Contemporary Satire: A Creative and Critical Journal.* 17 (1990): pp. 1–5.

Burhans, Clinton S. Jr., "Spindrift and the Sea: Structural Patterns and Unifying Elements in *Catch-22*." *Critical Essays on Joseph Heller.* Ed. James Nagel. Boston: G. K. Hall, 1984: pp. 40–51.

Craig, David M. "From Avignon to *Catch-22*." *War, Literature and the Arts.* 6:2 (Fall–Winter 1994): pp. 27–54.

———. "Joseph Heller's '*Catch-22* Revisited.'" *War, Literature and the Arts.* 1:2 (1989–1990): pp. 33–41.

Freeman, Roger A. *The Mighty Eighth: Units, Men and Machines (A History of the US 8th Army Air Force).* Garden City, NY: Doubleday, 1972.

Heller, Joseph. *Catch-22.* New York: Dell Paperback, 1961.

———. "*Catch-22* Revisited." *Holiday.* 41 (April 1967): pp. 45–60, 120, 141–142.

———. "Chronology 2/13/66." Unpublished manuscript, Joseph Heller Manusript Collection. Robert D. Farber University Archives and Special Collections Department, Brandeis University Library, Waltham, MA.

———. *Now and Then: From Coney Island to Here.* New York: Knopf, 1998.

———. "On Translating *Catch-22* into a Movie." *A Catch-22 Casebook.* Eds. Frederick Kiley and Walter McDonald. New York: Crowell, 1973: pp. 346–362.

Kiley, Frederick, and Walter McDonald, eds. *A Catch-22 Casebook.* New York: Crowell, 1973.

Merrill, Robert. *Joseph Heller.* Boston: G. K. Hall, 1987.

Merrill, Sam. "Playboy Interview: Joseph Heller." *Playboy.* 22:6 (June 1975): pp. 59–76.

Nagel, James. *Critical Essays on Joseph Heller.* Boston: G. K. Hall, 1984.

Nolan, Charles J. Jr. "Heller's Small Debt to Hemingway." *The Hemingway Review.* 9:1 (Fall 1989): pp. 77–81.

Ruderman, Judith. *Joseph Heller.* New York: Continuum, 1991.

Thompson, Scott. "The *Catch-22* Air Force." *Air Progress Warbirds International.* 9:5 (September–October 1990): pp. 18–29.

Joseph Heller Chronology

1923	Joseph Heller born 1 May in Brooklyn, New York.
1942	Joins U.S. Army Corps.
1944–1945	Stationed in Corsica with the 488th Squadron of the 340th Bombardment Group; flies 60 combat missions as a bombardier.
1945	Publishes his first short story, "I Don't Love You Anymore," in *Story.*
1948	Receives B.A. from New York University.
1949	Receives M.A. in English from Columbia University.
1950–1952	Teaches composition at Pennsylvania State University.
1952–1956	Advertising copywriter for *Time.*
1955	"Catch-18" published in *New Works Writing 7.*
1956–1958	Advertising manager at *Look.*
1958–1961	Promotion manager at *McCall's.*
1961	*Catch-22* published.
1967	*We Bombed in New Haven* produced and published.
1971	*Catch-22: A Dramatization* produced and published.
1972	*Clevinger's Trial* (from *Catch-22*): *A Play in One Act* published.
1974	*Something Happened* published.
1979	*Good as Gold* published.
1980	Ill with Guillain-Barré syndrome.
1984	*God Knows* published.

1985	*No Laughing Matter* (with Speed Vogel) published.
1988	*Picture This* published.
1994	*Closing Time* published.
1998	*Now and Then: From Coney Island to Here* published.
1999	12 December, death of Joseph Heller from heart attack at East Hampton, Long Island.
1999	*Portrait of an Artist, as an Old Man* published.
2003	*Catch as Catch Can: Collected Stories and Other Writings* published.

Contributors

HAROLD BLOOM is Sterling Professor of the Humanities at Yale University. He is the author of 30 books, including *Shelley's Mythmaking* (1959), *The Visionary Company* (1961), *Blake's Apocalypse* (1963), *Yeats* (1970), *A Map of Misreading* (1975), *Kabbalah and Criticism* (1975), *Agon: Toward a Theory of Revisionism* (1982), *The American Religion* (1992), *The Western Canon* (1994), and *Omens of Millennium: The Gnosis of Angels, Dreams, and Resurrection* (1996). *The Anxiety of Influence* (1973) sets forth Professor Bloom's provocative theory of the literary relationships between the great writers and their predecessors. His most recent books include *Shakespeare: The Invention of the Human* (1998), a 1998 National Book Award finalist, *How to Read and Why* (2000), *Genius: A Mosaic of One Hundred Exemplary Creative Minds* (2002), *Hamlet: Poem Unlimited* (2003), *Where Shall Wisdom Be Found?* (2004), and *Jesus and Yahweh: The Names Divine* (2005). In 1999, Professor Bloom received the prestigious American Academy of Arts and Letters Gold Medal for Criticism. He has also received the International Prize of Catalonia, the Alfonso Reyes Prize of Mexico, and the Hans Christian Andersen Bicentennial Prize of Denmark.

ROBERT BRUSTEIN is the founding director of the Yale Repertory and American Repertory Theatres and is Professor of English at Harvard and drama critic for *The New Republic*.

NELSON ALGREN wrote *The Man with the Golden Arm*, which received the 1950 National Book Award.

JOHN WAIN was Professor of Poetry at the University of Oxford; he wrote novels, verse, and criticism.

263

FREDERICK R. KARL taught at City College of CUNY at New York University; he wrote literary biographies.

MINNA DOSKOW teaches at Rowan College of New Jersey. She is the author of *William Blake's Jerusalem: Structure and Meaning in Poetry and Picture* (1982).

JAN SOLOMON taught at the University of Toledo.

DOUG GAUKROGER taught at the University of Waterloo, Ontario.

RICHARD LEHAN teaches at the University of California, Los Angeles. His books include *Realism and Naturalism: The Novel in an Age of Transition* (2005).

JERRY PATCH is currently the Dramaturg and a member of the artistic team at Southern California South Coast Repertory (SCR), as well as Resident Artistic Director at The Old Globe Theatre in San Diego.

JAMES L. MCDONALD taught at the University of Missouri at Kansas City.

THOMAS ALLEN NELSON teaches at San Diego State University. He is the author of *Kubrick: Inside a Film Artist's Maze* (2000).

CLINTON S. BURHANS teaches at Michigan State University. He has published widely on nineteenth- and twentieth-century American literature.

JAMES NAGEL, Edison Distinguished Professor of English at the University of Georgia, has edited several collections on the works of Joseph Heller, Ernest Hemingway, and Stephen Crane.

DAVID STREITFELD is a business reporter for the *Los Angeles Times*; he was previously a book reporter for the *Washington Post*.

CHRISTOPHER BUCKLEY is a political satirist. His novels include *The White House Mess* (1986), *Thank You for Smoking* (1994), *No Way to Treat a First Lady* (2002), and most recently, *Boomsday* (2007).

DAVID M. CRAIG is Professor of Humanities and Director of the Honors Program at Clarkson University.

DANIEL GREEN was formerly English Professor at Pittsburg State University. He has published critical articles and fiction.

NORMAN PODHORETZ, editor at large of *Commentary Magazine* and a senior fellow at the Hudson Institute, is the author of *Ex Friends* (2000), *My Love Affair With America*(2001), and *The Prophets: Who They Were, What They Are* (2002). In 2004, he was awarded the Presidential Medal of Freedom.

SANFORD PINSKER is the author and editor of more than a dozen books, including book-length studies of Philip Roth, Cynthia Ozick, Joseph Heller, and J. D. Salinger. He has retired from teaching at Franklin and Marshall College.

MICHAEL C. SCOGGINS is the historian for the Culture and Heritage Museums in York County, South Carolina, and is the author of several books on the Revolutionary War in the South.

Bibliography

Aldridge, John W., "'Catch-22' Twenty-Five Years Later," *Michigan Quarterly Review,* XXVI (Spring 1987): pp. 386–397.

Bruccoli, Matthew J. and Park Bucker, *Joseph Heller: A Descriptive Bibliography* (New Castle, Del.: Oak Knoll Press; Pittsburgh: University of Pittsburgh Press, 2002).

Eller, Jonathan R. "Catching a Market: The Publishing History of 'Catch-22,'" *Prospects,* 17 (1992): pp. 475–525.

———. "Catching Up": An Updated Bibliography of Joseph Heller's *Catch-22,* 1973–1988, *Bulletin of Bibliography,* 47 (1990): pp. 9–21.

Greenfield, Josh. "22 Was Funnier Than 14," *New York Times Book Review* (3 March 1961): pp. 49–51, 53.

Harris, Charles B., "*Catch-22:* A Radical Protest against Absurdity," *Contemporary American Novelists of the Absurd* (New Haven: College & University Press, 1971): pp. 33–50.

Kiley, Frederick, and Walter McDonald, eds. *A Catch-22 Casebook* (New York: Crowell, 1973).

Keegan, Brenda. *Joseph Heller: A Reference Guide* (Boston: G.K. Hall, 1978).

Merrill, Robert. *Joseph Heller* (Boston: Twayne, 1987).

———. "The Structure and Meaning of *Catch-22,*" *Studies in American Fiction,* 14 (Autumn 1986): pp. 139–152.

Nagel, James, "*Catch-22* and Angry Humor: A Study of the Normative Values of Satire," *Studies in American Humor,* Vol. 1 (1974): pp. 99–106.

———. "The *Catch-22* Note Cards," *Studies in the Novel,* 8 (1976): pp. 394–405.

———. ed. *Critical Essays on Joseph Heller* (Boston: G.K. Hall, 1984).

Pinsker, Sanford. "Reassessing 'Catch-22'," *The Sewanee Review* 108:4 (Fall 2000): pp. 602–611.

———. *Understanding Joseph Heller* (Columbia: University of South Carolina Press, 1991).

Potts, Stephen W., *Catch-22: Antiheroic Antinovel* (Boston: Twayne, 1989).

Protherough, Robert. "The Sanity of *Catch-22*," *Human World*, 3 (May 1971): pp. 59–70.

Richter, David H., "The Achievement of Shape in the Twentieth-Century Fable: Joseph Heller's *Catch-22*," *Fable's End: Completeness and Closure in Rhetorical Fiction* (Chicago: University of Chicago Press, 1974): pp. 136–165.

Ruderman, Judith. *Joseph Heller* (New York: Continuum, 1991).

Scotto, Robert M., ed. *Catch-22: A Critical Edition* (New York: Delta, 1973).

Seed, David. *The Fiction of Joseph Heller: Against the Grain* (New York: St. Martin's Press, 1989).

Sorkin, Adam J., ed. *Conversations with Joseph Heller* (Jackson: University of Mississippi Press, 1993).

Way, Brian. "Formal Experiment and Social Discontent: Joseph Heller's *Catch-22*," *Journal of American Studies*, 2 (October 1968): pp. 253–270.

Weixlmann, Joseph. "A Bibliography of Joseph Heller's *Catch-22*," *Bulletin of Bibliography*, 31 (1974): pp. 32–37.

Acknowledgments

Brustein, Robert. "The Logic of Survival in a Lunatic World," *New Republic*, 13 November 1961. © 1961 *The New Republic*. Reprinted by permission of the publisher.

Algren, Nelson. "The Catch," *The Nation* (4 Nov 1961): pp. 357–358. © 1961 *The Nation*. Reprinted by permission of the publisher.

Wain, John. "A New Novel About Old Troubles," *The Critical Quarterly*, Vol 5, Number 2 (Summer 1963): pp 168–173. © Blackwell Publishers.

Karl, Frederick R., "Joseph Heller's *Catch-22*: Only Fools Walk in Darkness," *Contemporary American Novelists*, ed. Moore (Carbondale: Southern Illinois University Press, 1965): pp. 134–142. Copyright © 1964 by Southern Illinois University Press. Reprinted by permission of Southern Illinois University Press.

Minna Doskow, "The Night Journey in *Catch-22*," *Twentieth Century Literature*, Vol. 12, No. 4 (Jan., 1967): pp. 186–193. © Hofstra University. Reprinted by permission of Hofstra University.

Heller, Joseph. "*Catch-22* Revisited," *Holiday* (April 1967): pp. 44–61, 120, 141–142, 145. © Joseph Heller. Reprinted by permission of the Estate of Joseph Heller.

269

Christopher Buckley, "Götterdämmerung-22," *The New Yorker*, Volume 70 (10 Oct 1994): pp. 104–109. Copyright © Condé Nast Publications. Reprinted by permission.

"From Avignon to Catch-22." *War, Literature & the Arts*, Volume 6, No. 2 (Fall–Winter 1994): pp. 27–54.

Green, Daniel. "A World Worth Laughing At: *Catch-22* and the Humor of Black Humor," *Studies in The Novel*, Volume 27, number 2 (summer 1995): pp. 186–196. Copyright © 1995 University of North Texas. Reprinted by permission of the publisher.

Nagel, James. "The Early Composition History of *Catch-22*," in *Biographies of Books: The Compositional History of Notable American Writings*, Barbour and Quirk (eds), (Columbia and London: University of Missouri Press, 1996), pp. 262–290. © 1996 University of Missouri Press. Reprinted by permission of the publisher.

Podhoretz, Norman, "Looking Back at 'Catch-22,'" *Commentary Magazine*, February 2000, pp. 32–37. Copyright © *Commentary Magazine*. Reprinted by permission of the publisher.

Pinsker, Sanford. "Once More Into the Breach: Joseph Heller Gives *Catch-22* a Second Act," *Topic: The Washington and Jefferson College Review*, Volume 50 (2000): pp. 28–39. Copyright © *Topic: The Washington and Jefferson College Review*. Reprinted by permission of the publisher.

Scoggins, Michael C., "Joseph Heller's Combat Experiences in *Catch-22*," *War, Literature & the Arts*, Volume 15 No. 1–2 (2003): pp. 213–227.

Index